Nicola Ferro (Ed.)

Bridging Between Information Retrieval and Databases

PROMISE Winter School 2013
Bressanone, Italy, February 4-8, 2013
Revised Tutorial Lectures

T0221609

 Springer

Volume Editor

Nicola Ferro
University of Padua
Department of Information Engineering
Via Gradenigo 6/a
35131 Padua, Italy
E-mail: ferro@dei.unipd.it

ISSN 0302-9743   e-ISSN 1611-3349
ISBN 978-3-642-54797-3   e-ISBN 978-3-642-54798-0
DOI 10.1007/978-3-642-54798-0
Springer Heidelberg New York Dordrecht London

Library of Congress Control Number: 2014935088

LNCS Sublibrary: SL 3 – Information Systems and Application,
incl. Internet/Web and HCI

Typesetting: Camera-ready by author, data conversion by Scientific Publishing Services, Chennai, India

Printed on acid-free paper

Springer is part of Springer Science+Business Media (www.springer.com)

Preface

The main mission of the PROMISE EU FP7 network of excellence is to advance the evaluation and benchmarking of multimedia and multilingual information access systems. Together with the ELIAS research network, funded by the European Science Foundation, on information access system evaluation, PROMISE organized a winter school on "Bridging between Information Retrieval and Databases"[1] as a week long event in Bressanone, Italy, during February 4–8, 2013.

The aim of the school was to give participants a grounding in the core topics that constitute the multidisciplinary area of information access and retrieval to unstructured, semi-structured, and structured information. The idea of the school stemmed from the observation that, nowadays, databases are more and more getting into techniques that have traditionally been typical of information retrieval and, viceversa, information retrieval is using more and more database-oriented techniques.

17 high quality lecturers from academia and industry were invited to speak on a large variety of topics from introductory talks on databases, information retrieval, experimental evaluation, metrics and statistics to advanced topics such as semantic search, keyword search in databases, semi-structured search, and evaluation both in information retrieval and databases. Focused lectures were devoted to bridging between information retrieval and databases and to the management and sharing of research data via evaluation infrastructures. Finally hot topics concerned evaluation with respect to usefulness, crowdsourcing, evaluation on social media, and moving from evaluation to applications.

52 participants from 16 countries attended the courses (17% MsC students, 63% PhD students, 10% post-docs, 10% academic) with a background mostly on databases (32%), information retrieval (40%), both (15%), natural language processing (9%), and other topics. 15 scholarships (supported by ELIAS) were granted to students to attend the school. The multidisciplinarity of the participants and lectures helped to create many lively discussions and a friendly atmosphere with many questions. Also most of the speakers stayed for the entire week and enriched the discussions as well. Interestingly enough, the school turned out to be a brainstorming and discussion opportunity also for the lecturers, since they had the occasion of meeting colleagues from a different field with their own perspectives on a ground of shared topics and issues.

To favor discussion and reciprocal knowledge, participants were asked to bring a poster describing their own research activities and plans. A Committee was set up to review the posters and the three best posters were awarded with a small

---

[1] http://www.promise-noe.eu/events/winter-school-2013/

prize and the winners were invited to contribute a short paper to the present volume.

Altogether the PROMISE winter school can be seen as a great success in connecting two research domains and allowing a large number of participants to get in contact with high quality lecturers. Hopefully an important outcome is that the participants now have a better view of the DB and IR research domains and also on the ways they can evaluate their own research and profit from available tools of visualization. An analysis of the evaluation forms compiled after the school highlighted that most students very much enjoyed it (97% of the participants) and the atmosphere among participants and lecturers. Most presentations were liked (95% of the participants with 77% highly appreciating the lectures) and the students were generally interested in the different topics offered by the school (95% of the participants with 76% highly interested).

December 2013   Nicola Ferro

Organization

The PROMISE Winter School 2013 was organized by the Department of Information Engineering of the University of Padua, Italy.

General Chair

Maristella Agosti   University of Padua, Italy

Program Chair

Nicola Ferro   University of Padua, Italy

Program Committee

Khalid Choukri   Evaluations and Language resources
                                     Distribution Agency (ELDA), France

Jussi Karlgren   Gavagai, Sweden

Henning Müller   University of Applied Sciences Western
                                     Switzerland (HES-SO), Switzerland

Maarten de Rijke   University of Amsterdam, The Netherlands

Giuseppe Santucci   Sapienza University of Rome, Italy

Poster Chair

Donna Harman   National Institute of Standards and Technology
                                     (NIST), Gaithersburg, USA

Poster Committee

Omar Alonso   Microsoft Bing, USA

Sonia Bergamaschi   University of Modena-Reggio Emilia, Italy

Fabio Crestani   University of Lugano, Switzerland

Publicity Committee

Pamela Forner   Centre for the Evaluation of Language and
                                   Communication Technologies (CELCT),
                                   Italy

Hèléne Mazo   Evaluations and Language resources
                               Distribution Agency (ELDA), France

Local Organization Chair

Gianmaria Silvello   University of Padua, Italy

Local Organization

Debora Leoncini   University of Padua, Italy
Ivano Masiero   University of Padua, Italy
Simone Peruzzo   University of Padua, Italy

Acknowledgements

We would like to warmly thank all the lecturers, participants, and people in the local organization who gave an extremely valuable contribution and made the PROMISE Winter School 2013 a success.

The PROMISE Winter School was supported by: the Department of Information Engineering of the University of Padua, Italy, the PROMISE[2] network of excellence (contract n. 258191), as part of the 7th Framework Program of the European Commission, and by the ELIAS[3] research networking programme of the European Science Foundation.

---

[2] http://www.promise-noe.eu/
[3] http://www.elias-network.eu/

Table of Contents

An Introduction to the Novel Challenges in Information Retrieval for Social Media

Giacomo Inches and Fabio Crestani

Faculty of Informatics
University of Lugano (USI)
Lugano, Switzerland
{giacomo.inches,fabio.crestani}@usi.ch

Abstract. The importance of the Internet as a communication medium is reflected in the large amount of documents being generated every day by users of the different services that take place online. This has caused a massive change in the documents being reached and retrieved. In this article we study how Information Retrieval models should change to reflect the changes that are happening to the documents being processed. We analyse the properties of the online user-generated documents of some of the most established services over the Internet (e.g. Kongregate, Twitter, Myspace and Slashdot) and compare them with a consolidated collection of standard information retrieval documents (e.g. Wall Street Journal, Associated Press, Financial Times). We study the statistical properties of these collections (e.g. Zipf's Law and Heap's Law) and investigate other important feature, such as document similarity, term burstiness, emoticons and part-of-speech analysis. We highlight the applicability and limits of traditional content analysis techniques to the new online user-generated documents and show the need for a specific processing for those documents in oder to be able to provide effective content analysis.

1 Introduction and Motivations

One of the most important needs of the human being is communication. Since ancient times he has expressed this necessity with verbal and written symbols, that later turned into letters, alphabets and then structured texts. Written texts, in fact, represented for hundreds of years the main way of communication for people, especially those separated by long distances. Letters were the main instrument for actively communicating and establishing a "dialog" between individuals that could not meet in person. Other forms of written communication included newspaper articles, to report recent events, and poems, books, or magazines, to spread in-depth events or thoughts. For this reason, scientists started to analyse this kind of texts when they first wanted to investigate written documents [1, 2]. They were, in fact, the only available texts.

With the advent of first computers and then the Internet, researchers could investigate year after year, larger and larger collections of written documents,

N. Ferro (Ed.): PROMISE Winter School 2013, LNCS 8173, pp. 1–30, 2014.
© Springer-Verlag Berlin Heidelberg 2014

until faced with the recent challenges posed by all the novel kinds of written data (e.g. websites, emails, blogs, chat transcripts, etc). The creation of these novel texts had been facilitated, in the latest years by the combination of Internet with the diffusion of small and smart devices, such as smartphones and tablets. In fact, innovations in the technology always influenced the production of text: Gutenberg and his printing machine completely changed the way people approached written texts and the same can be said for personal computers and Internet. However, the possibility of accessing Internet and related services "anytime" and "anywhere" with a portable device represents another step forward in the way people are communicating and producing texts. Most (if not all) of the available services for communicating online make use of a form of textual interaction, thus generating lots of interesting data for researchers. Among the various novel services born online we can mention:

- Blogs, in which a person writes short articles on topics of his interest and engaged readers can leave their comments;
- Chat messages, in particular those originating from the Internet Relay Chat (IRC) providers but also within other software, like Skype or Facebook;
- Twitter messages, born as an SMS based service and now a platform to share links, emotions, feelings or statuses more in general;
- Online fora, were communities of people discuss particular topics in an extensive way;
- Review websites, where users can share their experience of products or services;
- Email, used to communicate as in the traditional letters but with the possibility of reaching multiple interlocutors at the same time.

This novel set of documents calls for an in-depth analysis to understand their properties with respect to traditional written documents and the applicability of traditional Information Retrieval techniques. In this paper we aim at giving an overview on the properties of some relevant collections composed of novel documents and compare them with the properties of standard documents employed in IR. To this purpose, we present in the next section (Section 2) a brief introduction to the main components of an IR system, focussing on those parts that we will later employ for analysing the collections under investigation. These collections are presented in Section 3, while in Section 4 we analyse them in detail and identify the principal characteristics of novel and standard documents. In Section 6 we illustrate some challenges IR has to face with the advent of novel collections, in light of our previous analysis. In Section 7 we conclude summarising the main contributions of this paper.

2   A Classical Information Retrieval System

Information Retrieval (IR) is the research area "concerned with the structure, analysis, organization, storage searching, and retrieval of information" (according to a classical definition [3], recently recalled in [2]). IR has been involved with

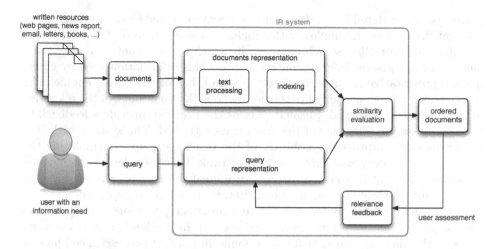

Fig. 1. From written resources to indexing, from a user need to the returned list of relevant documents: a classical IR system

the study of written documents since its early stages. In classical IR (Figure 1), textual documents are acquired generally using a system that automatically download them from Internet (crawler) or read them from a particular repository. The *documents* are therefore the "object" handled by an IR application and the software that process them is called IR system. The task of an IR system is to help users to find documents containing information he is looking for among a big collection of many ones. The IR system, therefore, provides an help to what is generally called an *information need.*

Generally the documents are processed and transformed into a simplified form, that reduces their dimensionality and provide a faster access to them. Some techniques of text processing to simplify documents are presented later (Section 2.1). Documents in this simplified form are then stored in an *index*, that represents the collection of documents. Generally the index stores an identifier per document and a set of terms contained in the document. This way it is relatively easy to obtain information on the collection given terms or documents. For example, given a term, one can find all the documents containing it (inverted index) or given a document, the list of terms is available (direct index). The index is generally the main source of data for any application based on an IR system. When a user submits a query to the IR system, for finding documents answering to an information need, this is transformed and reduced as in the indexing phase for the documents. This way documents representations (stored in the index) and query representation (computed on the fly) can be compared. Depending on the specific model adopted by the IR system, similarities between documents and queries representations are computed and the systems returns a list of relevant documents given the particular query issued by the user. The list of documents constitutes the answer to the user information need and it is generally ordered by relevancy to the query e.g. documents more relevant are displayed in higher positions. The ordered list of documents is always referred as the ranking list of relevant documents. Examples of this includes the classical ad-hoc search (i.e. Google, Yahoo or Bing search engines), in which a user what to retrieve web pages containing some information and express this information need by entering a representative set of terms into the search bar of the search engine. The search result is them presented to the user, who is the final judge of the relevancy of the documents returned. In some systems the user can provide a feedback to the system on the relevancy of the documents retrieved. The system might use the feedback to improve the accuracy of the results, e.g. by reformulating the original issued query and providing a new ranked list of relevant documents. This process might be iterated several times until the user is satisfied with the returned list of documents, that at each iteration should be improved.

In this paper we mainly focus on the text processing component (Figure 1) of the IR system, that we present in the next section. In Section 5, in particular, we focus on the major activities that can be found in the text processing component (i.e. parsing, stemming, stopwords removal) to study the properties of traditional and novel collections. Along with these activities we perform other analysis on the same collections using different techniques, in particular the Part-Of-Speech (POS) processing. In this study, in fact, we are interested in understanding how the techniques employed in the document representation component of an IR system should be adapted given the novel collections of documents produced online. Once identified the differences between collections of novel and traditional documents, we are also able to state how the techniques for the representation of documents in the IR system should be adapted. The same adaptation should also be applied to the query representation in the IR system, for maintaining the consistency between documents and query representations. For this reason we study in this work the differences between novel and traditional documents and how these differences influences the document representation in the IR systems only. We leave to future study the transposition of these differences to the query representation.

2.1 Text Processing

Parsing is the first activity performed by an IR system within the documents representation block (Figure 1). A program called parser reads the documents collected and splits their textual conten into terms, based on characters' boundaries like whitespace or punctuation, either preserving or not particular characters sequences (words but also links, markers, etc), numbers, punctuations or symbols. After that, a list of characters representing words or terms[1] is associated to each parsed text. All the terms that occur at least once in the text make up the *vocabulary*. Terms that appear just once in the text are called *singleton*, while the most frequent terms are inserted into the so-called *stopwords* list. Generally the most common terms in a text are function words e.g. propositions, connectors like "the" or "and" that do not contribute much to characterise the topicality

---

[1] Words and terms are used with the same meaning.

of the text and for this reason they can be removed. This procedure is called stopwords removal and has the benefit of reducing the size of the index. For particular applications, like authorship attribution, the functional words play an important role in characterising the style of the author of one text and for this reason the stopwords removal is not desired nor applied (e.g. POS analysis in Section 5). Moreover, term frequency is only one possible criteria for selecting stopwords and other strategies include the inverse document frequency of a term or its normalised version [4]. The last important operation conducted in the text processing block is *stemming*. Stemming is an operation carried out at term level that reduces all words to their root: for example win, winner, winning, are all reduced through stemming to a shorter form, in this case win. This also reduces the dimension of the index and it may improve the performances of the IR system since both the terms in the query and in the vocabulary are reduced to the same basic form. This is not always the case for novel documents, as it will be explained in Section 5.

2.2 Similarity Measures

To measure the degree of similarity between a document and a query or between two texts, different metrics can be applied, depending on the particular model assumed. One of the most common models used in the literature is the vector space model [3]. The vector space model assumes that each document is a vector and each term in the document is a component of this vector. With this assumption, the ordering of the words in each documents has no importance anymore and each word represents a dimension in the vector space [5]. Models that assume independence of the terms from their position in a document are often referred as using a *bag-of-words* approach. The measure of the distance in the case of the vector space model is the *cosine similarity*, that measures the angle between two vectors (documents) in the space, thus their degree of similarity. If the two vectors are overlapping, their similarity is 1, while if they are unrelated their similarity is equal to 0. We present in details the cosine similarity, showing its formulation in Section 5, where we employ it to measure the mutual similarity of documents belonging to the same collection. Other common approaches for measuring the distances between two texts are the probabilistic model, that assumes documents are generated according to a particular distribution of terms, modelled by a probability distribution [5]. A particular technique based on a probabilist approach is Language Models. One of the most common models employed is the Unigram Language Model, for which each term is estimated independently, as apposed to models that considers estimations for group of terms (e.g. two term - bigram, three terms - trigrams, ...) [5]. As in the case of the vector space model, this is another example of bag-of-words approach. In the case of Language Models the similarity between documents are computed with metrics derived from information theory or statistics. Measures of similarity from information theory are the Kullback-Leibler Divergence (KLD, and its particular case the Janson-Shannon divergence) and the Mutual Information (MI), while the χ^2 is an example of metric derived from statistics. It has to be noted that these metrics (KLD, MI, χ^2) are not similarity measures in a strict sense [6], but serve to this purpose only. Among other applications where they can be employed, we find features selection, that is the process of deciding the most representative features (e.g. terms) to use to represent an item (e.g. a document or user profile). These techniques might be used in problems of author identification [7, 8], clustering [9] or, more in general, different problems of IR [5] or machine learning and pattern recognition [10].

2.3 Further Readings

This simple and brief introduction of IR serves only to give the context where our work should be placed. It is not intended as a complete overview of IR, for which we suggest some books that covers all aspects of IR and related disciplines. One book that presents IR in its most general aspects and related fields is [11], that includes chapters on Digital Libraries, Interfaces, Visualization and Multimedia. Another one that presents in details the specific characteristics of search and search engines is [2]. A last book worth mentioning presents a nice overview of the principal IR concepts and can also be read in its free edition available online[2] [5].

3 Collections

In this section we present some of the most relevant collections containing novel documents as well as an extract of some traditional documents from standard collections. Some of the collections presented come from two of the main venues for standard as well as novel collections, the Text REtrieval Conference[3] (TREC) and the Conference and Labs of the Evaluation Forum[4] (CLEF). The ACM Special Interest Group on Information Retrieval[5] (SIGIR) and its associated conferences (CIKM[6], JCDL,[7], WSDM[8]) are, on the other hand, the main reference points for researches in IR.

The collections listed below include datasets that we use in our analysis in Section 4 and 5. Our aim is to give a good and relative complete picture of the existing collections in the literature, with a particular attention to conversational documents, that are of a great interest showing properties similar to the more trendy microblog ones. As representative of traditional collection of newspaper articles, we considered only a subset of those enclosed in TREC and CLEF, knowing that many other ones are available and interested readers should refers to TREC of CLEF website for this purpose.

---

[2] See: http://nlp.stanford.edu/IR-book/
[3] http://trec.nist.gov
[4] http://www.clef-initiative.eu//
[5] http://sigir.org
[6] Conference on Information and Knowledge Management, http://www.cikmconference.org
[7] Joint Conference on Digital Libraries http://www.jcdl.org
[8] Conference on Web Search and Data Mining, http://www.wsdm-conference.org/

Table 1. List of collections and their genre, with number of documents or posts per collection. In bold those used in our analysis.

Dataset	Type	# Posts
IRC Conversational	Chat	2K
NPS Chat Corpus	Chat	10K
CLEF-PAN 2012 SPI	Chat	125K
CAW 2.0 - Kongregate	**Chat**	**145K**
CAW 2.0 - Twitter	**Microblog**	**900K**
MS Twitter Conversations	Microblog	1.300K
TREC Microblog 2011	Microblog	16.000K
TREC Microblog 2013	Microblog	240.000K
NUS SMS Corpus	SMS	10K
CAW 2.0 - Ciao	Review	20K
CAW 2.0 - Myspace	**Blog**	**380K**
TREC Blogs06	Blog	3.200K
TREC Blogs08	Blog	29.000K
CAW 2.0 - Slashdot	**Forum**	**140K**
Enron Email Dataset	Email	600K
TREC Ad-Hoc - WSJ	**Newspaper**	**210K**
TREC Ad-Hoc - FT	**Newspaper**	**170K**
TREC Ad-Hoc - AP	**Newspaper**	**240K**
CLEF - Glasgow Herald	Newspaper	26K
CLEF - La Stampa	Newspaper	35K

3.1   Collections of Novel Documents

The CAW 2.0 Datasets. The first collection we present is the one developed for the Workshop for Content Analysis in Web 2.0 [12]. It is composed of documents crawled from different online sources and we use it as representative of the "novel documents" class in the analytic part of this article (Section 5): *Kongregate* (Internet Relay Chat -IRC- of online gamers), *Twitter* (short messages), *Myspace* (forum discussions) and *Slashdot* (comments on news-posts). The collection[9] is divided into training and testing set and for our experiments we used only the training part of the dataset, that was of sufficient size for our purposes. We present the actual statistics of the dataset in Section 4, while we analyse it in details in Section 5. One important aspect is its great novelty at time of creation. For example, in 2009 when the collection was released, Twitter was just emerging from the startups world but was already included in it. Moreover, we find in this collection both conversational documents and posts in blogs or fora, that, at that time, were just starting to capture the attention of the research community. For example, the Blog Track in TREC released the first corpus in 2006, while study on conversations started at the same time or later between 2008-2009 [13–15]. We can then conclude that this collection is

---

[9] Dataset and details available at `http://caw2.barcelonamedia.org/`

really the state-of-the-art and well suited for the kind of comparative study we are presenting.

Microsoft Conversation in Twitter Collection. This collection contains a corpus of 1.3 million Twitter conversations, which the authors made available in 2010 [16]. However, it was suddenly removed from the Internet[10], likely due to violations of Twitter's terms of service, that does not allow Twitter messages to be redistributed. In their work the authors [16] identified set of users "talking" together in the Twitter collection and studied this behaviour. They realise that "the proportion of posts on Twitter that are conversational in nature are somewhere around 37%", which is interesting and reinforce our interest for conversational documents [17].

IRC Conversational Dataset. This dataset was created with the purpose of developing algorithms able to automatically segment online conversations [13]. It was build recording all the messages on IRC channel #LINUX at `freenode.net` It was one of the first dataset of documents, together with the following NPS Chat corpus, containing conversations online . It is also quite popular among the Natural Language Processing (NLP) community [18]. One of the major weaknesses of this dataset is the relatively small number of documents contained and the fact that it is capturing only a single channel in the big panorama of IRC channels and providers. In fact, one would aim at a broader dataset, for example containing lot of channels with different topicalities [7].

The NPS Chat Corpus. This corpus[11] was developed for a study of online chat dialogs [19] and consists of a subset (about 10500 posts) out of approximately 500.000 posts the authors have crawled from various online chat services. It is distributed as part of the Natural Language Toolkit (NLTK)[12] or through the Linguistic Data Consortium.[13] Like the IRC Conversational Dataset, it contains a set of POS annotated posts divided by author characteristics (i.e. age and sex) but it does not contain information on the original source of such messages (i.e. from which online service were they originated) and on the exact extension in time of each chat. In fact, messages do not contain any timestamp information or any information about the length of the thread they are in. Finally, it is interesting to note that this dataset arose from one of the most active group in the field of conversational documents analysis. However, being this group strictly linked with organisations devoted to the national (U.S.) security, only limited information can be provided to the public. For example, some more detailed information on the larger NPS Chat dataset are only made available in [18] or [20], while the larger dataset is not made publicly available.

---

[10] A trace of the original page promoting the collections can still be found here: `http://web.archive.org/web/20100606154107/http://research.microsoft.com/en-us/downloads/8f8d5323-0732-4ba0-8c6d-a5304967cc3f/default.aspx`

[11] `http://faculty.nps.edu/cmartell/NPSChat.htm`

[12] `http://nltk.org`

[13] `http://www.ldc.upenn.edu` catalog id: LDC2010T05.

NUS SMS Corpus. This collection is slightly different from the other ones reported before because it does not include logs of IRC chats but only logs of SMS exchange. It was developed at the National University of Singapore (NUS) and contains hundreds of messages collected on a voluntary base between computer science students. After its creation in 2005, described by [21], it was left without any update for quite some time. In the last years (2012-1013), however, it has been updated on a regular basis and now it is growing every week, making it a live corpus online, as announced in [22].

The Blog Track in TREC and the Blog06 & Blog08 Collections. As part of the Blog Track[14] in TREC two collections were released, in 2006 (Blog06) and 2008 (Blog08) [23]. The two collections aim to be good representatives of the blogsphere, including both spam and non-blogs documents, like RSS feeds from news broadcasters. The contests organised in TREC from 2006 to 2010 were centred around these collections and covered different aspects of the blog analysis, from ad-hoc retrieval to top stories identification, from opinion finding to polarity detection. A complete survey [24] illustrates in-depth these tasks and collections, providing more details and references on each year's task edition.

The Microblog Track in TREC Corpus. The first Microblog collection[15] was released in 2011 as part of the first Microblog Track in TREC [25]. It represented the "evolution" of the previous Blog Track, that ceased in 2010 [24]. The organisers of TREC 2011 Microblog track released a tool for obtaining identifiers for approximately 16 million Tweets and each participant in the track had to autonomously download every Twitter message with the provided tool, in order not to violate the Twitter service agreement. The corpus was designed to be a reusable and representative sample of the twittersphere, including both important and spam tweets, therefore a must-have for all researchers interested in analysing documents from social media. This collection served primarily as testbed for the problem of ad-hoc retrieval, with attention to the temporal dimension, i.e. retrieval of important past tweets given a query and a certain date. In 2013 the track moved to an API based collections (collection-as-a-service), that allows users to query it and get tweets accordingly, instead of downloading a massive number of documents (around 240 millions, according to the organisers), as it was in the first edition. Unlike in the previous Twitter collection, these ones do not contain any grouping of the messages into conversations, moreover they really are huge collections. For these reasons the identification of the conversations and the filtering of non relevant messages (e.g. in a language other then English or spam messages) is complicated and computationally expensive. We employed in our experiments the previous Twitter collections (the one in the CAW 2.0 datasets) as representative of Twitter messages, because it was enough for our analysis. To conclude, the Twitter collections presented in this section are the most popular and the best suiting our experimental needs.

---

[14] http://ir.dcs.gla.ac.uk/wiki/TREC-BLOG
[15] http://trec.nist.gov/data/tweets/

In literature there are, however, several other collections of Twitter documents e.g. the one employed in the RepLab[16] as part of CLEF that interested users should investigate depending on their needs.

Enron Email Dataset. This dataset contains email from around 160 employee of the Enron company, made available during the legal investigation that followed the company bankruptcy in 2001. Different sources offer this collection as download but we mention here one of the most reliable[17], that is associated to publication [26] describing its properties. This is one of the few datasets containing emails and it is a good representative for those willing to study this kind of documents.

CLEF-PAN 2012 SPI. To conclude this overview of collections of novel documents, we mention one of the most recent and complete collections of online conversations we created in a previous work [27]. This collection incorporates 4 different dataset of IRC logs ("perverted justice", "krjin", "irclogs" and "omegle") and was originally designed to solve the problems of i) finding users that manifest unacceptable or illegal behaviour (such as a sexual predator) among a set of conversations and ii) to identify the lines of the conversations where this behaviour manifested. For this reason a small number of conversations between a predator and a victim are presents in the collection (around 1%) together with a relatively small set of false positive, represented by conversations between strangers (e.g. from `http://www.omegle.com`), while the vast majority of the collection contains homogeneous documents. These documents are centred on topics related to HTML 5 (e.g. html5, css, micro formats, accessibility, ...) or other field of informatics (e.g. java, gentoo, macosx, php, oracle, samba, ...). Despite this homogeneity of topics, however, in many cases users engaged in conversations that diverged from the expected technical topic, discussing, for example, about family's life, general interests and sometimes even anger.

3.2 Collections of Traditional Documents

Trec Ad-hoc (Tipster). The TREC ad-hoc collection [28] is the result of the earlier TREC conference series, originated from the TIPSTER project.[18] The ad-hoc collection contains different datasets, each with its own characteristics and a own set of topics (questions), and a corresponding set of relevance judgments (right answers). For the purpose of our studies, we are not interested in all the documents type present in the ad-hoc collection, like the Federal Register or the Congressional Record, but only at those that could contained factual

---

[16] `http://www.limosine-project.eu/events/replab2012` and
   `http://www.limosine-project.eu/events/replab2013`
[17] `http://www.cs.cmu.edu/~enron/`
[18] As from `http://trec.nist.gov/faq.html` "TIPSTER was a DARPA-sponsored project that encouraged the advancement of state-of-the-art technologies for text handling [...], successfully concluded in 1998", while TREC still continues nowadays.

or topical documents, like the Wall Street Journal (WSJ), the Associated Press (AP) and the Financial Times Limited (FT). We therefore considered only these three sets[19] of documents in our studies in Section 5.

CLEF 2004-2008. Another example of set with newspaper articles comes from the Cross-Language Evaluation Forum (CLEF),[20] in particular from the CLEF ad-hoc news Test Suites, for the years 2004-2008. This collection is similar in purpose to the TREC ones, containing both topics (queries) and relevance judgments (relevant documents). For this reason we only employed this later ones in our studies but we should mention the multi-language nature of the CLEF collections, that contains documents as articles from newspapers of different languages (from Bulgarian to Dutch, from Italian to Persian) [29].

4   General Properties of Novel Collections

In the previous section we presented different collections containing novel documents, from chat to microblog, from forum to newsgroup. In this section, instead, we select a representative subset of novel and traditional collection and present their overall properties, leaving the comparative analysis to the next section.

As representative of the novel type of collections, we use the documents from the CAW 2.0 collection, in particular those of chat (Kongregate), messages exchange (Twitter) and blog posting (Myspace and Slashdot). We compare these collections with the traditional newspaper collection of documents, in particular WSJ, AP (news article) and FT (markets and finance) from the TREC ad-hoc collection. We notice that these collections show a similar topicality to the collections of novel documents used for the comparison, in particular with Myspace and Slashdot. The Myspace dataset covers the themes of campus life, news & politics and movies, while the Slashdot dataset is limited to discussions of politics. The fact that the themes are similar to the news articles is important in order to make statistical comparison between the collections meaningful. As for the topicality of the Twitter and Kongregate datasets, due to their conversational and more unpredictable nature, we cannot state precisely what their topicality is [30–32].

In Figure 2 we display the average document length for the some popular collections of documents, including the ones employed in our analysis: CAW 2.0 and TREC ad-hoc. It is straightforward to identify a common trait of the CAW 2.0 documents, that is the relatively shortness compared to the traditional TREC ad-hoc collection. We list here below this and other important intuitive properties of the novel documents. They are:

– short: they have a length between few to 100 words per document as opposed to traditional newspaper articles of more then 400 words per document;

---

[19] Available at http://trec.nist.gov/data/docs_eng.html
[20] http://www.clef-initiative.eu//

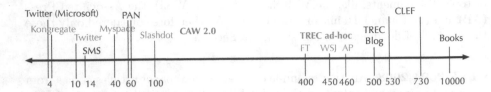

Fig. 2. Average document length (in number of words) for different collections. On the left (in red) the novel datasets analized (CAW 2.0); on the right (in blue) the standard newspaper datasets (TREC ad-hoc).

- user-generated: because they are produce directly by a person using a particular online service, without any review process as it happens to journalists or professional writers, who to the contrary generate "edited" content;
- "dirty", as a consequence of being user-generated and most of the time typed as fast as possible on the keyboard in emulating spoken acts, they contains spelling errors, domain specific terms or abbreviations.

We report in Table 2 some basic statistics about these datasets, where these properties can be seen. In particular, the difference in the average document length is evident: the novel collections contain documents that are 5 to 100 times shorter compared to the traditional newspaper articles. We will examine in Section 5 the implications of this property in terms of the document self-similarity and burstiness, where we will explain also the role of common and rare words.

5   Analysis of the Datasets

In performing the analysis of the chosen collections (see Table 1), we focus on the "text processing" block of Figure 1, employing some basics laws of IR, in particular the Zipf's Law and the Heap's Law and an elementary document's distance measure: the cosine similarity. We then make use of a simple information extraction technique to detect the structure of the documents in terms or their lexical categories (e.g. noun, verbs, adjectives, as well as emotions and "shoutings").

Some preliminary information about differences between novel and standard collections can be observed in inspecting the statistics presented in Table 2. To generate those statistics we first indexed the documents in each collection without employing any text processing techniques (e.g without removing any stopword or stemming), then we just used a standard stopword[21] list to filter

---

[21] Different standard stopword lists exist in literature, mostly generated taking into consideration the distribution of terms in classical books or newspaper collection. For the purpose of this work we made use of a standard stopword list from one on the most widely used IR platforms: Terrier (http://terrier.org).

Table 2. Statistics of datasets. All values were computed before stopword removal unless indicated.

Collection	Size # documents	avg. doc. length # words	avg. word length # characters
Kongregate	144.161	4,50	7,55
Twitter	977.569	13,90	7,30
Myspace	144.161	38,08	8,11
Slashdot	141.283	98,91	7,88
WSJ	173.252	452,00	7,57
AP	242.918	464,23	7,53
FT	210.158	401,22	7,26

(a)

Collection	Vocabulary	% terms in the vocabulary that are:				
		stopword	out-of-dictionary	singleton	common words	rare words
Kongregate	35.208	44,90	58,94	56,65	1,39	84,65
Twitter	364.367	44,99	68,37	66,95	0,20	97,19
Myspace	187.050	50,67	69,61	53,30	0,39	96,10
Slashdot	123.359	54,00	57,31	44,82	0,45	95,88
WSJ	226.469	41,45	67,57	34,33	0,44	96,85
AP	242.918	43,70	75,22	35,77	0,40	97,34
FT	210.158	42,45	61,22	36,45	0,36	97,23

(b)

them. For the novel collections we expected less terms to be discarded as stopword, since we assume short documents (in particular the ones used to "chat" as Kongregate or the Twitter microblog) to be written "quicker and dirtier", with no care for the syntactical structure of the sentences and using a lot of abbreviations. Surprisingly the quantity of stopword for novel collections is just slightly above the quantity of standard collections, with an increase for collections representing blog and fora (Myspace and Slashdot). A better evidence to support our hypothesis can be found in looking at the percentage of terms which occurred only once in the collection ("singleton terms"). The novel collections contain definitely more singleton terms, which we can consider as spelling mistakes or mistyped words. This is more evident when observing out-of-dictionary terms. These words are not contained in a standard dictionary and are identified as misspelled by a spelling checker algorithm. Although the percentage of out-of-dictionary terms is similar across all datasets, we noticed that for documents within the novel collections this value is closer to the number of singleton words (from 2% to 16%), while for traditional TREC collections the value is different (around 33%). This fact may indicate that in the novel collections the presence of more singleton words could be considered as an indicator of a greater number of mistyped words but also indicator of unique link identifier, e.g. shortened through services like `https://bitly.com` or `http://tinyurl.com` that were not removed during the indexing procedure. This is not the case of the traditional TREC collections, where the presence of singleton words is less evident and can be explained by the usage of particular terms such as geographical locations, foreign words or person names which are orthographically correct but not present in the spelling checker used. Different conclusions can be drawn when observing the percentage of common and rare terms. Common terms are defined as the most frequent words in the vocabulary, that account for more than 71% of the text in each collection, while rare terms are the least frequent words in the vocabulary, that account for just 8% of the text, as indicated in [33]. Common terms contribute more for Kongregate, which is a collection of conversational documents between online gamers, in which the language of the users repeats a lot and the topical words are fewer, compare to the other collections. On the opposite, the Twitter collection presents fewer common words, a behaviour that might indicate that Twitter documents are somehow more topical. This means that they also contain useful information for characterise them and better retrieve them, as opposed to Kongregate ones, in which a larger part of the vocabulary contains common words.

5.1 Zipf's Law (Frequency Spectrum)

The Zipf's Law as described in [11] is an empirical rule that describes the frequency of the text words and states informally that the frequency of any word in a collection is inversely proportional to its rank in the frequency table. It is described as follows [34], in the extend formulation of Mandelbrot:

$$\log f(w) = \log C - \alpha \, \log\left(r(w) - b\right) \tag{1}$$

where $f(w)$ denotes the frequency of a word w in the collection and $r(w)$ is the ranking of the word (in terms of its frequency), while C and b are collection specific parameters. As can be seen in Figure 3, in a log-log scale and for large values of $r(w)$, the relationship between frequency and rank of a word can be approximated with a descending straight line of slope $-\alpha$.

Two properties of the Zipf's law are particular interesting when we study collections of documents. In fact, if we assume that the terms in the collection follow the Zipf's law, we can derive the expected proportion of a term in the collection by its rank and we know that few words, generally the least informative ones, occupy a large amount of the vocabulary. The first observation is useful for scoring words, i.e. in the case of ad-hoc retrieval, while the second allows to define which words can be discarded before indexing, by identifying stopwords.

If we observe Figure 3, for both the novel and traditional documents a linear graph is observed. This is an interesting observation, that shows how the usage of terms in the novel collection is comparable to the traditional ones and, therefore, all the assumptions done in this context for the latter are also valid for the former. Moreover we noticed a dependence between the length of the documents and the slope: the collections containing longer documents tend to have a larger negative

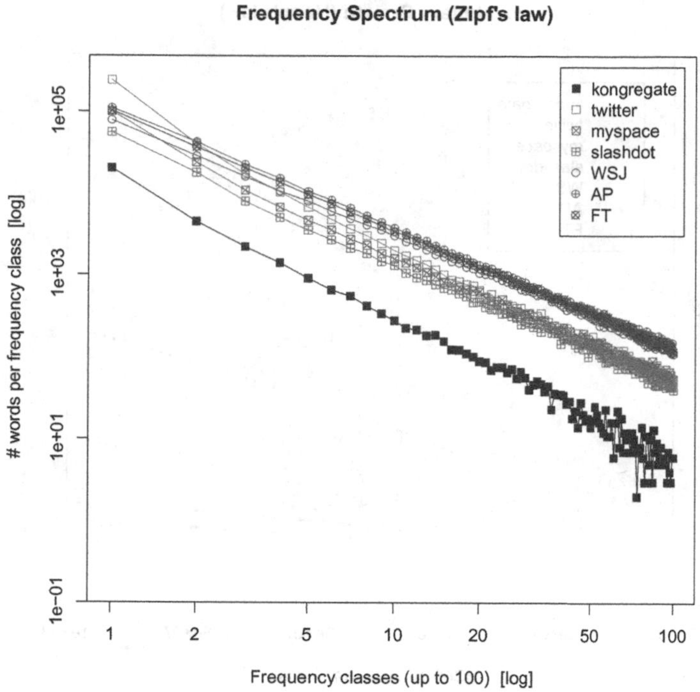

Frequency Spectrum (Zipf's law)

Fig. 3. Zipf's law for novel and traditional collections after stopword removal

slope, which may mean that the words in them are repeated more frequently, while the collections containing shorter documents are less repetitive. The same behaviour might be observed in the next section.

5.2 Heap's Law (Vocabulary Growth)

The Heap's law is an empirical rule which describes the vocabulary growth as a function of the text size, as described in [11]. Its formulation can be written as follow [2]:

$$v = k \cdot n^{\beta} \tag{2}$$

where v is the vocabulary size of n words, while k and β are collection's dependent parameters.

The Heap's law states informally that the vocabulary of a collection continues to grow with the addition of novel documents, although at a different rate with respect to the beginning. Figure 4 shows the vocabulary growth with respect to the size of the whole collection. We can observe that the vocabulary of collections of novel documents grows much faster in comparison with those containing standard documents. This suggests that conversations between users in Kongregate or broadcast messages of users in Twitter tends to vary greatly with the usage of ever more terms, according to the evolution of topics inside a

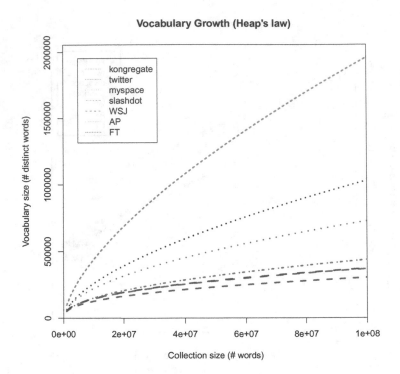

Fig. 4. Heap's law for novel and traditional collections after stopword removal

conversation or the sentiment of a Twitter user. This may be partially explained by the high percentage of singleton, out-of-dictionary, mistyped words, abbreviations or links that are continuously introduced during the production of such documents.

We also noticed a relationship between the decreasing value of the slopes of the Zipf's law and the growth of the vocabulary. Twitter has the minimum slope in the case of Zipf's law but the maximum vocabulary growth. To the contrary WSJ has the maximum slope and the minimum vocabulary growth. This could, again, be explained by the high frequency of mistyped terms in the vocabulary of novel collections in comparison to the standard collections.

5.3 Self-similarity

Another interesting property that can be used to characterise novel collections over standard collections is the self-similarity between documents. In IR there are different similarity measures that can be used to compute the distance between two texts (see Section 2.2), but the cosine correlation similarity proved to works better than others in particular for the task of ad-hoc retrieval. This similarity measure is generally applied to measure the distance between a text in a document (D) and a query (Q). The name is due to the measure used to calculate the similarity between the text and the query, which are represented as vector of terms. In determining the distance, the inner product between the two vectors is computed and the result of the product is between 1, if the two vector are identical, and 0, if they are completely disjoint (no terms in common). The formula of the cosine similarity is expressed by the following equation [2]:

$$cosine(D_i, Q) = \frac{\sum_{j=1}^{t} d_{ij} \cdot q_j}{\sqrt{\sum_{j=1}^{t} d_{ij}^2 \cdot \sum_{j=1}^{t} q_j^2}} \tag{3}$$

where D_i is a particular document in the collection with terms $(d_1, d_2, ..., d_t)$ and Q is a query with terms $(q_1, q_2, ..., q_t)$. In our case, we want to compute the similariy between two documents, therefore we should substitute Q with another document in the collection i.e D_k and q_j becomes consequently d_{kj}. At the numerator, for each matching term t the inner product is computed employing the score associated with each term, while at the denominator a normalisation depending on the length of the two vector is performed.

Traditionally the weight associated with each term for the cosine similarity is computed employing the *tf-idf* weighting. The *tf* component considers the relative frequency of a term in the document, while *idf* reflects the importance of the term in the collection.

$$tf_{ik} = \frac{f_{ij}}{\sum_{k=1}^{t} t_{ik}} \tag{4}$$

$$idf_k = \log \frac{N}{df_k} \tag{5}$$

In Equation 4 the formula for the *tf* is displayed, where f_{ij} is the number of occurrences of a term j in a particular document i, normalised by the length of the document. In Equation 5 the formula for the *idf* is illustrated, where N is the total number of documents in the collection and df_i is the number of documents in which term k occurs. The final score is obtained multiplying the two components together $tf_{ik} \cdot idf_k$, hence the name *tf-idf* score.

In this experiment, we computed the similarity for all the documents in each collection, to study how these documents are similar to each other. The computation of the cosine similarity employing *tf-idf* weighting was done after having removed the stopwords from the documents. We decided to display only WSJ as representative of the traditional collections, having observed a similar behaviour also for the other collections.

In Figure 5 we plot the frequency of each similarity class (from 0 to 1), interpolated by lines for visual purposes. A first observation at the general picture (Figure 5a) allows already to identify the most evident difference between the novel collections (Kongregate, Twitter, Myspace and Slashdot) and the traditional ones (represented by the WSJ) at the extremes of the similarity graph.

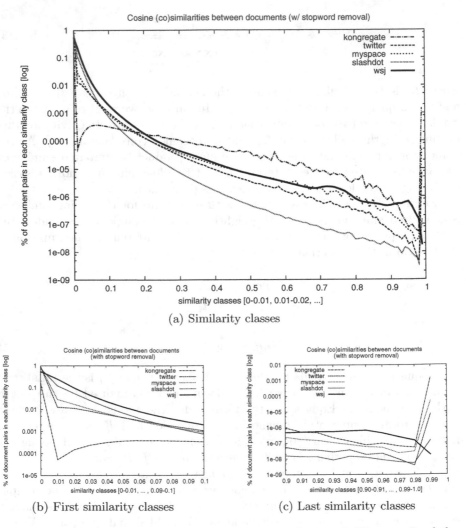

(a) Similarity classes

(b) First similarity classes

(c) Last similarity classes

Fig. 5. Self-similarity between documents after stopword removal. We normalized the count for document in each similarity class by the total number of comparisons.

For this reason we also zoom in to show only the percentage of document pairs with the lowest (Figure 5b) and highest (Figure 5c) similarity scores. The rest of the graph shows a similar trend for all the collections, although with lot of variations also among the novel collections.

In the first similarity class we observe that documents of novel collections appear less frequently with lower similarity values (0.01-0.09), as they become shorter (from Kongregate to Slashdot). To the contrary, they appear more frequently with higher similarity values (0.9-1.00), in contrast with the behaviour of the documents contained in traditional collections. This latter, in fact, drops down when we consider only the last similarity range (0.99-1.00).

This means that documents from novel collections seem to be more similar among themselves than longer ones. This can be explained with the length of the documents itself: short documents contain less words (less "information"). Therefore, given two short documents, there is an higher probability that they appear to be similar even if they are unrelated, just because they are short.

5.4   Burstiness

In this section we perform another analysis on the collections under collections, where we study the burstiness property of the words. There is not a unique and formal definition of burstiness in literature, but it is generally considered the property of a term to recur more often in documents or part of text where it is already mentioned rather than in other random places, thus characterising that particular document or part of text. In Figure 6 we display this property for a particular set of terms, common and rare, as defined at the beginning of Section 5. The plots display the percentage of documents in each collection that contains a certain number of common or rare words.

In each plot we show also the expected number of such documents if the words in the vocabulary were uniformly distributed (according to their overall frequency in the collection) across the documents in the collection. Differences between the curves for actual and expected number of documents indicates that terms in the different classes manifest the burstiness property.

Looking at the common terms plot for the three traditional collections (AP, FT, WSJ), we notice that the line denoting the actual number of documents with a certain number of common terms in them lies well below the expected number of such documents. This indicates that documents are bursty, since common terms are not spread evenly across the collection of documents, but are concentrated more in some documents than others. The same is true (although to a less extent) for the rare terms in these collections: the actual number of documents containing a certain number of rare words lies below the expected curve, again indicating that documents are bursty, since the rare words are not uniformly distributed across documents.

Comparing the plots for the novel collections (Kongregate, Twitter, Myspace and Slashdot) with those for the traditional collections, we observe that the difference between the expected and actual number of documents is far less pronounced (especially for the common terms) than it is for the traditional ones.

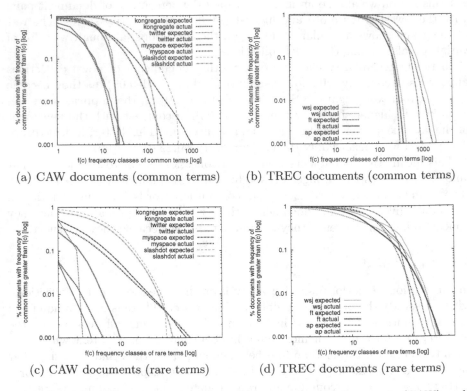

(a) CAW documents (common terms)   (b) TREC documents (common terms)

(c) CAW documents (rare terms)   (d) TREC documents (rare terms)

Fig. 6. Common and rare term burstiness for user-generated documents (CAW) and traditional ones (TREC)

This indicates that burstiness may not be an important issue for novel collection as it is for traditional collections.

The fact that the expected/actual curves for the different novel collections differ greatly from one another, positioning in different part of the plot, is due to the large difference in average document length in the different collections. The display of this curves, in fact, follow the same order as the average length of documents in each collection. The curves for the traditional collections, instead, line up quite well due to the fact that the average document length is very similar.

5.5 Part-Of-Speech Distribution

In this section we analyse the grammatical properties of the terms in each collection, i.e. looking at the number of noun, adjectives, verbs, etc present in each document. In order to do this, we employed a posting list where each word is assigned to

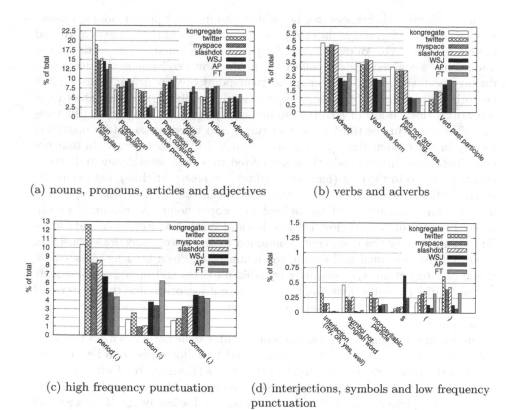

(a) nouns, pronouns, articles and adjectives

(b) verbs and adverbs

(c) high frequency punctuation

(d) interjections, symbols and low frequency punctuation

Fig. 7. POS analysis

one grammatical category: the framework GATE [22] and its component ANNIE[23] [35, 36] dedicated to this kind of analysis, called Part-Of-Speech (POS) analysis.

In Figure 7 we report the results of the POS analysis of the full text on 30% of the documents in the collection, selected at random (since we did not find significant variation in the distributions with an higher subset). We used the ANNIE default settings, which include a posting list based on newspaper articles, and report in Figure 7 only the most significant categories.[24]

If we observe in detail the results of Figure 7 we notice two different behaviours: first, some inter-collection variations, between the novel collections and the traditional collections, then an intra-collection variation within the novel collections, between chat-style and discussion-style documents.

---

[22] GATE: "General Architecture for Text Engineering", http://gate.ac.uk/

[23] ANNIE: "A Nearly-New Information Extraction System", http://gate.ac.uk/

[24] A complete list of the POS tag extracted by ANNIE can be found on http://tinyurl.com/gate-pos

Inter-collection differences can be seen in the usage of proper nouns, possessive pronouns and plural noun in Figure 7a as well as in the usage of verb and
adverb in Figure 7b. An explanation for this may be found in the nature of the
documents contained in each collection: in the novel collections the users producing the texts are willing to express their point of view or emotions against
the others (high usage of possessive pronouns), qualifying the amount of their
sensations (high usage of adverb), addressing directly in first person (high usage of verb not in the third person singular) and referring to action occurring
mostly in the present time (verb in base form). To the contrary, texts that are
contained in traditional collections are edited in a professional way and report
events occurred in the past (high usage of verb in past participle), not occurring
to the author itself (high usage of third person in the verb) or taking place in
a particular location (higher use of singular proper noun). Moreover, if we observe the usage of punctuation, interjection and symbols in Figure 7c and Figure
7d, we notice how the documents contained in the novel collections consist of
a more direct, personal and simple communication, given by a more extensive
usage of interjection, symbols, monosyllabic particles and periods. Documents
in the traditional collections, instead, are more descriptive, due to the usage of
colons and commas, which generally link together different concepts inside the
same sentence.

Intra-collection differences, on the other hand, can be noticed within the novel
collection, where some datasets (Myspace and Slashdot) appear to be more related to the traditional collections than the others (Kongregate, Twitter), which
highlight different properties. These properties are an high usage of proper singular nouns, periods, interjections and symbol, and a less usage of articles and
adjectives, which becomes the least among all the collection for verbs in the past
form and commas. These can be seen as attributes of an essential and immediate communication, such as the online-chat (Kongregate) or microblog (Twitter).
Despite that, for some POS categories the Myspace and Slashdot datasets are
similar to or just in-between with the traditional TREC datasets: this appear
for preposition and subordinative conjunction, adjectives (Figure 7a), verb in
the past partiple form (Figure 7b) as well as for periods, commas (Figure 7c)
and interjections (Figure 7d). We therefore label these collections (Myspace and
Slashdot) as containing discussion-style documents [37], opposed to the conversational ones (Kongregate, Twitter).

5.6   Emoticons and "Shoutings" Distributions

In this last section we complement the POS analysis of Section 5.5 by investigating the distribution of emoticons and "shoutings" among the different collections.
These features, in fact, can be very discriminative for identifying user-generated
content [38] and in particular conversational data [31].

We collected a list of the most common emoticons (mostly through Wikipedia)
and parsed each document by comparing each token separately with a regular
expression, thus identifying and counting only whitespace separated emoticons

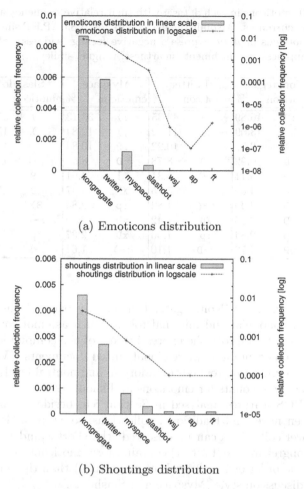

(a) Emoticons distribution

(b) Shoutings distribution

Fig. 8. Collection relative emoticons and shoutings distributions

(such as :) and :P).[25] In a similar way we the counted so-called "shoutings", that we define as whitespace separated tokens containing a succession of three-or-more consecutive instances of the same letter (e.g. zzzz and mmmmaybe). We did not include in this count tokens containing internet addresses (www and WWW) since they do not provide additional information on the collections being analysed.

In Figure 8 we report the distribution of the emoticons and shoutings for all the collections. The values represented are the relative collection frequency in both the linear and log scale. The behaviour of the distributions is similar and reflect the nature of the collections. The novel collections containing

---

[25] We experimented also with matching emoticons within sequences of characters like hello:)mum but obtained too many false positives to consider those results valid. For the same reason, we did not count emoticons containing whitespaces such as :⊔).

Table 3. Top 10 emoticons in each dataset with their relative frequency as a percentage of all emoticon occurrences. We omit the few counts for WSJ,AP,FT since they are not informative. Emoticons in *italic* express a negative feeling (sadness), all the others a positive one (happiness, astonishment, smartness, tongue, smiley,...).

	Kongregate emoticon	%	Twitter emoticon	%	Myspace emoticon	%	Slashdot emoticon	%
1	:P	16.89	:)	43.35	:)	33.13	:)	37.26
2	XD	13.09	;)	11.12	;)	12.84	;)	17.75
3	:)	12.72	:-)	10.22	:P	10.84	:-)	14.92
4	:D	10.92	:D	8.78	:D	8.93	;-)	10.56
5	-.-	5.11	;-)	5.31	:]	4.61	:P	5.42
6	xD	4.62	:P	5.15	XD	3.47	:D	2.94
7	:0	3.45	:-(	1.82	:p	2.84	B)	1.94
8	=D	2.95	XD	1.42	=P	2.39	:-(	1.36
9	:p	2.84	:p	1.36	xD	2.37	:p	1.19
10	=P	2.72	:-D	1.10	:-)	1.61	:-P	1.04

user-generated documents (Kongregate, Twitter, Myspace, Slashdot) present a large number of colloquial and informal tokens, such as emoticons and shoutings, that are used to improve the expressiveness of the communication. In the standard collections containing professional edited documents (WSJ, AP, FT), instead, the communication remains on a formal and neutral level (having these collection almost zero counts for emoticons and shoutings).

As for the POS features analysed in Section 5.5, beside the inter-class differences between novel and traditional collections, some intra-class differences among the novel collections can be observed: the shorter and more colloquial documents (Kongregate and Twitter) contain more emoticons and shoutings occurrences (on the order of 1 or 2 levels of magnitude) than the documents that are more of a discussion-style (Myspace and Slashdot).

5.7   Summary

In this section we studied the properties of novel collections of user-generated documents introduced recently in the literature. We compared them with traditional collections employed in IR. Our analysis was both qualitative and quantitative: different metrics were employed to compare the collections, including the Zipf's and Heap's law, the cosine similarity, the burstiness, a generic POS analysis and a specialised one to detect emoticons and shoutings. We selected four particular collections as representative of novel documents: conversational documents, microblog documents and documents from fora and blogs. We also made use of two standard collection of newspaper article as representative of traditional documents.

From the studies conducted we observed different properties of documents belonging to the novel collections with respect to the ones belonging to the

Table 4. A summary of the dimensions investigated and the different properties of each class of documents

Dimensions	Standard Documents	Novel documents	
		discussion-style	chat-style
Length of the documents	long		short
Zipf's law (slope in log-log scale)	linear		
Heap's law (convergence)	fast	slow	very slow
Self-Similarity (cosine)	always decreasing	increasing at the extremes	
Burstiness behaviour	evident	not so evident	
Part-of-Speech	structured text	poorly structured	no structure
Emoticons	none	few	lots
Shoutings	none	few	lots

standard collections, that we summarised in Table 4. In the next section we highlight these properties and illustrate techniques for making these novel documents suitable for standard IR systems. In particular we present approaches for dealing with spelling mistakes and emoticons, as part of the unconventional language present in the novel collections, as well as for treating short and casual documents contained in them. We concluded with a list of possible indicators to be combined with standard IR metrics to improve the characterisations of documents from social media.

6 Novel Challenges in Information Retrieval for Social Media

In the previous sections we presented a series of analysis to characterise collections of documents that are new to IR and compared them to traditional collections of newspaper articles or webpages. The novel collections contained documents of different kind, from online conversations to microblog, from blogs to fora, and are good representative of the so-called social media. The main question that arises after this analysis is: *what is the real applicability of these results in the field of IR?* We report some general observations in the following sections.

The techniques mentioned below are some basics examples of techniques that might be employed when dealing with documents originated from social media. These suggestions should serve as starting point for researchers wanted to start investigating this area as they constitutes building block for more complex and advanced systems. In fact, in all the different studies of collections generated from social media available in the literature in the latest year, at least one of the techniques mentioned in here is employed.

6.1 Documents Normalization

Document in the novel collections are dirty, containing a large and growing number of typos, spelling mistakes, grammatical errors and abbreviations (see beginning of Section 5, Sections 5.2 and 5.5). On the other hand, traditional techniques of IR assume the text in input to the IR system to be clean and consistent. For these reasons it is very important to be able to identify such "dirty" components in the texts and be able to "normalise" them. This "normalisation" process can be done at parser level, within the 'text processing' component of the IR system (Figure 1) in different ways. One possibility would be the corrections of the spelling mistakes with the help of a spelling checker. Another possibility might be the substitution of the abbreviations with their longer meaning, according to a posting list of most used expressions. In a last example, one might also decide to preserve those terms and consider them as neologism to be used to characterise a certain portion of a text, a specific document or a particular user associated with them. Emoticons, in particular, might be preserved and later used to detect the sentiment associated to the text they were attached to. We can conclude mentioning a useful tool that was designed specifically to parse and extract POS for Twitter [39] and that is able to parse and recognise, among others, emoticons, abbreviations and urls.

6.2   Documents Expansion

Documents in the novel collections are *short or very short*, in fact so short that they might be considered similar to each other even if they are part of a different context (see Section 5.3). This fact is interesting because it means that if we want to analyse documents from the novel collections, we cannot simply use the same techniques of traditional IR as if they were standard documents. In this latter case, in fact, if we process a single documents with traditional IR techniques, it is often long enough to extract meaningful information from it. In the first case, instead, a single document is generally too short to be able to provide enough information if it is processed with traditional IR techniques. For this reason, these short documents are often aggregated in a single longer document, to be later processed easier. There are different strategies for combining short documents into longer and more complex ones. One of the simplest methods is concatenating documents according to some proximity. Temporal proximity involves merging documents that were created close-in-time. Semantical proximity involves joining text with the same approximate content. Proximity based on the authorship implies concatenating documents produced by the same author. These operations, however, are not obvious and they are applications dependent. For example, it is relatively easy to concatenate documents of the same author if we want to profile and retrieve these documents based on their authors, like it is done for documents in traditional collections. It is, nevertheless, more difficult to decide which documents to concatenate if we want only those related to a certain topic, as characterising the content is not an easy problem. An approach based on simultaneous combination of different strategies might be of help in this case.

6.3   Documents Enrichment

Documens in the novel collections are less bursty, thus *less topically defined* (see Section 5.4), compared to the ones contained in traditional collections. As briefly stated before, a possibility would be to merge them according to some criteria. The idea is that from a longer text, the topical components would emerged easier and stronger than in a shorter text. However, sometimes this is not enough, therefore we should find other ways to better characterise them. One possibility is to expand their semantical content, starting from the few topical words contained in them and deriving from those additional text fragment from other sources. Having just few words to start with, the easiest thing to do would be to look in a standard dictionary and expand the single terms with their descriptions. This is however quite simplistic: a more refined possibility would be to substitute their dictionary entry with the Wikipedia definition, to have a richer and more diverse set of additional terms. Additionally one could employ conceptual-semantic networks like Wordnet, to navigate along related terms and find new concepts to be inserted in the original text or expanded iteratively. Moreover, since documents in the novel collections often contain links to webpages, another possibility would be to concatenate the text from these webpages to the original document, always to obtain a richer description of the underlined topic.

6.4   Language Analysis

Standard normalising techniques or scoring measures of IR (like the *tf-idf*) rely on the simple textual content of the documents. These methods can also be applied to documents in the novel collection only if some proper preprocessing is employed. The preprocessing techniques include all the steps indicated above, from errors correction, to documents merging and expansions. However, since documents in the novel collections are also more expressive than the ones in traditional collections (see Sections 5.5 and 5.6), it might be interesting and effective to combine standard IR scoring with scoring based on other different indicators based on language analysis.[26] We already mentioned emoticons as a way of complementing the standard textual informations in a documents. Emoticons indicate a particular emotion associated to the fragment of text and these can indeed be used to better characterise the text. Besides emotions, other indicators that can be derived and combined with standard textual information are polarity (if the text contains or not opinions), sentiment (if the opinion attached to the text is positive, negative or neutral) or other figurative expressions (like humour or irony).

---

[26] Another research area, Natural Language Processing (NLP), have been studying usage of language in written documents and this is the case where IR and NLP techniques are really effective if combined.

7   Conclusions

In this article we introduced some novel challenges of IR derived by the introduction of novel collections of user-generated documents. We first illustrated the purpose of an IR system and list some of the most popular novel collections in the literature. We then analysed the general properties of the documents belonging to the novel collections, concentrating on four particular collections: conversational documents, microblog documents and documents from fora and blogs. The studies presented in this article makes a comparison between these four classes of documents belonging to novel collections and a set of standard collections employed traditionally in IR containing professional edited documents (newspaper articles). Different metrics were employed to compare the collections, including the Zipf's and Heap's law, the cosine similarity, the burstiness and both a generic POS analysis and a specialised one to detect emoticons and shoutings. From these studies we observed different properties of documents belonging to the novel collections with respect to the ones belonging to the standard collections. In the last part of the article we highlight these properties and illustrated techniques for making these novel documents suitable for standard IR systems. In particular we presented methods for dealing with spelling mistakes and emoticons, as part of an unconventional language present in the novel collections, as well as for treating short and casual documents in there contained. We concluded with a list of possible indicators to be combined with standard IR metrics to improve the characterisations of documents from social media.

Acknowledgments. The authors would like to thank Dr. Mark James Carman, who contributed to the two papers this article is an extension of. The original work was partially supported by the Swiss National Science Foundation (SNSF) project Mining Conversational Content for Topic Modelling and Author Identification (ChatMiner) with grant nr. 200021_130208.

References

1. Mendenhall, T.C.: The characteristic curves of composition. Science, 237–246 (1887)
2. Croft, B., Metzler, D., Strohman, T.: Search Engines: Information Retrieval in Practice. Addison Wesley (2009)
3. Salton, G.: Automatic Information Organization and Retrieval. McGraw Hill Text (1968)
4. Lo, R.T.W., He, B., Ounis, I.: Automatically building a stopword list for an information retrieval system. JDIM 3(1), 3–8 (2005)
5. Manning, C.D., Raghavan, P., Schutze, H.: Introduction to Information Retrieval. Cambridge University Press (2008)
6. Cover, T., Thomas, J.: Elements of Information Theory. Wiley Series in Telecommunications and Signal Processing. John Wiley & Sons (2006)
7. Inches, G., Harvey, M., Crestani, F.: Finding participants in a chat: Authorship attribution for conversational documents. In: ASE/IEEE International Conference on Social Computing, Washington, DC, USA, pp. 272–279 (September 2013)

8. Savoy, J.: Authorship Attribution Based on Specific Vocabulary. ACM Transactions on Information Systems 30(2), 1–30 (2012)
9. Bader, B.W., Chew, P.A.: Algebraic Techniques for Multilingual Document Clustering. In: Text Mining: Applications and Theory, pp. 21–36. John Wiley & Sons, Ltd. (2010)
10. Bishop, C.M.: Pattern Recognition and Machine Learning. Springer-Verlag New York, Inc. (2006)
11. Baeza-Yates, R., Ribeiro-Neto, B.: Modern Information Retrieval: The Concepts and Technology behind Search, 2nd edn. Addison-Wesley Professional (2011)
12. Codina, J., Kaltenbrunner, A., Grivolla, J., Banchs, R.E., Baeza-Yates, R.: Content analysis in web 2.0. In: 18th International World Wide Web Conference (2009)
13. Elsner, M., Charniak, E.: You Talking to Me? A Corpus and Algorithm for Conversation Disentanglement. In: Proceedings of ACL 2008: HLT, pp. 834–842 (2008)
14. Wang, L., Oard, D.W.: Context-based message expansion for disentanglement of interleaved text conversations. In: NAACL 2009, pp. 200–208 (2009)
15. Layton, R., McCombie, S., Watters, P.: Authorship attribution of irc messages using inverse author frequency. In: 3rd Cybercrime and Trustworthy Computing Workshop (CTC), pp. 1–8 (2012)
16. Ritter, A., Cherry, C., Dolan, B.: Unsupervised Modeling of Twitter Conversations. In: Human Language Technologies: The 2010 Annual Conference of the North American Chapter of the Association for Computational Linguistics, pp. 172–180 (2010)
17. Inches, G., Crestani, F.: Online conversation mining for author characterization and topic identification. In: Proceedings of the 4th Workshop for Ph.D. Students in Information & Knowledge Management - PIKM 2011 (2011)
18. Lin, J.: Automatic Author Profiling of Online Chat Logs. PhD thesis, Naval Postgraduate School, Monterey, USA (2007)
19. Forsythand, E.N., Martell, C.H.: Lexical and Discourse Analysis of Online Chat Dialog. In: International Conference on Semantic Computing (ICSC), pp. 19–26 (2007)
20. Durham, J.S.: Topic detection in online chat. Master's thesis, Naval Postgraduate School, Monterey, USA (2009)
21. How, Y., Kan, M.: Optimizing predictive text entry for short message service on mobile phones. In: Human Computer Interfaces International (HCII 2005), Las Vegas (2005)
22. Chen, T., Kan, M.Y.: Creating a live, public short message service corpus: the nus sms corpus. Language Resources and Evaluation 47(2), 299–335 (2013)
23. Macdonald, C., Santos, R.L.T., Ounis, I., Soboroff, I.: Blog track research at trec. SIGIR Forum 44(1), 58–75 (2010)
24. Santos, R.L.T., Macdonald, C., McCreadie, R., Ounis, I., Soboroff, I.: Information retrieval on the blogosphere. Foundations and Trends in Information Retrieval 6(1), 1–125 (2012)
25. Ounis, I., Macdonald, C., Lin, J., Soboroff, I.: Overview of the trec-2011 microblog track. In: Proceeddings of the 20th Text REtrieval Conference, TREC 2011 (2011)
26. Klimt, B., Yang, Y.: The enron corpus: A new dataset for email classification research. In: Boulicaut, J.-F., Esposito, F., Giannotti, F., Pedreschi, D. (eds.) ECML 2004. LNCS (LNAI), vol. 3201, pp. 217–226. Springer, Heidelberg (2004)
27. Inches, G., Crestani, F.: Overview of the International Sexual Predator Identification Competition at PAN-2012. In: CLEF (Online Working Notes/Labs/Workshop) (2012)

28. Voorhees, E.M., Harman, D.: Overview of the eighth text retrieval conference (trec-8). In: NIST Special Publication 500-246: The Eighth Text REtrieval Conference (TREC 8), pp. 1–24 (2000)
29. Peters, C., et al. (eds.): CLEF 2008. LNCS, vol. 5706. Springer, Heidelberg (2009)
30. Ramage, D., Dumais, S., Liebling, D.: Characterizing microblogs with topic models. In: ICWSM (2010)
31. Dong, H., Hui, S., He, Y.: Structural analysis of chat messages for topic detection. Online Information Review, 496–516 (2006)
32. Tuulos, V.H., Tirri, H.: Combining topic models and social networks for chat data mining. In: WI 2004: Proceedings of the 2004 IEEE/WIC/ACM International Conference on Web Intelligence, pp. 206–213 (2004)
33. Serrano, M., Flammini, A., Menczer, F.: Modeling statistical properties of written text. PLoS ONE 4(4), 1–8 (2009)
34. Manning, C.D., Schutze, H.: Foundations of Statistical Natural Language Processing. MIT Press, Cambridge (1999)
35. Cunningham, H., Maynard, D., Bontcheva, K., Tablan, V.: GATE: A framework and graphical development environment for robust NLP tools and applications. In: Proceedings of the 40th Anniversary Meeting of the Association for Computational Linguistics (2002)
36. Wilcock, G.: Introduction to linguistic annotation and text analytics. Synthesis Lectures on Human Language Technologies 2(1), 1–159 (2009)
37. Yin, D., Xue, Z., Hong, L., Davison, B.D., Kontostathis, A., Edwards, L.: Detection of harassment on web 2.0. In: CAW 2.0 2009: Proceedings of the 1st Content Analysis in Web 2.0 Workshop (2009)
38. Balog, K., Bron, M., He, J., Hofmann, K., Meij, E.J., de Rijke, M., Tsagkias, E., Weerkamp, W.: The University of Amsterdam at TREC 2009: Blog, Web, Entity, and Relevance Feedback. In: TREC 2009 Working Notes (2009)
39. Owoputi, O., O'Connor, B., Dyer, C., Gimpel, K., Schneider, N., Smith, N.A.: Improved part-of-speech tagging for online conversational text with word clusters. In: Proc. of NAACL (2013)

Semantic Search over Documents and Ontologies

Kalina Bontcheva, Valentin Tablan, and Hamish Cunningham

University of Sheffield, Regent Court, 211 Portobello, UK
Initial.Surname@sheffield.ac.uk

1 Introduction

Semantic search over documents is about finding information that is not based just on the presence of words, but also on their meaning [1, 2]. This task is a modification of classical Information Retrieval (IR), but documents are retrieved on the basis of relevance to ontology concepts, as well as words. Nevertheless the basic assumption is quite similar – a document is characterized by the bag of tokens constituting its content, disregarding its structure. While the basic IR approach considers word stems as tokens, there has been considerable effort towards using word-senses or lexical concepts (see [3, 4]) for indexing and retrieval. In the case of semantic search, what is being indexed is typically a combination of words, ontological concepts conveying the meaning of some of these words (e.g. Cambridge is a location), and optionally relations between such concepts (e.g. Cambridge is in the UK) [1]. The latter enable somebody searching for documents about the UK to find also documents mentioning Cambridge.

Cambridge however (as well as many other names and words) has multiple meanings, i.e. is ambiguous. The token "Cambridge" may refer to the city of Cambridge in the UK, to Cambridge in Massachusetts, the University of Cambridge, etc. Similarly, different tokens may have the same meaning, e.g. New York and the Big Apple. Therefore, semantic search tries to offer users more precise and relevant results, by using semantics. Frequently this semantics is encoded in ontologies, which can be defined as "a formal specification of a shared conceptualisation" [5]. Alternatively, Google refers to such semantics as *knowledge graphs* and to semantic search as "searching for things, not strings" [6].

Semantic search requires some natural language processing techniques for understanding word meaning. Since some of the most frequently used searches are for persons, locations, organisations, and other named entities [7], one of the most widely used techniques for interpreting this meaning are named entity recognition [8] and semantic annotation [9].

From a retrieval perspective, content annotated with named entities (i.e. PERson, LOCation, etc.) enables semantic search queries such as "LOC earthquake" which would return all documents mentioning a location and the word earthquake. Semantic annotation, on the other hand, goes one step further by differentiating, among other things, which specific real-world location is mentioned in the text (e.g. Cambridge, UK vs Cambridge, Mass.). This enables even more

N. Ferro (Ed.): PROMISE Winter School 2013, LNCS 8173, pp. 31–53, 2014.

powerful searches for documents, based on knowledge and relationships that are external to those documents. For example, a query on flooding in the UK would retrieve a document about floods in Sheffield, even if the latter does not explicitly mention the UK.

As can be seen from these example, what is required here is a source of knowledge that there are several cities called "Cambridge", one in the UK (which is a country) and one in Massachusetts, which is a state in the USA. Semantic annotation typically uses ontologies which contain such semantic knowledge, not just about the concepts (e.g. country, city) and instances (e.g. UK, USA) but also about relationships between concepts (e.g. cities are located within countries) and relations between instances (e.g. Cambridge_UK is located within England, which in turn is located within the UK).

Some semantic annotation methods have used Wikipedia as the large-scale source of such knowledge, e.g. [10–12]. However, recent semantic annotation and search methods have increasingly turned towards exploiting the massive, inter-linked cloud of Linked Open Data (LOD)[1], which contains hundreds of billions of statements about entities and relations between them. Some LOD datasets cover general knowledge (e.g. DBpedia (automatically derived from Wikipedia), YAGO, Freebase), whereas others focus on domain-specific knowledge (e.g. Mu-sicBrainz, PubMed, GeoNames). Some state-of-the-art methods for semantic an-notation (and consequently search) utilise only one LOD resource, (e.g. DBpedia Spotlight[13]), YAGO (e.g. [14]), MusicBrainz (e.g. [15]), whereas others create a larger knowledge resource, mixing several different LOD datasets. For instance, LDSR is a collection of several LOD datasets, comprising 440 million explicit statements about entities, derived from DBpedia, Geonames, Wordnet, the CIA Factbook, lingvoj, and UMBEL [16]. Similarly, Google's knowledge graph con-tains 500 million entities and is derived from Wikipedia, the CIA Factbook, and Freebase [6].

The rest of this chapter is structured as follows. Section 2 introduces semantic search in more detail, followed by a discussion on why semantic search is neces-sary (Section 3). Next Section 4 discusses where does document semantics comes from and how it is indexed. Semantic search query languages and available se-mantic search engines are discussed in Section 5. Due to the complexity of the underlying query languages, user-friendly interfaces to semantic search are key (see Section 6). Next Section 7 discusses evaluation, followed by a conclusion, which outlines outstanding challenges in this area.

2   What Is Semantic Search

In order to understand better what semantic search is, it is useful to consider two aspects: (i) what is being searched; and (ii) what are the results. We discuss these in turn next.

With respect to what is being searched, there are three main kinds of content to consider:

---

[1] http://linkeddata.org/

- *Documents*: This is traditional full-text search, where queries are answered on the basis of word co-occurrence in text content. For example, a query for "Cambridge university" returns all documents that contain the words Cambridge and/or university somewhere. This does not mean the results are only documents about that university. This kind of search has problems answering entity-type queries, e.g. which cities in the UK have population less than 100,000.
- *Ontologies and other semantic knowledge, e.g. LOD*: This is search over structured formal data, typically expressed as RDF [17] or OWL [18], and stored in a database or a semantic repository. Consequently, such formal queries are expressed in structured query languages, such as SPARQL [19] or SQL. This kind of search is often referred to as semantic search, because it uses semantics and inference to find the matching formal knowledge. In this chapter, we will refer to this kind of search as *ontology-based search*. This kind of search is particularly suited to answering entity-type queries, such as our example above.
- *Both documents and formal knowledge*: This is what this chapter refers to as semantic search over documents, or multi-paradigm [2], or semantic full-text search [20]. This kind of search draws both on document content and on semantic knowledge, in order to answer queries such as: "flooding in cities in the UK" or "flooding in places within 50 miles of Sheffield". In this case information about which cities are in the UK or within 50 miles of Sheffield is the result of ontology-based search (e.g. against DBpedia or GeoNames). Documents are then searched for the co-occurrence of the word "flooding" and the matching entities from the ontology-based search. In other words, what is being searched here are the document content for keywords, the index of semantically annotated entities that occur within these documents, and the formal knowledge.

With respect to the kinds of results returned by searches, there are four main kinds:

- *Documents*: The search returns a ranked list of documents, typically displayed with their title and optionally, some additional metadata (e.g. author). This kind of results are typically produced by full-text searches, although some do also include snippets.
- *Documents + highlighted snippets*: In addition to document titles, one or more snippets are returned, where the query hits are highlighted, in an attempt to make it apparent to users why this document is relevant to their query. Semantic search systems typically return matching documents in this way, e.g. the KIM system [1], Mímir[2], Broccoli [21].
- *Information summary*: This is a human-readable rendering of formal knowledge, returned by ontology-based searches for entities. For instance, a search in Google for "Tony Blair" would display on the right a summary showing several photos and basic facts, such as date of birth, generated automatically from their formal knowledge graph representation [6].

- *Structured results*: Ontology-based searches, which results are a list of entities, are often shown like that, e.g. a list of UK city names. See for example
the KIM entity searches[2] [1] or Brocolli [21].

3   Why Semantic Full-Text Search

As argued by [20], full-text search works well for precision-oriented searches,
when the relevant documents contain the keywords that describe the user need.
However, there are many cases when recall is paramount and, also, implicit
knowledge is needed in order to answer parts of the query. A frequent class
of such queries are entity-based ones, e.g. "plants with edible leaves" [20]. In
this case, most likely there is no one document containing the answer, and also,
documents most likely refer to the specific plants by name (e.g. broccoli), instead
of using the generic term "plants".

Environmental science is another example, where there is a strong need to go
beyond keyword-based search [22]. The British Library carried out a survey of
environmental science researchers and analysed the kinds of information needs
they struggled to satisfy through keyword search [23]. The top requirement was
for geographically specific queries, including proximity search (e.g. "documents
about flooding within 50 miles of Sheffield") and implied locations (e.g. the
query "documents about flooding in South West England" needs to return a
document about flooding in Exeter, even though South West England is not
mentioned explicitly).

One more example is patent search [24], where recall is crucial, since failure to
find pre-existing, relevant patents may result in legal proceedings and financial
losses. Examples of hard to find information using keywords alone are searches
for references to papers cited in a specific section of the patent and also searches
for measurements and quantities (e.g. in chemical patents). Measurements in
particular are numeric and can show great variation – the same value can be
expressed using different measurement systems, e.g. inches or centimetres, or
different multipliers even when using the same measurement system, e.g. mm,
cm, or metres.

Implementing semantic full-text search poses four key challenges [20]:

1. The automatic recognition of entities in full text, since most content is not
   pre-annotated.
2. Indexing efficiently words, entity occurrences, and formal knowledge in ontologies.
3. Need for semantic interpretation of document content and search query.
4. Easy to use and transparent user interfaces for semantic full-text search.

Next we discuss the first three challenges in more detail, while the last challenge is covered in Section 6.

---

[2] http://ln.ontotext.com/KIM

4   Indexing Document Semantics

As can be seen from our discussion above, understanding the meaning of documents is the key enabler of semantic search. Two main approaches have been explored so far: (i) asking document creators to encode semantics in a machine-readable format at publishing time; (ii) deriving semantics automatically.

The advantage of the first approach is that it relies on human intelligence and could thus be more accurate. The disadvantages are that humans need to learn and adopt these metadata encoding formats and do that for a sufficiently large number of documents. Lastly, already published content would need to be tagged retrospectively, which is not always possible.

Conversely, the advantage of automatic approaches is that machine readable semantics can be generated for every document, even already published ones, regardless of their publication format. The disadvantage is loss of accuracy, since semantic annotation methods tend to perform with between 80 and 90% precision and recall.

Next we discuss in some detail each of the two approaches.

4.1   Human-Encoded Semantics

Human-embedded semantics in web documents typically conforms to one of two standards: RDFa (http://rdfa.info/) and Schema.org.

In brief, RDFa (or Resource Description Framework in attributes) is a W3C standard. It adds a set of attribute-level extensions to HTML and XHTML, to describe rich metadata, embedded within Web documents.

Schema.org is a similar endeavour, which is supported by many of the web search engines, including Bing, Google, Yahoo, and Yandex.

This additional metadata has enabled search engines to enrich their result presentation, by adding richer information, e.g. a restaurant's phone number and address [25]. Even though useful for some queries, such metadata nevertheless falls short of enabling the kinds of semantic queries discussed above.

4.2   Automatic Semantic Annotation

The process of tying semantic models and natural language together is referred to as *semantic annotation*. It may be characterised as the dynamic creation of interrelationships between *ontologies* and unstructured and semi-structured documents in a bidirectional manner [1]. From a technological perspective, semantic annotation is about annotating in texts all mentions of concepts from the ontology (i.e. classes, instances, properties, and relations), through metadata referring to their URIs in the ontology.

Figure 1 shows an example text on the left. The automatically added semantic annotation on the phrase "South Gloucestershire" is shown on the right. As can seen, the entity mention has now been linked to the corresponding DBpedia (the value of the inst attribute) and GeoNames URIs (the value of the geonamesURI attribute). Additional semantic knowledge has been brought in from these LOD

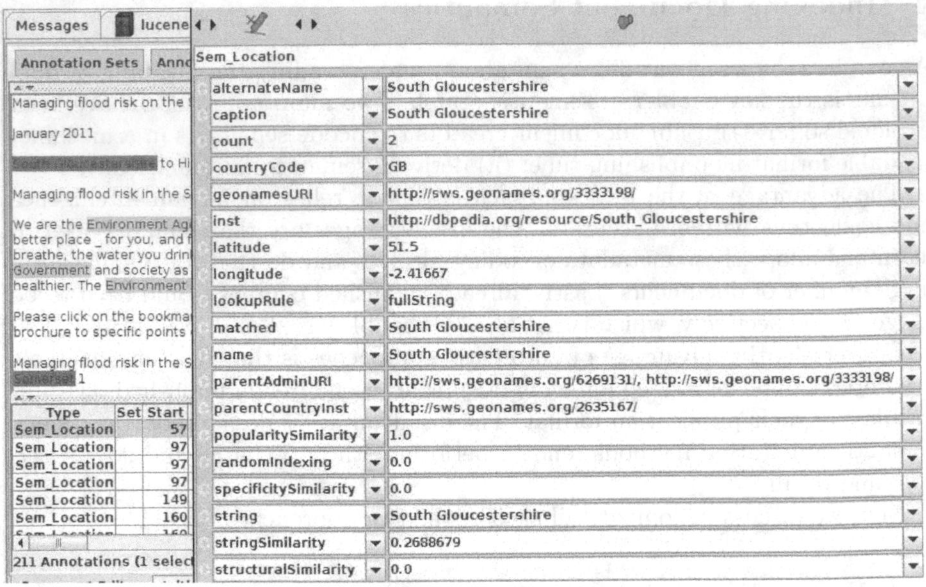

Fig. 1. Example Semantic Annotation in GATE [26]

resources, including latitude and longitude, the URI of the parent country, and the URIs of the relevant NUTS administrative regions.

Information Extraction (IE), a form of natural language analysis, has become the natural language processing technology of choice, for bridging the gap between unstructured text and formal knowledge expressed in ontologies. Ontology-Based IE (OBIE) is IE which is adapted specifically for the semantic annotation task [27]. One of the important differences between traditional IE and OBIE is in the use of a formal ontology as one of the system's inputs and as the target output. Some researchers (e.g. [28]) call ontology-based any system which specifies its outputs with respect to an ontology, however, in our view, if a system only has a mapping between the IE outputs and the ontology, this is not sufficient and therefore, such systems should be referred as *ontology-oriented*.

Another distinguishing characteristic of the ontology-based IE process is that it not only finds the type of the extracted entity (i.e. Location for South Gloucestershire), but it also disambiguates it, by linking it to its semantic description in the target knowledge base, typically via a URI (see Figure 1). This allows entities to be traced across documents and their descriptions to be enriched during the IE process, as shown. In practical terms, this requires automatic recognition and disambiguation of named entities, terms, and relations and also co-reference resolution both within and across documents. These more complex algorithms are typically preceded by some shallow linguistic pre-processing (tokenisation, Part-Of-Speech (POS) tagging, etc.) In our example, entity recognition and disambiguation have been carried out by the open-source GATE natural language toolkit [26, 29].

Linking Open Data resources, especially DBpedia, YAGO and Freebase, have become key sources of ontological knowledge for semantic annotation, as well as being used as target entity knowledge bases for disambiguation. These offer: (i) cross-referenced domain-independent hierarchies with thousands of classes and relations and millions of instances; (ii) an inter-linked and complementary set of resources with synonymous lexicalisations; (iii) grounding of their concepts and instances in Wikipedia entries and other external data. The rich class hierarchies are used for fine-grained classification of named entities, while the knowledge about millions of instances and their links to Wikipedia entries are used as features in the OBIE algorithms.

Due to space limitations, we are not able to discuss semantic annotation methods and approaches in more details, but see [30] for details.

5 Semantic Search Approaches: A High-level Overview

As discussed already, semantic annotations enable users to find all documents that mention one or more instances from the ontology and/or relations. The queries can also mix free-text keywords, not just the semantic annotations. Most retrieval tools provide also document browsing functionality as well as search refinement capabilities. Due to the fact that documents can have hundreds of annotations (especially if every concept mention in the document is annotated), annotation retrieval on a large-document collection is a very challenging task.

Annotation-based search and retrieval is different from traditional information retrieval, because of the underlying graph representation of annotations, which encode structured information about text ranges within the document. The encoded information is different from the words and inter-document link models used by Google and other search engines. In the case of semantic annotations, the case becomes even more complex, since they also refer to ontologies via URIs. While augmented full-text indexes can help with efficient access, the data storage requirements can be very substantial, as the cardinality of the annotation sets grows. Therefore different, more optimised solutions have been investigated.

The main difference from semantic web search engines, such as Swoogle [31], is the focus on annotations and using those to find documents, rather than forming queries against ontologies or navigating ontological structures. Similarly, semantic-based facet search and browse interfaces, such as /facet [32], tend to be ontology-based, whereas annotation-based facet interfaces (see KIM below) tend to hide the ontology and instead resemble more closely "traditional" string-based faceted search.

Before discussing several representative semantic search approaches in more detail, let us first discuss query languages for semantic search.

5.1 Semantic Search Queries

Since semantic search queries need to contain both text-based keywords and formal SPARQL-like queries over the ontology, they are often referred to as hybrid queries. The Semplore system [33], for example, uses conjunctive hybrid query graphs, similar to SPARQL, but enhanced with a "virtual" concept called keyword concept W. A similar approach has been taken in the Broccoli system [21], which has a special *occurs – with* relation, the value of which is the free text keyword.

Mímir[3] [2] has an even richer query language, which also supports the inclusion of linguistic annotations in queries. For example, a Mímir query "PER says" will return documents where an entity of type Person is followed by the keyword says. Morphological variations for keywords are also supported (e.g. "PER root:say"), as are distance restrictions (e.g. "Person [0..5] root:say" which matches text such as "Sebastian James of Dixons Group said"). Additional semantic restrictions based on knowledge from the ontology are expressed by adding a SPARQL query. For examples, this query is for documents mentioning people born in Sheffield:

```
{Person sparql = "SELECT ?inst
    WHERE { ?inst :birthPlace <http://dbpedia.org/resource/Sheffield>}"}
```

5.2   Relevance Scoring and Retrieval

In the context of semantic full-text search, [34] propose a modification of TF.IDF, based on the frequency of occurrence of instances from the semantic annotations in the document collection. They also combine semantic similarity with a standard keyword-based similarity for ranking, in order to cater for cases when there are no sufficiently relevant semantic annotations.

The Mímir semantic full-text search framework (see Section 5.3) supports different ranking functions and new ones can easily be integrated. In addition to TF.IDF, it already implements ranking based on hit length and the BM25 algorithm.

The CE^2 system goes one step further and uses a graph-based approach to compute the ranking of the hybrid search results [35]. The graph structure comes from the formal semantic knowledge.

With respect to ranking individuals returned via knowledge base search, [36] propose ObjectRank – a PageRank-based approach.

5.3   Semantic Search Full-Text Platforms

Due to limited space, the focus of this section is on extensible semantic search full-text frameworks (namely KIM and Mímir), which are available to download and experiment with freely for research. There is other relevant research, mostly at the level of proof-of-concept prototypes, some of which are introduced briefly next.

GoNTogle [37] is a search system that provides keyword, semantic and hybrid search over semantically annotated documents. The semantic search replaces

---

[3] A set of example queries and several test Mímir indexes are available for experimentation at: http://demos.gate.ac.uk/mimir/

keywords with ontological classes. Results are obtained based on occurrences of the ontological classes from the query within the annotations associated with a document. Finally, the *hybrid search*, comprises a standard boolean AND or OR operation between the result sets produces by a keyword search and a semantic search. The only type of annotation supported is associating an ontology class with a document segment. Another similar system is Semplore [33] which uses conjunctive hybrid query graphs, similar to SPARQL, but enhanced with a "virtual" concept called keyword concept W. However, both GoNTogle and Semplore do not have support for searches over document structure, nor for searches over other types of linguistic annotations.

The Broccoli system [21] also provides a user interface for building queries, combining text-based and semantic constraints (encoded as entity mentions in the input text, with URIs). The association between text and semantics is encoded by means of the *occurs-with* relation which is implied whenever mentions of words and ontological entities occur within the same *context*. The *contexts* are automatically extracted at indexing time, and rely mainly on shallow syntactic analysis of the document and extraction of syntactic dependency relations. The *occurs-with* relation provides access to the underlying phrase structure of the input document. However, the system is designed to only use this particular relation, so indexing other kinds of document structure (e.g. abstract, sections) is likely to prove problematic. Consequently, there is no support for richer linguistic annotations, such as part-of-speech or morphology, document metadata, or structural search other than based on co-occurrences within *contexts*.

The KIM. (Knowledge and Information Management) platform [1, 38], was among the first systems to implement semantic search, both over RDF knowledge bases via SPARQL, and over semantically annotated document content, including hybrid queries mixing keywords and semantic restrictions. KIM has a number of user interfaces for semantic search and browsing and can be customized easily for specific applications. It is freely available for research use from http://www.ontotext.com/kim/getting-started/download.

KIM is an extendible platform for knowledge management, which offers tools for semantic annotation, indexing, and semantic-based search (referred to as multi-paradigm search in KIM). Figure 2 shows KIM's architecture, which also includes a web crawler for content harvesting; a knowledge ETL component which interfaces to thesauri, dictionaries, and LOD resources; and a set of web-based user interfaces for entity-based and semantic-based full text search (see 6.1 for details on the KIM faceted search).

Semantic annotation in KIM is based on the open-source GATE NLP framework [29]. The essence of KIM's semantic annotation is the recognition of named entities with respect to the KIM ontology. The entity instances all bear unique identifiers that allow annotations to be linked both to the entity type and to the exact individual in the instance base. For new (previously unknown) entities, new identifiers are allocated and assigned; then minimal descriptions are added to the semantic repository. The annotations are kept separately from the content, and an API for their management is provided.

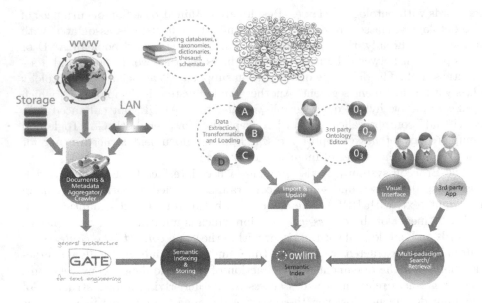

Fig. 2. KIM Architecture

KIM can also use Linked Data ontologies for semantic annotation and search. At present it has been tested with DBPedia, Geonames, Wordnet, Musicbrainz, Freebase, UMBEL, Lingvoj and the CIA World Factbook. Those datasets are preprocessed and loaded to form an integrated dataset of about 1.2 billion explicit statements. Forward-chaining is performed to materialise another 0.8 billion implicit statements.

Mímir [4] [2] is an integrated semantic search framework, which offers indexing and search over full text, document structure, document metadata, linguistic annotations, and any linked, external semantic knowledge bases. It supports hybrid queries that arbitrarily mix full-text, structural, linguistic and semantic constraints. A key distinguishing feature from previous work are the containment operators, that allow flexible creation and nesting of full-text, structural, and semantic constraints.

Figure 3 shows the Mímir semantic query UI. In this case the goal is to find documents, mentioning locations in the UK, where the population density is more than 500 people per square km. In this case the knowledge about population density is coming from DBpedia. The documents being searched in this case are metadata descriptions of government reports on climate change and flooding, created by the British Library as part of the EnviLOD project[5].

The high-level concept behind Mímir is that a document collection is processed with NLP algorithms, typically including semantic annotation using Linked

---

[4] http://gate.ac.uk/mimir/
[5] http://gate.ac.uk/projects/envilod

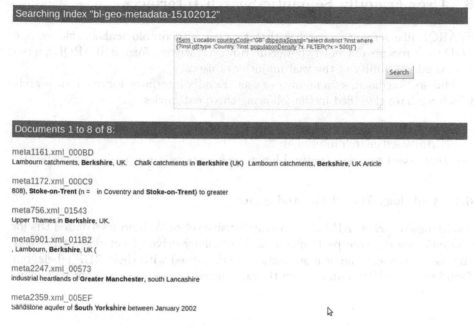

Fig. 3. Mímir's Semantic Search UI showing a formal query, the retrieved documents, and short text snippets showing in bold the matched locations

Open Data accessed via a triple store, such as OWLIM [39] or Sesame. The annotated documents are then indexed in Mímir, together with their full-text content, document metadata, and document structure markup (the latter can also be discovered automatically via the NLP tools). At search time, the triple store is used as a source of implicit knowledge, to help answer the hybrid searches that combine full-text, structural, and semantic constraints. The latter are formulated using a SPARQL query, executed against the triple store.

Mímir uses inverted indexes for indexing the document content (including additional linguistic information, such as part-of-speech or morphological roots), and for associating instance of annotations with the position in the input text where they occur. The inverted index implementation used by Mímir is based on MG4J [40]. Beside document text, the other main kind of data are the structural and NLP-generated annotations. In Mímir both kinds are represented in the same data structure, comprising a start and end position, an annotation type (e.g. Location, p), and an optional set of attributes (called features in the GATE framework).

Mímir is highly scalable. 150 million web pages were indexed successfully, using two hundred Amazon EC2 Large Instances running for a week to produce a federated index [41]. Since Mímir runs on GateCloud.net [42], building Mímir semantic indexes on the Amazon cloud is straightforward.

6   User Friendly Semantic Search Interfaces

SPARQL-like semantic searches that tapping into ontological knowledge and LOD resources are extremely powerful. However, writing formal SPARQL queries is beyond the ability of the vast majority of users.

This section discusses a number of user-friendly interfaces for semantic search, which we have classified in the following three categories:

- Ontology-based faceted search interfaces;
- Form-based search interfaces;
- Text-based searches (natural language interfaces for semantic search).

6.1   Ontology-Based Faceted Search

As discussed earlier, KIM has a comprehensive set of Web browser-based UIs for semantic search. One particular kind is ontology-driven faceted search, where the user can select one or more instances (visualised with their RDF labels, but found via their URIs) and obtain the documents where these co-occur. Timeline and entity-centric views are also supported.

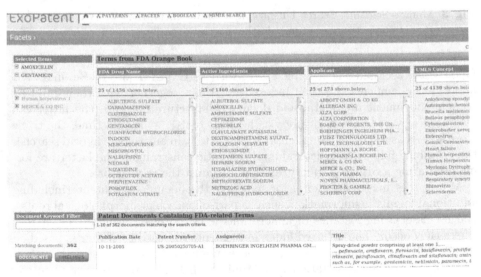

Fig. 4. KIM's entity-based faceted search UI

Figure 4, for example, shows a case where the user is searching for patents mentioning amoxicillin and gentamicin. This example is taken from the ExoPatent online KIM demo[6], which uses the the FDA Orange Book (23,000 patented drugs) and Unified Medical Language System (UMLS – a database

---

[6] Available online at http://exopatent.ontotext.com

of 370,000 medical terms) to annotate documents with semantic information. The demo runs on a small set of 40,000 patents. ExoPatent supports semantic search for diseases, drug names, body parts, references to literature and other patents, numeric values, and ranges.

In the faceted search UI, as new entities are selected as constraints (see left column), the number of matching documents is updated dynamically. Optional keyword constraints can also be specified in the keyword filter field on the left. At the bottom of the figure, one can see the titles of the retrieved documents and some relevant content from them. The titles are clickable, in order to view the full document content and the semantic annotations within it. The entities/terms listed in the entity columns (i.e. Drug name, ingredients, applicant, and UMLS concept) are also updated, to show only entities co-occurring with the already selected entity constraints.

The Broccoli system [21] has a similar interactive query building UI, which updates dynamically as the user is typing concepts or keywords to search for. What is being searched are Wikipedia articles, indexed with classes and instances from the YAGO ontology. Figure 5 shows an example query for documents mentioning UK cities, which also contain the keyword "flood". The semantic query is displayed as a graph on top, making explicit the relations between the searched for concepts. Keywords have a special relation "occurs-with", whereas all other semantic relations come from the YAGO ontology. As the user starts typing a query term (e.g. City), the lists of matching classes, instances, and relations on the left are updated dynamically. For instance, once City is selected, only relations applicable to this class are shown in the list of relation candidates. Due to the entity-centric queries, the result list is structured as a list of entities, where relevant information from the YAGO ontology is provided for each returned entity, as well as documents from Wikipedia about this entity, which also contain the given keyword(s).

6.2 Natural Language Queries

NL queries allow users to perform semantic search through written language (e.g. English). In general, natural language search interfaces, while potentially useful for naive users, are still fairly experimental. The majority of work on natural language interfaces for semantic search has focused on the problem of querying ontologies (e.g. [43–45]) or ontology authoring (e.g. [46, 47]). Using language-based queries for retrieving semantic annotations and associated documents is a somewhat different task, since the queries need to go beyond the ontology and into documents as well.

The QuestIO system [48], for example, has an ontology modelling documents and the semantic annotations in them and uses it to help naive users to search through RDF annotations and get a list of matching documents back. The example domain is software engineering where over 10,000 different artefacts (software code, documentation, user manuals, papers, etc.) were annotated semantically with respect to a domain ontology.

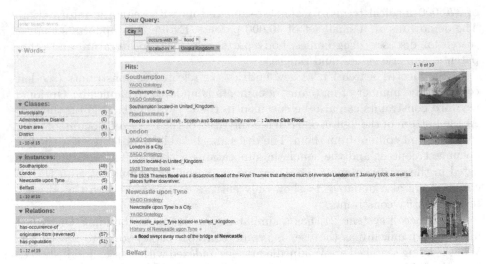

Fig. 5. The Broccoli Interactive Query Building UI

Figure 6 shows a query where the user has typed the word "ontology", which in GATE can refer to various concepts in the GATE domain ontology of Java classes and their documentation. Due to this ambiguity, the results are first a list of candidate concepts. Once the user selects the intended GATE concept, a list of matching documents is displayed, listed by type (Java code, forum post, etc). Their titles are clickable, which then shows the document content with the query terms highlighted (see the example Java code in the bottom right corner of Figure 6).

QuestIO interprets the queries as follows. First it tries to match some or all of the contained words to ontology concepts. Then any remaining textual segments are used to deduct property names and act as context for disambiguation. The sequence of concepts and property names can then be converted into a formal query that is executed against the semantically annotated documents. Throughout the process, metrics are used to score the possible query interpretations, allowing the filtering of low scoring options, thus reducing ambiguity and limiting the search space.

Another similar system is SemSearch [49] which is based on Sesame for indexing the semantics and Lucene for indexing the texts. Queries can be a combination of keywords (e.g. news) and connectors such as "and" and "or" (see Figure 7 for an example). The system performs semantic matching between words in complex queries and semantic entities by exploring different plausible combinations between the keywords. For longer queries this could compromise the performance of the search engine and more efficient strategies are needed.

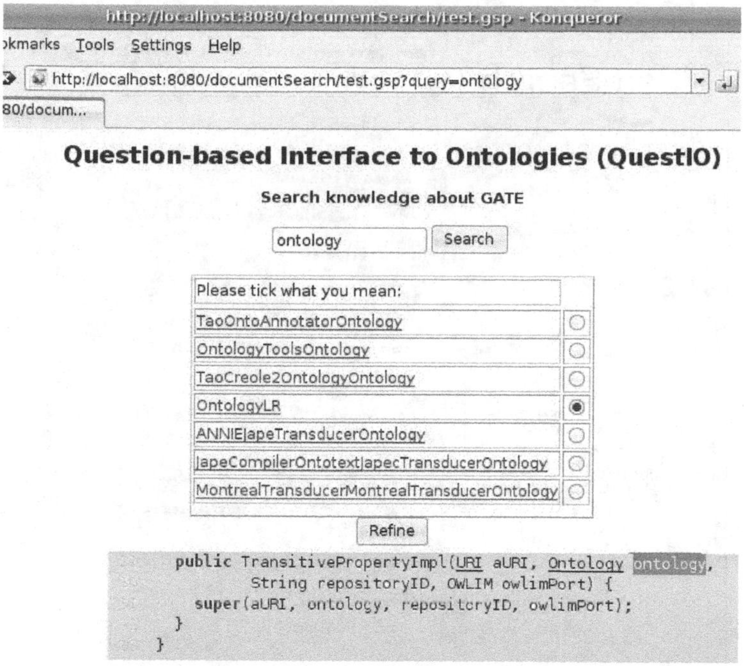

Fig. 6. A semantic search example in QuestIO

6.3   Form-Based Semantic Search Interfaces

One of the challenges faced by semantic search interfaces, especially in subject-specific cases, is to indicate to users what they can search for. A form-based interface makes this explicit, in a manner similar to the facet-based UIs discussed above.

One example of such interface is the EnviLOD UI (see Figure 8), which was developed as a user-friendly semantic search front end to a Mímir index of environmental science documents, terms, and LOD entities (DBpedia and GeoNames were used for this purpose).

There is a keyword search field, complemented with optional semantic search constraints, through a set of inter-dependent drop-down lists. In the first list, users can search for specific entity types (Locations, Organisations, Persons, Rivers, Dates) and Document – for specifying constraints on document-level attributes, etc. More than one semantic constraint can be added, through the plus button, which inserts a new row underneath the current row of constraints.

For instance, if Location is chosen as a semantic constraint, then, further constraints can be specified by choosing an appropriate property constraint (see Figure 8). Population allows users to pose restrictions on the population number of the locations that are being searched for. Similar numeric constraints can be imposed on the latitude, longitude, and population density attribute values.

Fig. 7. Example SemSearch query results

Restrictions can also be imposed in terms of location name or the country it belongs to. For string-value properties, if "is" is chosen from the third list instead of none, then the value must be exactly as specified (e.g. Oxford), whereas "contains" triggers sub-string matching, (e.g. Oxfordshire is matched as a location name containing Oxford). In this way, a user searching for documents mentioning locations with name containing Oxford, will be shown not only documents mentioning Oxford explicitly, but also documents mentioning Oxfordshire and other locations in Oxfordshire (e.g. Wytham Woods, Banbury). In the latter case, the knowledge from DBpedia and GeoNames will be used to identify which other locations are in Oxfordshire, in addition to Oxford.

One problem with an EnviLOD-style UI is that it hides from users information about what instances of these classes occur in the indexed document collection, (e.g. which UK counties are mentioned). In order to provide such high-level entity-based overviews of the documents, one approach is to list all instances, for each class, as done in the KIM and Broccoli interfaces.

An alternative is to use tag clouds and other visualisations of entity co-occurrences. Mímir has recently been extended with such a user interface, called GATE Prospector (see Figure 9). The top half of the UI shows ontology classes and instances (UMLS in this example) and the user selects the desired ones. Additional search restrictions could be imposed via document metadata filters. The bottom half of Figure 9 shows the matching instances (terms in the case of

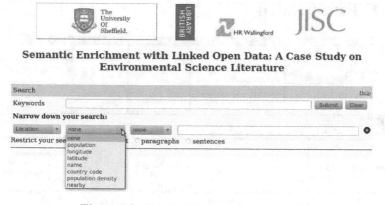

Fig. 8. The EnviLOD semantic search UI

UMLS) as well as the number of times they occur in the document collection. A frequency-based term cloud is also shown. The set of terms/instances can be saved for later use, e.g. to generate entity/term co-occurrence visualisations.

Figure 10 shows an example co-occurrence visualisation, where the most frequently mentioned instances of diseases are plotted against the most frequently mentioned instances of pathogens. Examples from other domains include plotting which sentiment terms co-occur most frequently with which political parties or politicians, given a large collection of tweets about an election.

7   Evaluation

In the context of evaluating semantic search over RDF triples, a repeatable and generic evaluation framework has emerged recently [50]. However, due to its focus purely on structured data, it is not directly reusable for evaluation of semantic full-text search.

Another example is [51], who again evaluate search over RDF facts, compared against web search. In this case, 200 queries are used and 12,000 relevance judgements are collected from human judges. Relevance feedback from a web-based keyword search is used to improve the results, however, the two types of search are kept entirely separate, instead of combined as in semantic full-text search. Therefore, again this dataset cannot be reused directly.

Specifically with respect to evaluating semantic full-text search, [34] use a TREC collection, 20 semantic search queries adapted from two TREC evaluations and the corresponding judgements, as well as a number of relevant ontologies and knowledge bases. Semantic search is compared against Lucene and TREC-based systems, evaluated using mean average precision. Query time performance is also reported.

The CE^2 system is evaluated using Wikipedia for the documents and DBpedia as the semantic knowledge base, thus directly exploiting the connection

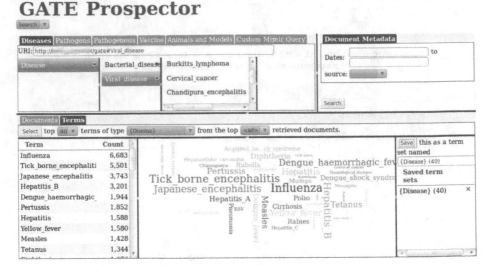

Fig. 9. The GATE Prospector semantic search UI

between the two [35] (links in Wikipedia articles are easily mapped to DBpedia URIs). The collection contains 2.1 million documents and 42 million annotations. The textual data and annotations are stored in Lucene, whereas the DBpedia triples (4.3 million) are stored in a relational database. 5 kinds of semantic full-text search queries are evaluated: retrieving documents containing an annotation with a specified instance URI; retrieving documents mentioning classes of annotations (e.g. companies); conjunctive queries requiring some reasoning with the RDF triples (e.g. institutions of scientists mentioned in a given document); user-created questions of the previous 3 types; questions based on Wikipedia list pages. Relevance judgements were produced for the fourth kind of queries by 20 researchers.

The most comprehensive and publicly available dataset (including queries and relevance judgements) is the one created for the evaluation of the Broccoli semantic full-text search system [21].[7] Similar to the previous system, it uses Wikipedia, but combined with the YAGO ontology, instead of DBpedia. A total of 61 queries were used (including 15 from a TREC benchmark), as well as 10 Wikipedia lists (similar to those used in the evaluation of CE^2). Traditional IR evaluation metrics are used, but no comparison against an IR baseline or another semantic search system is made on their dataset.

To summarise, evaluation of semantic full-text search is still in nascent stages, due to the lack of a shared evaluation task on which different approaches can be evaluated independently, in a reliable manner. Keyword-based IR systems are sometimes used as baselines, but, at the time of writing, no in-depth comparisons between semantic full-text search systems have been published.

---

[7] http://broccoli.informatik.uni-freiburg.de/repro-corr/

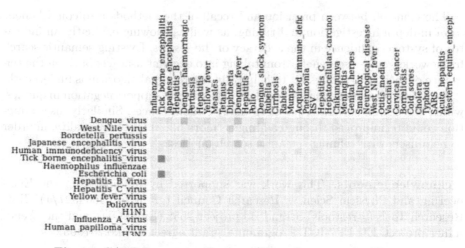

Fig. 10. GATE Prospector: Instance/Term Co-occurrence View

8 Conclusions and Future Work

This chapter provided a high-level introduction to semantic search over documents and ontologies. Semantics is needed in particular in cases where the correct interpretation of the search query requires knowledge not contained explicitly in the full text documents. For example, documents about flooding in UK cities with population under 50,000 people.

In summary, there seems to be an emerging consensus that current keyword-based, full-text search does not cater sufficiently well for information discovery. Semantic search and Linked open data offer much promise, but require significant development effort to implement in a way, which makes them accessible to end-users. Present prototypes typically require some understand of the underlying ontological relations, which give rise to the semantic search properties, which is a limitation to wider take-up.

Evaluations of semantic search (e.g. [52]) have demonstrated the need to show more feedback on why a certain document was matched, especially when this is a result of using implicit semantic knowledge from external knowledge resource. For example, in the EnviLOD interface, if a population or a distance-based constraints are used, relevance was not always obvious to the user.

One of the challenges with adopting semantic search is making the user interfaces as intuitive as possible, in order to reduce the initial learning curve. Particular attention needs to be paid to usability and design details, especially consistency with keyword-based general-purpose search engines, such as Google, Yahoo. These details should not be underestimated, even in research prototypes, since they can influence heavily the evaluation results.

Secondly, scalability and computational efficiency of semantic search are non-trivial, especially combining large volumes of content and entities from large LOD datasets.

The trade-off between precision and recall of the methods also could benefit from in-depth investigation and tuning, as well as showing explicitly an indicator of system confidence in the accuracy of the results. Existing semantic search frameworks could also benefit from taking into account user feedback on the relevance of each returned result, to help train the retrieval algorithms underneath.

Fourthly, current semantic query languages do not support negation in queries, which is a search feature required in many circumstances. Similarly, user adoption could be improved through adding a "more like this" functionality, in order to help users with refining semantic search queries.

Acknowledgements. This work was supported by funding from the Engineering and Physical Sciences Research Council (grant EP/I004327/1), JISC Research Tools (#restools) Strand B3 project 2658 (EnviLOD), and the Trendminer project, EU FP7-ICT Programme, grant agreement no.287863.

References

1. Kiryakov, A., Popov, B., Ognyanoff, D., Manov, D., Kirilov, A., Goranov, M.: Semantic annotation, indexing and retrieval. Journal of Web Semantics, ISWC 2003 Special Issue 1(2), 671–680 (2004)
2. Cunningham, H., Tablan, V., Roberts, I., Greenwood, M.A., Aswani, N.: Information Extraction and Semantic Annotation for Multi-Paradigm Information Management. In: Lupu, M., Mayer, K., Tait, J., Trippe, A.J. (eds.) Current Challenges in Patent Information Retrieval. The Information Retrieval Series, vol. 29, pp. 307–327. Springer, Heidelberg (2011)
3. Mahesh, K., Kud, J., Dixon, P.: Oracle at TREC8: A Lexical Approach. In: Proceedings of the Eighth Text Retrieval Conference, TREC-8 (1999)
4. Voorhees, E.: Using WordNet for Text Retrieval. In: Fellbaum, C. (ed.) WordNet: An Electronic Lexical Database. MIT Press (1998)
5. Gruber, T.R.: A Translation Approach to Portable Ontologies. Knowledge Acquisition 5(2), 199–220 (1993)
6. Singhal, A.: Introducing the knowledge graph: things, not strings (May 2012)
7. Pound, J., Mika, P., Zaragoza, H.: Ad-hoc object retrieval in the web of data. In: Proceedings of the 19th International Conference on World Wide Web, pp. 771–780. ACM (2010)
8. Ratinov, L., Roth, D.: Design challenges and misconceptions in named entity recognition. In: Proceedings of the Thirteenth Conference on Computational Natural Language Learning, pp. 147–155. Association for Computational Linguistics (2009)
9. Bontcheva, K., Cunningham, H.: Semantic annotations and retrieval: Manual, semiautomatic, and automatic generation. In: Domingue, J., Fensel, D., Hendler, J. (eds.) Handbook of Semantic Web Technologies, pp. 77–116. Springer, Heidelberg (2011)
10. Milne, D., Witten, I.H.: Learning to link with Wikipedia. In: Proc. of the 17th Conf. on Information and Knowledge Management (CIKM), pp. 509–518 (2008)
11. Rao, D., McNamee, P., Dredze, M.: Entity linking: Finding extracted entities in a knowledge base. In: Multi-source, Multi-lingual Information Extraction and Summarization. Springer (2013)

12. Ji, H., Grishman, R.: Knowledge base population: Successful approaches and challenges. In: Proc. of ACL 2011, pp. 1148–1158 (2011)
13. Mendes, P.N., Jakob, M., García-Silva, A., Bizer, C.: DBpedia Spotlight: Shedding light on the web of documents. In: Proceedings of the 7th International Conference on Semantic Systems, pp. 1–8 (2011)
14. Shen, W., Wang, J., Luo, P., Wang, M.: LINDEN: Linking named entities with knowledge base via semantic knowledge. In: Proceedings of the 21st Conference on World Wide Web, pp. 449–458 (2012)
15. Gruhl, D., Nagarajan, M., Pieper, J., Robson, C., Sheth, A.: Context and Domain Knowledge Enhanced Entity Spotting in Informal Text. In: Bernstein, A., Karger, D.R., Heath, T., Feigenbaum, L., Maynard, D., Motta, E., Thirunarayan, K. (eds.) ISWC 2009. LNCS, vol. 5823, pp. 260–276. Springer, Heidelberg (2009)
16. Kiryakov, A., Ognyanoff, D., Velkov, R., Tashev, Z., Peikov, I.: Ldsr: Materialized reason-able view to the web of linked data. In: OWL: Experiences and Directions workshop (OWLED 2009) (2009)
17. Klyne, G., Carroll, J.: Resource description framework (RDF): Concepts and abstract syntax. W3C recommendation, W3C (2004), http://www.w3.org/TR/rdf-concepts/
18. Bechhofer, S., van Harmelen, F., Hendler, J., Horrocks, I., McGuinness, D.L., Patel-Schneider, P.F., Stein, L.A.: OWL web ontology language reference. W3C recommendation, W3C (February 2004), http://www.w3.org/
19. Prud'hommeaux, E., Seaborne, A.: SPARQL Query Language for RDF. W3C recommendation — 15 January 2008, W3C (2008), http://www.w3.org/, http://www.w3.org/TR/rdf-sparql-query/.
20. Bast, H., Bäurle, F., Buchhold, B., Haussmann, E.: A case for semantic full-text search. In: Proceedings of the 1st Joint International Workshop on Entity-Oriented and Semantic Search, JIWES 2012, pp. 4:1–4:3. ACM (2012)
21. Bast, H., Bäurle, F., Buchhold, B., Haussmann, E.: Broccoli: Semantic full-text search at your fingertips. CoRR abs/1207.2615 (2012)
22. Kieniewicz, J., Sudlow, A., Newbold, E.: Coordinating improved environmental information access and discovery: Innovations in sharing environmental observations and information. In: Pillman, W., Schade, S., Smits, P. (eds.) Proceedings of the 25th International EnviroInfo Conference (2011)
23. Kieniewicz, J., Wallis, M.: User requirements. Technical Report, EnviLOD project deliverable (2012), http://gate.ac.uk/projects/envilod/EnviLOD-WP2-User-Requirements.pdf
24. Lupu, M., Hanbury, A.: Patent retrieval. Foundations and Trends in Information Retrieval 7(1), 1–97 (2013)
25. Haas, K., Mika, P., Tarjan, P., Blanco, R.: Enhanced results for web search. In: Proceeding of the 34th International ACM SIGIR Conference on Research and Development in Information Retrieval (SIGIR), pp. 725–734 (2011)
26. Cunningham, H., Tablan, V., Roberts, A., Bontcheva, K.: Getting more out of biomedical documents with gate's full lifecycle open source text analytics. PLoS Computational Biology 9(2), e1002854 (2013)
27. Li, Y., Bontcheva, K., Cunningham, H.: Hierarchical, Perceptron-like Learning for Ontology Based Information Extraction. In: 16th International World Wide Web Conference (WWW 2007), pp. 777–786 (May 2007)
28. McDowell, L.K., Cafarella, M.: Ontology-Driven Information Extraction with OntoSyphon. In: Cruz, I., Decker, S., Allemang, D., Preist, C., Schwabe, D., Mika, P., Uschold, M., Aroyo, L.M. (eds.) ISWC 2006. LNCS, vol. 4273, pp. 428–444. Springer, Heidelberg (2006)

29. Cunningham, H., Maynard, D., Bontcheva, K., Tablan, V.: Gate: an architecture for development of robust hlt applications. In: Proceedings of the 40th Annual Meeting on Association for Computational Linguistics, ACL 2002, July 7-12, pp. 168–175. Association for Computational Linguistics, Stroudsburg (2002)

30. Bontcheva, K., Cunningham, H.: Semantic annotation and retrieval: Manual, semi-automatic and automatic generation. In: Domingue, J., Fensel, D., Hendler, J.A. (eds.) Handbook of Semantic Web Technologies. Springer (2011)

31. Ding, L., Finin, T., Joshi, A., Pan, R., Cost, R.S., Peng, Y., Reddivari, P., Doshi, V.C., Sachs, J.: Swoogle: A Search and Metadata Engine for the Semantic Web. In: Proceedings of the Thirteenth ACM Conference on Information and Knowledge Management (2004)

32. Hildebrand, M., van Ossenbruggen, J., Hardman, L.: /facet: A Browser for Heterogeneous Semantic Web Repositories. In: Cruz, I., Decker, S., Allemang, D., Preist, C., Schwabe, D., Mika, P., Uschold, M., Aroyo, L.M. (eds.) ISWC 2006. LNCS, vol. 4273, pp. 272–285. Springer, Heidelberg (2006)

33. Zhang, L., Liu, Q., Zhang, J., Wang, H., Pan, Y., Yu, Y.: Semplore: An IR approach to scalable hybrid query of semantic web data. In: Aberer, K., et al. (eds.) ISWC/ASWC 2007. LNCS, vol. 4825, pp. 652–665. Springer, Heidelberg (2007)

34. Fernández, M., Cantador, I., López, V., Vallet, D., Castells, P., Motta, E.: Semantically enhanced information retrieval: An ontology-based approach. Web Semantics 9(4), 434–452 (2011)

35. Wang, H., Tran, T., Liu, C., Fu, L.: Lightweight integration of ir & db for scalable hybrid search with integrated ranking support. Web Semantics: Science, Services and Agents on the World Wide Web 9(4) (2011)

36. Fazzinga, B., Gianforme, G., Gottlob, G., Lukasiewicz, T.: Semantic web search based on ontological conjunctive queries. Web Semantics: Science, Services and Agents on the World Wide Web 9(4) (2011)

37. Bikakis, N., Giannopoulos, G., Dalamagas, T., Sellis, T.: Integrating keywords and semantics on document annotation and search. In: Meersman, R., Dillon, T., Herrero, P. (eds.) OTM 2010. LNCS, vol. 6427, pp. 921–938. Springer, Heidelberg (2010)

38. Popov, B., Kiryakov, A., Kirilov, A., Manov, D., Ognyanoff, D., Goranov, M.: KIM – Semantic Annotation Platform. In: Fensel, D., Sycara, K., Mylopoulos, J. (eds.) ISWC 2003. LNCS, vol. 2870, pp. 834–849. Springer, Heidelberg (2003)

39. Kiryakov, A.: OWLIM: balancing between scalable repository and light-weight reasoner. In: Proceedings of the 15th International World Wide Web Conference (WWW 2006), Edinburgh, Scotland, May 23-26 (2006)

40. Boldi, P., Vigna, S.: MG4J at TREC 2005. In: Voorhees, E.M., Buckland, L.P. (eds.) Proceedings of the Fourteenth Text REtrieval Conference (TREC 2005), November 15-18. Special Publications, NIST, vol. 500, pp. 266–271 (2005), http://mg4j.dsi.unimi.it/

41. Maynard, D., Greenwood, M.A.: Large Scale Semantic Annotation, Indexing and Search at The National Archives. In: Proceedings of LREC 2012, Turkey (2012)

42. Tablan, V., Roberts, I., Cunningham, H., Bontcheva, K.: Gatecloud.net: a platform for large-scale, open-source text processing on the cloud. Philosophical Transactions of the Royal Society A 371(1983) (2013)

43. Damljanovic, D., Agatonovic, M., Cunningham, H.: Natural Language Interfaces to Ontologies: Combining Syntactic Analysis and Ontology-Based Lookup through the User Interaction. In: Aroyo, L., Antoniou, G., Hyvönen, E., ten Teije, A., Stuckenschmidt, H., Cabral, L., Tudorache, T. (eds.) ESWC 2010, Part I. LNCS, vol. 6088, pp. 106–120. Springer, Heidelberg (2010)

44. Lopez, V., Uren, V., Motta, E., Pasin, M.: AquaLog: An Ontology-driven Question Answering System for Organizational Semantic Intranets. Web Semantics: Science, Services and Agents on the World Wide Web 5(2), 72–105 (2007)
45. Kaufmann, E., Bernstein, A.: How Useful Are Natural Language Interfaces to the Semantic Web for Casual End-Users? In: Aberer, K., et al. (eds.) ISWC/ASWC 2007. LNCS, vol. 4825, pp. 281–294. Springer, Heidelberg (2007)
46. Funk, A., Tablan, V., Bontcheva, K., Cunningham, H., Davis, B., Handschuh, S.: CLOnE: Controlled Language for Ontology Editing. In: Aberer, K., et al. (eds.) ISWC/ASWC 2007. LNCS, vol. 4825, pp. 142–155. Springer, Heidelberg (2007)
47. Bernstein, A., Kaufmann, E.: GINO - A Guided Input Natural Language Ontology Editor. In: Cruz, I., Decker, S., Allemang, D., Preist, C., Schwabe, D., Mika, P., Uschold, M., Aroyo, L.M. (eds.) ISWC 2006. LNCS, vol. 4273, pp. 144–157. Springer, Heidelberg (2006)
48. Damljanovic, D., Bontcheva, K.: Enhanced Semantic Access to Software Artefacts. In: Workshop on Semantic Web Enabled Software Engineering (SWESE), Karlsruhe, Germany (October 2008)
49. Lei, Y., Uren, V.S., Motta, E.: SemSearch: A Search Engine for the Semantic Web. In: Staab, S., Svátek, V. (eds.) EKAW 2006. LNCS (LNAI), vol. 4248, pp. 238–245. Springer, Heidelberg (2006)
50. Blanco, R., Halpin, H., Herzig, D.M., Mika, P., Pound, J., Thompson, H.S., Tran, T.: Repeatable and reliable semantic search evaluation. Web Semantics: Science, Services and Agents on the World Wide Web (in press)
51. Halpin, H., Lavrenko, V.: Relevance feedback between hypertext and semantic web search: Frameworks and evaluation. Web Semantics: Science, Services and Agents on the World Wide Web 9(4) (2011)
52. Bontcheva, K., Kieniewicz, J., Aswani, N., Wallis, M., Andrews, S.: User feedback report on the envilod semantic search interface. Technical Report, EnviLOD project deliverable (2012), http://gate.ac.uk/projects/envilod/EnviLOD-user-feedback-report.pdf

Keyword Search over Relational Databases: Issues, Approaches and Open Challenges

Sonia Bergamaschi[1], Francesco Guerra[1], and Giovanni Simonini[2],*

[1] Dipartimento di Ingegneria "Enzo Ferrari"
Università di Modena e Reggio Emilia, Italy
firstname.lastname@unimore.it
[2] International Doctorate School in ICT
Università di Modena e Reggio Emilia, Italy
firstname.lastname@unimore.it

Abstract. In this paper, we overview the main research approaches developed in the area of Keyword Search over Relational Databases. In particular, we model the process for solving keyword queries in three phases: the management of the user's input, the search algorithms, the results returned to the user. For each phase we analyze the main problems, the solutions adopted by the most important system developed by researchers and the open challenges. Finally, we introduce two open issues related to multi-source scenarios and database sources handling instance not fully accessible.

1 Introduction

There is a large amount of structured data currently available on the Internet, mainly in relational and RDF formats. The technology is moving from a "web of documents" where the information is published to be directly human-consumed in a "web of data", where the information is provided in a structured form, like the data you find in databases. The European Commission is contributing to this process: several EU FP7 projects are dealing / dealt with tools enabling the publication, the interlinking of data on the web (see for example, LATC[1], PlanetData[2], LOD2[3], etc). The "Digital Agenda for Europe 2010-2020"[4] is promoting the publication and the reuse of public sector information (PSI) in the form of open data, publicly accessible by other Institutions and Enterprises (See Digital Agenda for Europe 2010-2020, Action 3). The economic potential in using these data is enormous. A recent study[5] estimated the total market for public sector information in 2008 at €28 billion across the EU. The same study indicates that the overall economic gains from further opening up public sector information

---

* Phd Student.
[1] http://latc-project.eu/
[2] http://www.planet-data.eu/
[3] http://lod2.eu/Welcome.html
[4] http://ec.europa.eu/information_society/digital-agenda/index_en.htm
[5] http://europa.eu/rapid/pressReleasesAction.do?reference=MEMO/11/891

N. Ferro (Ed.): PROMISE Winter School 2013, LNCS 8173, pp. 54–73, 2014.
© Springer-Verlag Berlin Heidelberg 2014

by allowing easy access are in the order of €40 billion a year for the EU and the total direct and indirect economic gains from easier PSI re-use across the whole EU economy would be in the order of €140 billion annually.

However, open data represent only a fraction of the structured data available on the web. Data-intensive websites (product catalogs, scientific databases, e-commerce systems) typically publish on the web data extracted from structured databases. The collection of these databases constitutes the *deep web* (invisible web), which has been considered the largest collection of the data available. The dimension of the data in the deep web has been the subject of several studies. Among them, [29] claims that the deep web size is up to 500 times larger than the Surface Web of static HTML pages.

To access structured data, users and applications need to formulate queries in the native query language of the specific structured source. This makes data access a difficult task, for users, since the formulation of structured queries needs strong knowledge of a query language (such as SQL for relational databases and SPARQL for RDF collections) and of the schema of the source. In a dynamic and distributed environment understanding the semantics of the source instance and schema could be very difficult for a user.

Keyword-based Search has become the de-facto standard for finding information on the Web (everyone uses a search engine). The Information Retrieval community has already developed advanced techniques for keyword search over documents, but direct application of these solutions to relational data sources, where information is typically fragmented in multiple tables, is neither efficient nor effective. Full-text inverted indexes, typically used in IR approaches, can be useful to associate keywords to tuples in tables, but cannot say anything about how tables have to be joined to form a meaningful answer to the keyword query as a whole. As a matter of fact, it could happen that no meaningful join-path might exist among the tuples containing the keywords in the query. Even if this issue can be partially addressed by applying IR techniques to the "universal relation", building and keeping up-to-date such a relation is not feasible in practice. Furthermore, IR techniques do not take into account the structural semantics conveyed by the source schemas, which could largely improve the quality of the results. These limitations have led to the development of techniques for effectively and efficiently querying structured databases through keywords.

For this reason, Keyword Search on Databases has become a hot research direction, and attracted researchers in DB, IR, theory, etc. Between 2002 and 2009, more than 50 different research approaches from both research labs and universities have been published in major database conferences/journals [7]. The trend shows an increasing number of proposals are expected in the following years. the simplicity of formulating queries with keywords is the main reason for its popularity.

In this paper, we give an overview of the current approaches to address the problem of keyword search over relational databases, proposed in the prototypal systems developed by researchers.

Most approaches build a special index on the contents of the database (instance) and to use that index to find the attribute values matching the keywords. Once the terms have been located in a index, a path discovery algorithm is used to find the different parts of the schema/tuples where these terms are located and the different links connecting these parts/tuples (e.g., finding minimal joining networks or Steiner trees).

In the following sections, we analyze the process adopted for solving keyword queries by following the typical three phases of keyword based search: a) the user keyword input; b) the matching of keywords and database schema/values; and c) the query result. An extensive study of the characteristics of all the proposed systems is out of the scope of the paper (see [30] for a good survey). Here, we limit our focus on some systems (DBXPLORER [2], BANKS [1], BANKS II [15], DISCOVER [14], DISCOVER II [13], DPBF [9], PRECIS [24], BLINKS [12], STAR [16], SQAK [25], and KEY-MANTIC [3] / KEYRY [5]) that for some reason have been considered as "pioneering" and innovative for some features.

Our analysis of the process individuates three ideal components (for the three phases) related to: understanding the meaning of the users' queries, matching keywords with the schema/tuples, returning the results. For each component, we analyze the main issues, the solutions proposed in the literature and the open issues. The component for analyzing the keyword queries is introduced in Section 2, where we address issues concerning the ambiguity of keyword queries and the need of techniques for discovering the intended meaning of keywords. Section 3 introduces the techniques for associating keywords to corresponding elements in the datasources. Typically these techniques can be divided in two steps: the first concerns the discovery of the database structures/tuples that can be associated to the keywords; the second one concerns the selection of the paths, connecting the database structures identified in the previous step. Section 4 discusses issues related to the completeness, ranking and visualization of the results. Finally, in Section 5, we introduce some open challenges related to the capabilities of querying databases with limited access (i.e., scenarios where fullt-text indexes are not allowed) and the ability of managing multi-source queries, i.e., queries where the answer is obtained by merging the solutions provided by different queries against different data sources.

2   Understanding the Meaning of the Users' Queries

2.1   Issues to Address

Describing his information needs by means of keyword queries is easy for a user, but comes with a price: keywords are inherently ambiguous and their intended meaning needs to be discovered [27]. Two kinds of possible queries are distinguished in [11]: *navigational searches*, where the user provides the search engine a phrase or combination of words which he expects to find in the documents, and *research searches*, where the user provides the search engine with a phrase which is intended to denote an object about which the user is trying to gather/search information. Typically, keyword search in Information Retrieval addresses the first type of query, looking for documents containing the user keywords. The same happens for the existing keyword search systems over structured databases, where tuples containing the user keywords are retrieved.

Roughly speaking, the process for understanding the intended meaning of a user query consists in associating to each keyword a specific concept in a reference ontology. A large number of techniques relies on ontologies and disambiguation techniques to discover the users' intended meaning of a keyword query. These techniques aim to associate meanings to terms labels, by matching the text strings labels with elements belonging to reference ontologies / knowledge base thesauri(see [20] for a survey). Among the existing approaches, in [26] Description Logics techniques are exploited for checking the proximities and consistencies of the meanings associated to the keywords in a query through ontologies; in [21] a probabilistic framework supports the selections of possible meanings associated to schema labels. Identifying the meaning of terms composing a keyword query separately is in general insufficient for understanding the intended meaning of a keyword query; context information can be very useful. In particular, in [17], a clustering approach is proposed to categorize and personalize search results according to user interests. A large body of works exploits query context to improve ranking, where the goal is usually better capturing the user intent [32].

Nevertheless, even if we assume that the right meaning of the keywords has been computed, different interpretations of a query are still possible. Let us consider, for example, the query "George Clooney Italy", where the meaning associated to each term is unambiguous. Nevertheless, the two keywords may refer to different queries: the movies acted by the actor, the houses that the actor owns in Italy, the awards that received in Italy, etc. In structured data sources, the possible interpretations of a keyword query correspond to the different ways by which their respective tuples are connected, forming the so-called "joining network" of tuples or tuple trees or Steiner tree, that often become the information unit returned to the user. In Section 3, the problem of computing all the possible interpretations for a keyword query is discussed and the approaches developed in the literature presented.

Finally, the overall meaning of keyword queries composed of more terms depends on the meaning associated to the connectors between the keywords. Boolean connectives (AND, OR, NOT) are typically supported by keyword search engines over structured databases. More complex operators, such as aggregation, filter and proximity functions are in most cases not supported and we observe that can be extremely useful to better specify the intended meaning of users' keyword queries.

2.2 Existing Approaches

To evaluate the main existing proposal for discovering the meaning of keyword queries, we reviewed the approaches of current systems following two perspectives: one user-oriented, aiming to check whether and how it is possible for a user to specify the information he is looking for, and the other application-oriented, evaluating the techniques (if any) exploited by the application for analyzing the user's input.

Concerning the user-oriented perspective, the analysis considers three dimensions:

1. Query language adopted. Users can formulate queries by means of keywords specifying values they want to retrieve, sentences in natural language describing what they are looking for, controlled terms (taken from an ontology / thesaurus).
2. Ability to search for metadata (i.e., schema descriptions).
3. Supported operators in the formulations (e.g., boolean, logical and arithmetical operators).

The results of our user-oriented analysis are summarized in Table 1. For almost all the approaches analyzed, only the instances are the target for the keyword queries and the applications allow the management of exact keyword queries only.

Table 1. Techniques for understanding the Keyword Queries

	User-oriented		
	Query Language	Querying Metadata	Operators
DBXPLORER	Exact keyword search	No	AND
BANKS / BANKS II	Exact keyword search	Yes (schema ele-ments)	AND
DISCOVER	Exact keyword search	No	AND
DISCOVER II	Exact keyword search	No	AND / OR
DPBF	Exact keyword search	No	AND
PRECIS	Exact keyword search	No	AND / OR / NOT
BLINKS	Exact keyword search	No	AND
STAR	Exact keyword search	No	AND
SQAK	Approximate string match	Yes (schema ele-ments)	Boolean and aggre-gate functions
KEYMANTIC - KEYRY	Exact keyword search	Yes (schema ele-ments)	AND

Concerning the application-oriented perspective, the analysis concerned the following three dimensions:

1. Existence of techniques for query disambiguation. We analyzed which technique (if any) has been adopted for understanding the correct meanings of the terms used in the queries;
2. Existence of techniques for input enrichment and transformation. We checked if any technique has been implemented for transforming the user's input into a similar one (with hypernym / hyponym / related terms) to obtain better results;
3. Existence of techniques for relaxing constraints, i.e. techniques for transforming the user's input into a less selective one to obtain more results.

The majority of the systems does not implement any specific technique for disambiguating and enriching keywords or for relaxing constraints. Only KEYMANTIC and KEYRY adopt a disambiguation approach based on the lexical database WordNet and, PRECIS, tries to provide possible interpretations for the query based on the data retrieved in the database.

2.3   Open Issues

Understanding the meaning of the keyword queries needs to address a number of issues which are still open.

First of all, new paradigms for querying data sources have to be investigated. The way queries have to be entered by users, e.g. by means of incremental refinements of an initial query [31] or by exploiting query suggestions made by the system based on previous searches or results, have a large impact on the quality perceived by the user of the interaction with the system. These paradigms have also to consider the various standards and constraints of mobile devices. For example, limited CPU performance, display size, and keyboard input possibilities have to be taken into account – as well as natural language interfaces with speech.

Moreover, one of the strength points of keyword search approaches resides in their capability of allowing users to easily formulate queries. This capability represents at the same time a limitation: the query engines holding the structured data sources could allow the execution of complex queries, including aggregation functions, application of constraints, and selection filters, which are difficult to be expressed by means of simple keyword queries. The development of a standard easy to use language for enriching keyword queries with advanced operators can be useful for overcoming this limitation.

Finally, the heterogeneity of the sources available impose the development of semantic functions to enrich user keywords. Among them, the availability of *conceptualisation functions*, i.e. functions transforming data to metadata by associating a keyword to the most related database structure, *lexical transformations functions*, translating keyword queries into semantically-similar queries, with different terms (by using synonyms, hypernyms, hyponyms, etc.), would be very useful.

3   Matching Keywords into the Database

3.1   Issues to Address

In keyword search over textual documents, documents are treated as a "bag of words": each word is indexed separately from the others (in most of the approaches, the semantics represented by the order of the words is completely lost), and at query time, the indexes built are used to retrieve all the documents that contain keywords.

Also tuples in relational databases (RDBs) can be viewed as textual documents and indexed in the same way; indeed, most of current commercial relational database management systems (RDBMS) provide facilities to support keyword queries, i.e. full-text indexes built and automatically maintained on textual attributes of relations. At query time, indexes are used to efficiently retrieve and rank tuples that contain keywords. The most important RDBMS capabilities and techniques discovering the database structures that can be associated to the keywords existing in the literature are introduced in section 3.2. However, the use of IR-style search is not effective because it considers tuples as unstructured data, while in RDBs information to be retrieved is spread among tables. Unlike textual documents, tuples are semantically connected by *foreign-primary key references*. Thus, foreign-primary key paths connecting tuples that contain keywords represent an essential ingredient for solving a keyword query over a database. Hence, the need of defining representation models of databases to be exploited for retrieving these paths is mandatory.

Finally, techniques to rank paths (once obtained) are needed for providing the generated results in order of relevance.

3.2   Existing Approaches

The approaches can be categorized into two broad categories [24,9,30]:

- *Schema-based approach*

  The Schema-based approach models the database schema as a graph (schema graph) where nodes represent database relations and edges represent primary key - foreign key dependencies. The generation of an answer is based on the graph and involves two generic phases. First, the relations that contain a query keyword and the schema graph are taken as input and the possible paths are generated. The second phase generates appropriate queries that retrieve the actual tuples from the database following each path [24]. This kind of approaches aims at processing a keyword query by using the schema information to generate SQL queries in RDBMS. Systems modeled as schema-based approach are: DBXPLORER, DISCOVER, DISCOVER II, PRECIS, STAR, SQAK, KEYMANTIC, and KEYRY.

- *Tuple-based approach*

  Tuple-based approaches model the databases as a data graph, where nodes are tuple identifiers and edges represent foreign key references between two tuples. Only one phase is needed in these approaches to generate the query answer, where the tuple retrieval task and the answer schema extraction are combined: the system analyzes the data graph for building trees of joining tuples that meet the query specification, e.g., trees containing all keywords for queries with AND semantics [24]. In the data graph, nodes and edges are typically weighted. A node that has many links with others has a relative small possibility of having a close relationship to any of them, thus the weights of edges incident on it have to be properly set [9]. Unlike an undirected graph, the fact that an object u can reach another object v in a directed graph does not necessarily mean the vice-versa, i.e., that the object u is reachable from v. In this context, a returned structure is directed. Such direction handling provides users with more information on how the objects are interconnected. On the other hand, it requests higher computational cost to find such structures [30]. Systems modeled as tuple-base approach include: BANKS, BANKS II, DPBF, BLINKS.

Table 2 compares the main approaches of the current systems on the basis of the following dimensions:

1. **Representation Model**

   This perspective aims at evaluating how the data source is represented for the keyword search purpose. The problem here is to model the schema in an effective way in order to find the possible paths connecting tuples containing the keywords.

2. **Keyword Matching Process**

   This perspective analyzes techniques for computing keyword matches on the database.

   There are several techniques. Many systems exploit IR-styled search supported by commercial RDBMS (DB2[6], Oracle[7], SQL Server[8], Postgres[9] and MySQL[10]),

---

[6] http://www.ibm.com/developerworks/data/tutorials/dm-0810shettar/index.html

[7] http://docs.oracle.com/

[8] http://msdn.microsoft.com/it-it/library/ms142571.aspx

[9] http://www.postgresql.org/docs/9.1/static/textsearch-intro.html

[10] http://dev.mysql.com/doc/internals/en/full-text-search.html

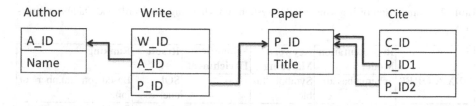

Fig. 1. Portion of the DBLP Database Schema [22]

in which a built-in keyword search engine builds full-text indexes over text attributes, and uses them to retrieve which attributes in the relations contain the specified keywords.

3. **Semantic Enrichment of the Model by means of External Ontologies**
   External ontologies, taxonomies and knowledge bases can be used for improving the searching algorithm by allowing the discovering of semantic relationships among tuples and schema elements in the database.

4. **Ranking techniques**
   This perspective compares the ranking functions used to generate the potentially best results first.

   The ranking algorithm plays an important role in the efficiency of the system, and it strongly depends on the data model adopted to represent the database. Indeed, as explained for PRECIS [24], one advantage of tuple-based techniques over schema-based ones is the possibility of a finegrained tuple ranking. In the directed graph model, an answer to a keyword query is a minimal rooted direct tree, embedded in the data graph, and containing at least one node matching a keyword, for each keyword.

   Its overall score is defined by specifications of:

   (a) overall edge score of the tree based on individual edge weights
   (b) overall node score of the tree, obtained by combining individual node scores
   (c) combination of the tree edge score and the tree node score

   Otherwise, schema-based approaches cannot fully make use of node/edge weights at tuple level. Thus, Discover [14], ranked the tuples (the output generated by the system) by the number of joins, based on the idea of proximity.

Schema-Based Approach

In the schema-based approach, the model of the database schema is represented as a direct graph $G = (V, E)$ *(schema graph)*, where V is the set of relations of the schema $\{R_1..R_n\}$ and E is the set of primary key to foreign key relationships between two relations R_i and R_j, formally: $(R_i, R_j) \in E$. We define G_u to be the undirected version of G.

An example *schema graph* is shown in Fig. 1. Fig. 2 shows an example of database instance that conforms to the schema in Fig. 1

Table 2. Comparison of Keyword Search Systems on Matching Keywords and Database Structures

	Representation Model	Keyword Matching	Semantic Enrichment	Result	Ranking
DBXPLORER	Schema-based	Symbol Tables	-	SQL queries	Based on number of joins
BANKS BANKS-II	Tuple-based	Double index	-	Tuples	Based on proximity and prestige of node *weight at tuple level*
DISCOVER	Schema-based	RDBMS full-text index	-	SQL queries	Based on number of join
DISCOVER-II SPARK	Schema-based	RDBMS full-text indexi	-	SQL queries	Top-k *based on attribute level ranking*
DPBF	Tuple-based	RDBMS full-text index	-	Tuples	Top-k with Cost Function *weight at tuple level*
PRECIS	Schema-based (both relations and attributes are nodes)	Full-text index in Oracle PLSQL	-	DB Subset	Cost Function *weight at schema level*
BLINKS	Tuple-based	Bi-level index	-	Tuples	Top-k with Cost Function *weight at tuple level*
SQAK	Schema-based	*Apache Lucene*	Ontology based normalization	SQL queries	Cost Function *weight at schema level*
KEYRY KEYMAN-TIC	Schema-based	Regular expressions and semantic similarity measures	Metadata enrichment via WordNet	SQL queries	Manually selected by the user

*Definition 1. **Joining Network of Tuples***
A joining network of tuples (JNT) is a connected tree of tuples, where for each pair of adjacent tuples t_i, t_j, where $t_i \in r(R_i), t_j \in r(R_j)$, $r(R_i)$ instance of R_i and $r(R_j)$ instance of R_j, there is an edge $(R_i, R_j) \in E$ and $(t^i \bowtie t^j) \in (R_i \bowtie R_j)$

Given a keyword query of size i, every *JNT* that satisfies the following two conditions is defined as **Minimal Total Join Network of Tuples** (*MTJNT*):

- the *JNT* contains every keyword at least in one of its tuples.
  (*Totality Condition*)
- removing any tuples from the *JNT*, the *JNT* no longer satisfies the *Totality Condition*.
  (*Minimality Condition*)

TID	Name
a_1	Charlie Carpenter
a_2	Micheal Richardson
a_3	Michelle

(a)

TID	Title
p_1	Contributions of Michelle
p_2	Keyword Search in XML
p_3	Pattern Matching in XML
p_4	Algorithm for TopK Query

(b)

TID	AID	PID
w_1	a_1	p_1
w_2	a_1	p_2
w_3	a_2	p_2
w_4	a_3	p_2
w_5	a_3	p_4
w_6	a_3	p_3

(c)

TID	PID1	PID2
C_1	P_2	P_1
C_2	P_3	P_1
C_3	P_2	P_3
C_4	P_3	P_4
C_5	P_2	P_4

(d)

Fig. 2. Portion of the DBLP Database. (a)Author (b)Paper (c)Write (d)Cite [22].

The set of all possible *MTJNTs* for a given *l*-keyword query represents the result of that query. The number of joins involved in the *MTJNT* determines its *size*.

The process to generate the set of MTJNTs begins with the retrieving of all the tuples that contain keywords, by means of full-text indexes, grouped in *tuple sets*. A *tuple set* $R_i^{k_j}$ groups all tuples of relation R_i that contain a certain keyword k_j. Then, *tuple sets* are processed to produce **keyword relations** R_i^K, where K is a subset of the keywords of the query $Q = \{k_1, \ldots, k_m\}$:

$$R_i^K = \{t | t \in r(R_i) \land \forall k \in K, t \text{ contains } k \land \forall k \in Q - K, t \neg contains \, k\} \quad (1)$$

If $K = \emptyset$, we call the relation *free tuple set*, denoted as $R^{\{\}}$.

From the *keyword relations* we can now define *candidate networks*:

Definition 2. **Candidate Network**
A candidate network (CN) is a connected tree of keyword relations, where for each pair of adjacent keyword relations R_i^K, R_j^M there is an edge (R_i, R_j) in G_u, and the CN satisfies the following two conditions:

1. (Total) each keyword in the query must be contained in at least one keyword relation of the CN
2. (Minimal) the total condition is not satisfied anymore if any keyword relation is removed

CNs produce the set of all possible MTJNTs and correspond to a relational algebra expression that joins a sequence of relations to obtain MTJNTs over the relations involved [30]. In Fig. 3 an example of CNs is shown for the query

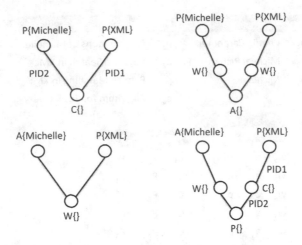

Fig. 3. CNs for the query Q={"Michelle", "XML"} [22]

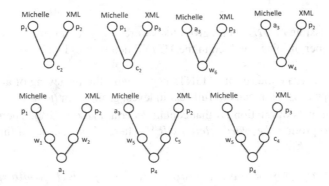

Fig. 4. MTJNTs for the query Q={"Michelle","XML"}. Maximum number of allowed tuples in a MTJNT: 5. [22]

$Q = \{$ "$Michelle$","XML"$\}$, considering the schema graph in Fig. 1. Fig. 4 shows a set of possible MTJNTs obtained from those CNs.

To produce *CNs*, DBXPLORER does not consider solutions that include two tuples from the same relations, while DISCOVER and DISCOVER-II do it, in order to exploit the reusability opportunities of the joining trees [14].

The two main steps to process a keyword query with a RDBMS are: *candidate network generation* and *candidate network evaluation*

Candidate Network Generation
First, a naïve algorithm to generate all CNs (this process is called *candidate network generation*) was proposed in DISCOVER. It takes as input all the keyword relations generated in the previous step, and recursively expands them with adjacent keyword

relations (also empty ones). Pruning rules ensure that all CNs generated are duplication-free, complete and minimal. This algorithm has high computational costs, thus, to improve the performance, the *rightmost* algorithm was proposed in [19]; it avoids pruning rules by assigning a proper expansion order to the partial trees.

Candidate Network Evaluation and Result Ranking
CNs naturally correspond to database queries, hence a set of SQL queries must be generated and executed in order to get final results. In DBXPLORER and DISCOVER, all CNs are evaluated by specifying a proper execution plan. The results so obtained are ranked by the number of joins involved. Since it represents a closer association, based on the idea of proximity, the smaller is that number, the higher is the score.

DISCOVER-II and SPARK propose several algorithms to output *top-k* MTJNTs basing on score functions. The aim is to find a proper order of execution, to stop early before all results are generated.

The *Sparse* algorithm, the *Single-pipelined* algorithm and the *Global-pipelined* algorithm are based on attribute level ranking functions: for each tuple of a MTJNT, a tuple level ranking function assigns for each text attribute of the tuple a score exploiting single-attribute relevance-ranking of an RDBMS that supports text-indexes capabilities (e.g. Oracle 9.1 in DISCOVER). Finally, the final score is obtained combining individual scores together.
A brief overview:

- the *Sparse* algorithm does not execute queries for non promising CNs, thus it does not produce effective top-k results; it leverages the highly optimized execution plans the underlying RDBMS can produce when a single query is issued for each CN, thus is more efficient for queries with few results;
- the *Single-Pipelined* algorithm first gets the top-k MTJNTs for each CN, and then combines them together to get the final result;
- the *Global-Pipelined* algorithm progressively evaluates a small prefix of each CN, in order to retrieve only the top-k results, hence it is more efficient for queries with a relative large number of results.

In an attribute-level ranking function, each text attribute of a tuple is considered as a virtual document. Alternatively, a whole MTJNT can be viewed as a virtual document, as proposed in tree-level functions (*Skyline-sweeping* and *Block-pipelined* algorithm) proposed in SPARK , based on IR-styled function (*TF-IDF*).

Other schema based approaches
A notable variant of the schema graph G_u representation is proposed in PRECIS [24], where in the database schema graph $G(E, V)$ there are two types of nodes: (a) a relational node R for each relation in the schema and (b) an attribute node A for each attribute in the schema. Hence, there are two types of edges: (a) projection edges Π, one for each attribute node emanating from its container relation node, and (b) join edges J between relational nodes. Thus $V = R \cup A$ and $E = \Pi \cup J$. Edges in Π are undirected with weights associated; while the ones of J have a weight for each direction (from node $R_i \in R$ to node $R_j \in R$ and vice-versa).

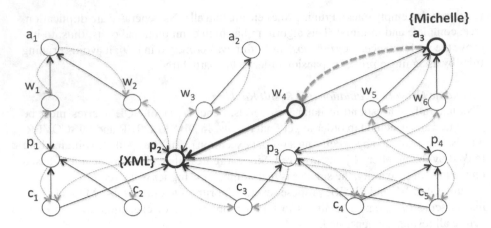

Fig. 5. Example of tuple graph, based on the portion of the DBLP Database in Figure 2. Solid lines represent foreign-primary key relationships (direct edges), while dashed lines are backward edges. The bold lines represent a possible path for the query Q={"Michelle", "XML"} [22].

This model allows to support a finer-grained ranking to rank answers according to their relevance, which is determined basing on the weight at the schema level.

Current commercial RDBMS are powerful enough to support keyword queries in RDBs efficiently without any additional new indexing to be built and maintained [22].

However, early approaches proposed in the literature exploited different full-text indexing techniques, such as *symbol tables*. Symbol tables store information at row level granularity, i.e. for each keyword they keep the list of rows that contains the keyword. Alternative symbol table designs are possible where RDBs have columns with index. In this case, the system only stores the list of columns where keywords occur.

SQAK uses an inverted index built on all the text columns of the DB with *Lucene*. This inverted index returns all the table names and the columns in which a keyword occurs. Matching keywords, SQAK also tries to find out what keywords may refer to some table of the DB, in order to better address the user's query. For example in a movie database with *movies, actors and directors* tables, given the query "*film with Nicolas Cage*" the keyword "film" is interpreted by the system as a synonym of the name of the table *movies*. Synonymous terms in the query may be automatically matched using ontology-based normalization [25].

Tuple-Based Approach

Tuple-based approaches model the database as a direct graph $G_d(E, V)$, in which nodes V represent tuples and (forward) edges E represent primary to foreign key dependencies between tuples. Forward (u, v) edges have weights. For each of them, a backward edges (v, u) is defined with a weight proportional to the number of links to v from nodes of the same type as u. Also nodes may have a weight to reflect the prestige of the link [1].

In Figure 5 an example of tuple graph $G_d(E, V)$ is shown.

Under this representation model, an answer to a keyword query is represented by a set of connected subtrees of G_d containing all the keywords in its nodes.

If we consider a subset of E where each node contains a specific keyword, and a group E for each keyword of the query, an answer to a query is represented by sets of connected subtrees of the weighted graph G_d that contains at least one node for each group and with minimal cost (only *top-k* ranked results are returned). This is the classical Steiner tree problem [10].

To address the Steiner tree problem and find the *top-k* results, BANKS emulates the *distance network heuristic* (DNH) [16] by running single source shortest paths iterators from each node in each of the $V_i s$, where V_i is the set of nodes which contain the keyword k_i. The iterators are expanded in a best-first strategy and follow the edges backwards (*backward search*).

In BANKS, the tuple-graph G_d is materialized and supposed to fit in memory (as in other tuple-based approaches). This assumption is not unreasonable, even for relative large databases, because the in-memory node representations[11] needs only to store TIDs[12]. Another only in-memory structure needed is an index to map TIDs to the graph nodes. This technique is called *double indexing*.

BLINKS uses a variant of the backward search strategy of BANKS, but one of the the most interesting difference between the approaches is the *bi-level indexing*. Two kinds of indexes are built to speed up the search. The first index maintains, for each keyword, a list of nodes that can reach the keyword and the distances of these nodes from it. The second one maintains a list of reachable keywords for each node. However, the proposed indexes may be too large to be stored, thus the tuple graph is partitioned in *blocks*, and a high level keyword-block is built and exploited in backward searching within blocks.

3.3 Open Issues

A general consideration about the open challenges is about scalability. As a matter of fact, almost all the presented approaches are not able to grow as quickly as data grow in relational databases. This is due to the costs for managing full-text indexing and ensuring (at least near) real-time generation of responses. Typically, this is a NP-complete problem (e.g. this can be modeled as a Steiner tree problem).

4 Returning the Results

4.1 Issues to Address

The ways in which results are returned to the user is a critical aspect of keyword search engines. In this context, the main issues concern the identification of the granularity of the results and the time performance of the techniques developed for retrieving the results.

The granularity of the results might vary from a simple list of data sources (as it happens usually for keyword search engines that retrieve documents related to the keywords of interest), to a set of records satisfying the keywords (as it happens for results

---

[11] G_d may be materialized using dynamically two hash structures: one for the nodes, the other one for the edges.

[12] Tuple identifiers.

of structured queries). The list of data sources relevant for a specific keyword query is computed by the application of techniques for query-routing. Query-routing approaches are able to identify the relevant domain(s) of a query and then to map the keywords in the query to the fields of the virtual schema for that domain [18]. Typically, structured queries formulated over a database return a list of tuples satisfying the constraints and according to the database. A similar mechanism for specifying the structure and the granularity of the results is not defined in the keyword query paradigm. Consequently, techniques for identifying what the user is really expecting as a result have to be developed. Moreover, due to the data models adopted for representing structured data sources which fragment the data into several structures (e.g., tables in relational schemas), there are multiple paths connecting the same data structures, thus leading to several possible answers for a query. In this case, it is important to show not only the results, but also the paths generating the results that can "explain" the actual meaning of each answer [4].

The time performance represents one of the main drawbacks of the approaches developed in the literature. [8] proposes an experimental comparison of some important systems against three datasets: Mondial[13], IMDB[14] and a relational version of Wikipedia. The three datasets have different features: Mondial is small, but the tables are connected by multiple foreign-key relationships, IMDB is a very large dataset with a flat structure, and Wikipedia features represent a "middle point" between the other datasets. For comparing the approaches, the authors computed the time needed for answering fifty queries against the three datasets. The result of the experiments shows that even if we consider the smaller dataset, the majority of the approaches need some seconds for providing results. The response times dramatically increase if we consider the other datasets, where in some cases few thousand seconds are required for solving the queries.

4.2 Existing Approaches

To provide a synoptic view about how the results are returned to the users, we reviewed the existing approaches according to two different perspectives: the first concerns the management of the process and results, and the second the evaluations of the performances.

In the first perspective, we are interested in the interactions needed and the modalities adopted by the systems to provide the results to the users. For this reason, we analyzed the following dimensions:

- User interaction. The searching process may be automatic, or it may require any user's feedback for improving/refining the query.
- Data visualization. The systems may visualize only the tuples satisfying the keyword queries or provide more information for supporting the user in understanding the results retrieved (e.g., the results can be annotated with respect to an external reference ontology, part of the data source schema can be shown, ...).

The second perspective analyzes how the performances of the search engines are evaluated in terms of datasets and indicators. In particular:

---

[13] http://www.dbis.informatik.uni-goettingen.de/Mondial/
[14] http://www.imdb.com/

– Datasets/Queryset. Due to the absence of standard well-known benchmarks for the evaluation and comparison of the approaches, the existing techniques have been evaluated against different datasets (both real and synthetic databases) and with different query sets. This leads to the impossibility of a fair comparison of the performances on the basis of the experimental results published. Moreover, as stated in [28], the evaluation of the approaches performed by the own proposers may be unfair, since, in some cases, the number of queries analyzed and the quality of the queries (self-formulated by the authors of the approach) do not guarantee the absence of bias in the evaluation.

– Effectiveness / Efficiency indicators. The approaches are typically evaluated in terms of efficiency and effectiveness. Nevertheless, there is no agreement among the approaches about the metrics adopted for measuring these performance features.

Table 3 shows the results of our analysis. Most of the approaches of current systems do not allow users to specify / refine previously formulated queries or do not provide any mechanism for managing the interactions with the users during this phase. Moreover, the approaches typically show only the tuples resulting from the query processing (no metadata). Schema information that could support the user in understanding the results retrieved are in most cases omitted. Finally, our analysis confirmed what was stated in [28]: the approaches are compared against different datasets, with different querysets and by means of different metrics.

4.3 Open Issues

The main open issues in this phase of the query answering process concern the development of techniques for a better visualization / exploration of the results. The large diffusion of mobile devices requires the development of techniques for visualizing query results with devices having small screens and limited access to the Internet. The use of summarization and graphical representations of the results may support the overcoming of the issue. The same problem may occur also with standard devices dealing with big data sources. Also in this case, the large amount of data and possible results make indispensable the development of specific algorithms and techniques for retrieving and visualizing the results.

Finally, the development and application of machine learning techniques exploiting the results of previous queries can largely improve the results of the existing approaches.

5 Open Issues in Keyword Search over Relational Databases

Apart from the specific issues concerning the process for solving the keyword queries showed in the previous sections, we think that there are two important general issues the research community has to face. The first concerns the development of techniques in cases where it is not possible to use indexes for retrieving the data structures containing the keywords, and the second is related to multi source scenarios, where the answer of a query is possible uniquely by merging partial results provided by several partial queries over different sources.

Table 3. How Keyword Search Systems return the Results to the users

	Interactions		Performances	
	User Interaction	Data Visual-ization	Datasets / Queryset	Indicators
DBXPLORER	Search ASP page	Standard web browser	Dataset: synthetic (TPC-H)	efficiency (response time)
BANKS - **BANKS II**	Web Interface for browsing the data (with Group-By) and following FK relationships	Tuples and Database Metadata	Dataset: real (DBLP, an Internal DB (BANKS), IMDB(BANKSII)).	BANKS qualitative; BANKS II efficiency (# of node explored, touched and time performance considering the last relevant result)
DISCOVER	-	Tuples	Dataset: synthetic (TPC-H)	efficiency (Dimension of CN and processing time)
DISCOVER II	-	Tuples	Dataset: real (DBLP)	efficiency (response time)
DPBF	-	Tuples	Dataset: real (DBLP and MDB). Queryset: 20 random queries	efficiency (processing time, memory consumption, tree dimension)
PRECIS	Weights for customizing answers / Refinement of previous answers (against the returned database)	A subset of the database	Dataset: real (IMDB, gastronomia.gr). Queryset: 14 users formulating 10 queries each one	efficiency (response time); effectiveness (user satisfaction)
BLINKS	-	Tuples	Dataset: real (IMDB, DBLP). Queryset: 10 queries selected by authors	efficiency (time performance and impact on internal parameters)
STAR	-	Tuples	Dataset: real (DBLP and IMDB). Queryset: 3 querysets of 60 queries (3, 5, 7 keywords)	efficiency (tree dimension, processing time)
SQAK	Users are alerted if the accuracy of results could be low	Tuples	Dataset: real (internal), synthetic (TPC-H). Queryset: 15 queries for each database	efficiency (processing time); effectiveness (accuracy of the generated sql query)
KEYMANTIC - KEYRY	KEYMANTIC: user is required to select the path in a list of suggested ones	Tuples and Schema elements	Dataset: real (DBLP, MONDIAL, IMDB). Queryset: 10000 queries generated from 100 queries as a template	efficiency (response time); effectiveness (position of the correct answer)

5.1 Dealing with Not Accessible Database Extensions

In the previous sections, we showed that the majority of the existing approaches for keyword-based search are based on the construction of specialized content indexes. Unfortunately, such techniques cannot be applied in all contexts. Databases on the Deep Web, for instance, do not typically expose their full contents, but only a part of them, often through predefined web forms. The same happens for sources behind wrappers in Data Integration Systems. Furthermore, for sources that are typically under the responsibility of different owners, their contents may change at any time without a notice to update an index structure. In all these cases, the application of an index based approach is not possible (when the extensions of the databases are not accessible) or a hard task (when the frequent updates in the database contents require to update frequently the indexes).

To the best of our knowledge, only few approaches deal with this scenarios. All these approaches (KEYMANTIC, KEYRY and SODA [6]) exploit metadata for generating SQL queries (in SODA by using also aggregate functions) from keyword queries.

5.2 Multi-source Scenarios

Solving keyword queries in multi source scenarios implies the development of techniques for selecting among the available sources the ones suitable for each keyword query, for dividing the user query into a set of sub-queries, and for performing "on the fly" fusion of the results returned by the partial queries over the different sources. A simple solution to this problem can be obtained thanks to the application of some data integration techniques over the databases to be queried. Nevertheless, this solution is not practical when the number of databases is large or the sources are subject to frequent updates. Moreover, typical approaches for data integration build a virtual view of a set of databases. This means that the data extensions are typically not involved in the process (only the schemas are integrated) and consequently the existing approaches are not applicable due to the impossibility to build indexes over the data (see Section 5.1).

To the best of our knowledge, the problem of solving keyword queries over multiple databases is addressed only in [23] where the Kite system is presented. Kite exploits the joins, i.e. a sort of discovered automatically foreign keys relationships between different databases, to enable fast and effective querying over the distributed data.

6 Conclusion

In this paper we overviewed the main existing approaches for supporting keyword queries over relational databases. We divided the process for solving keyword queries in three main phases: understanding the meaning of the keyword query, matching the keyword query and the database, returning the results. For each steps, we analyzed the main issues to address, the solutions proposed by the existing systems and the issues which are still open. Finally, we sketched out two problems which are only partially addressed by the current research: how to query databases where the extension is only partially accessible and how to solve queries where the solutions require to merge partial results obtained by querying multiple sources.

The absence of any industrial grade business application for keyword search over relational database shows that further research effort is needed to deal with the still open research issues.

References

1. Aditya, B., Bhalotia, G., Chakrabarti, S., Hulgeri, A., Nakhe, C., Parag, Sudarshan, S.: Banks: Browsing and keyword searching in relational databases. In: VLDB Conference, pp. 1083–1086 (2002)
2. Agrawal, S., Chaudhuri, S., Das, G.: Dbxplorer: A system for keyword-based search over relational databases. In: ICDE Conference, pp. 5–16. IEEE Computer Society (2002)
3. Bergamaschi, S., Domnori, E., Guerra, F., Lado, R.T., Velegrakis, Y.: Keyword search over relational databases: a metadata approach. In: SIGMOD Conference, pp. 565–576. ACM (2011)
4. Bergamaschi, S., Domnori, E., Guerra, F., Orsini, M., Lado, R.T., Velegrakis, Y.: Keymantic: Semantic keyword-based searching in data integration systems. PVLDB 3(2), 1637–1640 (2010)
5. Bergamaschi, S., Guerra, F., Rota, S., Velegrakis, Y.: A hidden markov model approach to keyword-based search over relational databases. In: Jeusfeld, M., Delcambre, L., Ling, T.-W. (eds.) ER 2011. LNCS, vol. 6998, pp. 411–420. Springer, Heidelberg (2011)
6. Blunschi, L., Jossen, C., Kossmann, D., Mori, M., Stockinger, K.: Soda: Generating sql for business users. PVLDB 5(10), 932–943 (2012)
7. Chen, Y., Wang, W., Liu, Z., Lin, X.: Keyword search on structured and semi-structured data. In: SIGMOD Conference, pp. 1005–1010. ACM (2009)
8. Coffman, J., Weaver, A.: An empirical performance evaluation of relational keyword search techniques. IEEE Transactions on Knowledge and Data Engineering (99), 1 (2012)
9. Ding, B., Yu, J.X., Wang, S., Qin, L., Zhang, X., Lin, X.: Finding top-k min-cost connected trees in databases. In: ICDE Conference, pp. 836–845. IEEE (2007)
10. Dreyfus, S.E., Wagner, R.A.: The steiner problem in graphs. Networks 1(3), 195–207 (1971)
11. Guha, R.V., McCool, R., Miller, E.: Semantic search. In: WWW, pp. 700–709 (2003)
12. He, H., Wang, H., Yang, J., Yu, P.S.: Blinks: ranked keyword searches on graphs. In: SIGMOD Conference, pp. 305–316. ACM (2007)
13. Hristidis, V., Gravano, L., Papakonstantinou, Y.: Efficient ir-style keyword search over relational databases. In: VLDB Conference, pp. 850–861 (2003)
14. Hristidis, V., Papakonstantinou, Y.: Discover: Keyword search in relational databases. In: VLDB Conference, pp. 670–681 (2002)
15. Kacholia, V., Pandit, S., Chakrabarti, S., Sudarshan, S., Desai, R., Karambelkar, H.: Bidirectional expansion for keyword search on graph databases. In: VLDB Conference, pp. 505–516. ACM (2005)
16. Kasneci, G., Ramanath, M., Sozio, M., Suchanek, F.M., Weikum, G.: Star: Steiner-tree approximation in relationship graphs. In: ICDE Conference, pp. 868–879. IEEE (2009)
17. Ma, Z., Pant, G., Sheng, O.R.L.: Interest-based personalized search. ACM Trans. Inf. Syst. 25(1) (2007)
18. Madhavan, J., Halevy, A.Y., Cohen, S., Dong, X.L., Jeffery, S.R., Ko, D., Yu, C.: Structured data meets the web: A few observations. IEEE Data Engineering Bulletin 29(4), 19–26 (2006)
19. Markowetz, A., Yang, Y., Papadias, D.: Keyword search on relational data streams. In: SIGMOD Conference, SIGMOD 2007, pp. 605–616. ACM (2007)
20. Navigli, R.: Word sense disambiguation: A survey. ACM Computing Surveys 41(2) (2009)

21. Po, L., Sorrentino, S.: Automatic generation of probabilistic relationships for improving schema matching. Information Systems 36(2), 192–208 (2011)
22. Qin, L., Yu, J.X., Chang, L.: Keyword search in databases: the power of rdbms. In: SIGMOD Conference, pp. 681–694. ACM (2009)
23. Sayyadian, M., LeKhac, H., Doan, A., Gravano, L.: Efficient keyword search across heterogeneous relational databases. In: ICDE Conference, pp. 346–355. IEEE (2007)
24. Simitsis, A., Koutrika, G., Ioannidis, Y.E.: Précis: from unstructured keywords as queries to structured databases as answers. VLDB Journal 17(1), 117–149 (2008)
25. Tata, S., Lohman, G.M.: SQAK: doing more with keywords. In: SIGMOD Conference, pp. 889–902. ACM (2008)
26. Trillo, R., Gracia, J., Espinoza, M., Mena, E.: Discovering the semantics of user keywords. Journal of Universal Computer Science 13(12), 1908–1935 (2007)
27. Wang, H., Zhang, K., Liu, Q., Tran, T., Yu, Y.: Q2Semantic: A lightweight keyword interface to semantic search. In: Bechhofer, S., Hauswirth, M., Hoffmann, J., Koubarakis, M. (eds.) ESWC 2008. LNCS, vol. 5021, pp. 584–598. Springer, Heidelberg (2008)
28. Webber, W.: Evaluating the effectiveness of keyword search. IEEE Data Engineering Bulletin 33(1), 55–60 (2010)
29. Wright, A.: Searching the deep web. Communications of ACM 51(10), 14–15 (2008)
30. Yu, J.X., Qin, L., Chang, L.: Keyword Search in Databases. Synthesis Lectures on Data Management. Morgan & Claypool Pub. (2010)
31. Zenz, G., Zhou, X., Minack, E., Siberski, W., Nejdl, W.: From keywords to semantic queries-incremental query construction on the semantic web. Journal of Web Semantics 7(3), 166–176 (2009)
32. Zhuang, Z., Cucerzan, S.: Exploiting semantic query context to improve search ranking. In: ICSC Conference, pp. 50–57. IEEE Computer Society (2008)

Semistructured Data Search

Krisztian Balog

University of Stavanger
NO-4036 Stavanger, Norway
krisztian.balog@uis.no

Abstract. This paper presents a selection of methods for searching in heterogeneous data collections where some amount of structure is available. We start with a general retrieval framework, based on generative probabilistic modeling, for ranking unstructured document representations. Then, we consider structure at two different levels: documents and queries. For documents, the internal structure is captured through the use of multiple document fields, and various approaches to setting field weights are discussed. For queries, the focus is on effectively utilizing additional input data that the user might provide along with the keyword query, such as target categories or example documents. We place a particular emphasis on methods that are robust with respect to the availability of structured data and are able to deal with inconsistent or incomplete information.

Keywords: Semistructured data, generative probabilistic models, document modeling, query modeling.

1 Introduction

Traditionally, information retrieval (IR) systems have dealt with the problem of search in unstructured text collections. Database (DB) systems, on the other hand, have aimed at querying structured data that is highly organized and follows a strict schema. While this distinction still exists, it is not as sharp as a decade ago and some convergence between the two fields has occurred. To a large extent, this can be attributed to changes in the data landscape; over the past few years, alongside the document-oriented web, the Web of Data has emerged [8, 9]. This resulted in increased availability of (semi)structured data and made it possible to respond to users' queries with specific entities and objects, as opposed to merely a ranked list of documents. The Web has also changed users' expectations about how search applications should function; the single-search-box paradigm has become widespread, and ordinary users have little incentive to formulate structured queries (which would require the knowledge of the underlying schema as well as that of the query language). However, users might supply additional input data beyond the keyword query, such as target categories or example documents, provided that it is made sufficiently effortless for them to do so (for example, through specialized interfaces or query assistance services). This tutorial introduces a selection of methods that are able to effectively utilize structure that is present on the document side or arise on the query side.

N. Ferro (Ed.): PROMISE Winter School 2013, LNCS 8173, pp. 74–96, 2014.
© Springer-Verlag Berlin Heidelberg 2014

1.1 Scope

For a long time, semistructured search was taken to be synonymous with XML retrieval. This paper offers a different perspective. Our unit of retrieval is documents, more precisely, document-based representations of entities or objects, which are assumed to be readily available. Unlike in XML retrieval, we do not provide responses beyond this level. Further, we assume that there is no separate schema; in XML, structure can be enforced by the XML schema with virtually the same rigor as in a relational database. Our approaches are primarily text-based; in Section 5.2 we introduce methods for modeling categories associated with documents, an idea that could be conceptualized further as an IR equivalent of categorical attribute values in databases. However, we do not support query operators, for example, for handling numerical values. Also, the methods we present in this chapter work with flat structures (but often with multiple ones); this stands in contrast with XML retrieval where much of the modeling efforts revolve around hierarchical structures. We particularly aim for methods that are robust with respect to the availability of structure and can be applied to a wide range of document types, from web documents written in HTML to entities described in RDF. Our general attitude towards query-side structure is that any additional input the user might provide beyond the keyword query is to be seen as complementary descriptions of the underlying information need and to be considered as "structural hints" as opposed to rigid formal constraints. For an excellent overview on XML retrieval we refer the reader to [26].

1.2 Organization

In Section 2 we explain what we mean by semistructured data search. Next, in Section 3 we present our general retrieval framework, based on generative probabilistic modeling techniques. This provides a common ground for methods that follow later and a principled way of accounting for the inherent uncertainty and heterogeneity involved with searching in this type of data. Section 4 starts with unstructured document retrieval and discusses methods for capturing internal document structure using multiple document fields. It also deals with questions related to setting field weights. Section 5 considers scenarios where the user can optionally complement the keyword query with additional information, such as target categories or example documents. Utilizing this extra input requires changes both on the query and on the document side. We conclude with a summary of our findings in Section 6.

2 Semistructured Data

In this section we briefly explain what we mean by *semistructured data* in the context of this tutorial. It is best understood in contrast to unstructured and structured data. The key characteristics are summarized in Table 1.

Unstructured data can be found in many different forms, including documents, spreadsheets, web pages, emails, blogs, tweets, and medical records. Generally

Table 1. Comparison of unstructured, semistructured, and structured data search

	Unstructured	Semistructured	Structured
Unit of retrieval	documents	objects	tuples
Schema	no	self-describing	fixed
Queries	keyword	keyword++	formal languages

speaking, it also includes non-textual data like images, video, and audio, however, our focus here is limited to textual data. There is little uniformity among the different forms, so content is utilized in an unstructured manner without making any further assumptions about the format. Retrieval in unstructured text collections is often referred to as *full-text search*.

Structured data is typically highly organized and tabular, such as the information stored in relational databases. The semantics of the data are captured in a data model and are mapped to a database schema. The schema describes various elements of the database, including tables, fields, and relationships, and imposes constraints to ensure the consistency of the data. Querying of the data is done using formal languages, like SQL.

Semistructured data is characterized by the lack of rigid, formal structure, such as the data models associated with relational databases. This means that there is no single schema to the data. Instead, the schema is contained within the data and is evolving together with the content, thereby making it "self-describing." Parts of the data yield little structure or lack structure altogether (e.g., plain text). Even when structural annotations are present, they are often ignored (e.g., full-text search). It is important to note that our take on semistructured data is somewhat different from the traditional view, especially when it comes to XML (cf. Section 1.1). Throughout this paper we will simply refer to the task of ranking documents. What we really mean by that is ranking document-based representations of objects or entities. Our queries are primarily keyword-based, which, optionally, can be complemented with additional components; hence, we refer to these as keyword++.

3   Retrieval Framework

The task we address is *ad-hoc retrieval*: answering a one-off query, representing the user's underlying information need, with a ranked list of documents. (Note that by documents we mean the document-based representations of objects or entities.) We approach this task in a generative probabilistic modeling framework. Generative models are attractive from both theoretical and empirical perspectives, and have been successfully applied to a wide range of retrieval problems [27, 44]. Importantly for us, generative models allow for a sound incorporation of structural clues into the retrieval model and are particularly well-suited for settings where training data is not available in large quantities. Another pragmatic consideration behind this choice is that it enables us to present the material that follows in this chapter in a coherent and consistent manner. At the same time, we would like to emphasize that our main focus is on developing approaches for dealing with structure effectively and efficiently, and that generative models represent one possible solution for implementing general retrieval strategies; the same ideas may also be expressed in other retrieval frameworks.

Ranking documents given an input query q is done according to probability $P(d|q)$, computed for each document d in the collection. Instead of estimating this probability directly, a more accurate estimate may be obtained by applying Bayes' theorem:

$$P(d|q) = \frac{P(q|d)P(d)}{P(q)} \stackrel{\text{rank}}{=} P(q|d)P(d).$$ (1)

Notice that $P(q)$ in the denominator is the same for all documents, therefore, it is ignored for the purpose of ranking. We are then left with two main components: the *query likelihood* $P(q|d)$ and the *prior* probability of the document $P(d)$. Under this formulation the ranking of documents may be viewed as the following generative process. First, a particular document d is chosen with probability $P(d)$. Then, we subsequently attempt to draw the query q from this document with probability $P(q|d)$.

The simplest and most common way of estimating $P(q|d)$ is using multinomial unigram language models. Indeed, this is what we will be discussing first in the next section, then gradually moving to more complex estimation schemes based on document structure. In Section 5 we will move from keyword-only queries to semistructured queries containing semantic annotations, target types, or example documents. Making effective use of such additional information often necessitates query representations that go beyond the term level, breaking the query likelihood into multiple components. The prior probability of the document, $P(d)$, is often assumed to be uniform (and, as such, it can be ignored since it does not influence the ranking). Alternatively, it can be used encode query-independent evidence based on document length, authority, popularity, link structure, etc. [21, 22, 32].

4 Modeling Documents

This section is concerned with the modeling of internal document structure. We start with an unstructured "flat text" representation in Section 4.1. Then, we continue in Section 4.2 with an approach, which has been the predominant to date, to dealing with document structure: through the use of multiple document fields. Without exception, the models we discuss in this section are based on generative language modeling techniques. Language models, as the name suggests, represent language usage as statistical information associated with a vocabulary. A language model θ_d is built for each document d and then used to describe how likely this document would generate the query q, $P(q|\theta_d)$. We will cover this process in more detail next. Our presentation is self-contained, but the interested reader is referred to [45] for a full account on language modeling.

t	$P_{ML}(t|d)$	t	$P_{ML}(t|d)$
query	0.0150	language	0.0046
document	0.0135	field	0.0046
documents	0.0081	structure	0.0043
equation	0.0080	films	0.0036
data	0.0070	terms	0.0035
probability	0.0066	information	0.0035
model	0.0065	modeling	0.0033
retrieval	0.0058	example	0.0033
fields	0.0058	using	0.0031
term	0.0046	representation	0.0031

Fig. 1. Top terms with the corresponding term probabilities from the language model of this article (after stopword removal)

Fig. 2. Language model of this article, visualized as a tag cloud

4.1   Unstructured Document Representation

The simplest form of document representation is to ignore any structural clues or elements and take the whole document to be a bag of words. In this view of the document the exact ordering of terms is ignored and the importance of a term within the document is proportional to its number of occurrences (but is independent of where in the document those occurrences take place). Language models provide an elegant way of capturing this notion of term importance by representing each document as a multinomial probability distribution over the vocabulary of terms. We write θ_d to denote the model of document d, and the probability of a term t in the document's model is $P(t|\theta_d)$. This probability tells us how likely we would see t if we sampled a term randomly from d. Much of our efforts in this section will revolve around the estimation of this model.

The most straightforward way of obtaining the document language model is by using the *maximum likelihood* (ML) estimation:

$$P(t|\theta_d) = P_{ML}(t|d) = \frac{n(t,d)}{|d|}, \tag{2}$$

where $n(t,d)$ denotes the number of times term t occurs in document d and $|d|$ is the length of the document (i.e., $\sum_t n(t,d)$). This effectively means that the probability of the term equals to its relative frequency in the document. Figure 1 illustrates the idea of a document language model by listing the top terms (i.e., the ones with highest probabilities) given the language model of this article. A language model could be plotted as a histogram, like it is done in Figure 12, where bars correspond to terms and their heights are proportional to term probabilities. A visually more exciting alternative is to display it as a word cloud, such as the one shown in Figure 2. The document model θ_d is then used to estimate the probability of a given query q by taking the product of individual term probabilities as follows:

$$P(q|\theta_d) = \prod_{t \in q} P(t|\theta_d)^{n(t,q)}, \tag{3}$$

where $n(t,q)$ denotes the number of times term t is present in query q. Assuming uniform document priors (cf. Eq. 1) this probability can be used directly to produce a document ranking. To prevent numerical underflows, this computation, in practice, is performed in the log domain. We rewrite Eq. 3 as follows:

$$\log P(q|\theta_d) = \sum_{t \in q} n(t,q) \log P(t|\theta_d). \tag{4}$$

The document model constructed using the ML estimator has a severe limitation: unseen words in the document would get a zero probability. Moreover, because of the multiplication of individual term probabilities in Eq. 3, the whole query would be assigned a zero probability in such cases. Obviously, this is undesired behavior. The main purpose of *smoothing* is to assign a non-zero probability to the unseen words and to improve the accuracy of word probability estimation in general. This is typically achieved by discounting the probabilities of the words seen in the text and then assigning the extra probability mass to unseen words according to a background language model estimated using the entire collection:

$$P(t|\theta_d) = (1 - \lambda)P_{ML}(t|d) + \lambda P_{ML}(t|C), \tag{5}$$

where the interpolation parameter λ controls the influence of the collection model, $P_{ML}(t|C)$, which is taken to be a maximum likelihood estimate:

$$P_{ML}(t|C) = \frac{\sum_d n(t,d)}{\sum_d |d|}. \tag{6}$$

This representation of the document as a mixture between the document and the collection is usually referred to as the *standard language modeling approach*.

The linear interpolation in Eq. 5 is also known as *Jelinek-Mercer smoothing*. Notice that the amount of smoothing applied is the same for all documents. Intuitively, longer documents may require less smoothing (as they already have a richer representation, through having more terms). The Bayes smoothing method, often referred to as *Dirichlet smoothing*, implements this idea by setting

$$\lambda = \frac{\mu}{|d| + \mu} \qquad (1 - \lambda) = \frac{|d|}{|d| + \mu}, \tag{7}$$

where μ is a parameter. Smoothing plays an important role in language modeling and the choice of the smoothing method and smoothing parameter can have a considerable impact on retrieval performance [47]. As a general rule of thumb, Dirichlet smoothing with μ set to the average document length in the collection is usually a reasonable starting point.

Despite its relative simplicity, the standard language modeling approach is a very powerful one; the overall idea of representing "things" by the language associated with them is intuitive and works well in many application scenarios.

4.2 Fielded Document Representation

Documents are rarely just flat text. For example, email messages have from, to, subject, and body fields; news articles are divided into title, lead, and body elements; web documents are annotated with structural markup using HTML. A common way to incorporate the internal structure of documents into the retrieval model is through the usage of *document fields*. Generally speaking, a field is made up of specific parts or segments of the document. We do not impose strict constraints on document fields. Specifically, we do not require each term occurrence to be assigned to exactly one field, i.e., fields can be overlapping. Also, fields do not necessarily have to cover the entire document, i.e., there may be parts of a document that are not associated with any specific field. In practical terms, fields usually correspond to the contents of particular markup tags provided by the structural annotation. In web document retrieval, for example, title, headings, meta keywords and descriptions, anchor text, and body text may be regarded as document fields [33]. Figure 3 shows an excerpt from a HTML file, with the corresponding field based document representation presented in Figure 4. When searching in the Web of Data, entities are described in the form of subject-predicate-object (SPO) triples of the RDF data model; a natural way of building a document-based representation of a particular entity is to consider all triples with the given subject, create separate fields for each predicate, and associate the corresponding object values with those fields; Figure 5 displays an example.

Next, we present an extension to our generative language modeling approach that makes us able to deal with multiple fields. Rather than using the language model estimated from a single document representation, this method estimates a mixture language model based on a combination of language models created from the various document fields [33]. We will refer to this approach as the *mixture of language models* (MLM).

```
<html>
   <head>
      <title>Winter School 2013</title>
      <meta name="keywords" content="PROMISE, school, PhD, IR, DB" />
      <meta name="description" content="PROMISE Winter School 2013" />
   </head>
   <body>
      <h1>PROMISE Winter School 2013</h1>
      <h2>Bridging between Information Retrieval and Databases</h2>
      <h3>Bressanone, Italy 4 - 8 February 2013</h3>
      <p>The aim of the PROMISE Winter School 2013 on "Bridging
      between Information Retrieval and Databases" is to give
      participants a grounding in the core topics that constitute the
      multidisciplinary area of information access and retrieval to
      unstructured, semistructured, and structured information.</p>
      [...]
   </body>
</html>
```

Fig. 3. Excerpt from a HTML page

Field	Content
title	Winter School 2013
meta	PROMISE, school, PhD, IR, DB
	PROMISE Winter School 2013
headings	PROMISE Winter School 2013
	Bridging between Information Retrieval and Databases
	Bressanone, Italy 4 - 8 February 2013
body	The aim of the PROMISE Winter School 2013 on "Bridging
	between Information Retrieval and Databases" is to give
	participants a grounding in the core topics that constitute
	the multidisciplinary area of information access and retrieval to
	unstructured, semistructured, and structured information.

Fig. 4. Fielded document representation based on HTML markup for the document shown in Figure 3

Formally, let F be the set of possible fields, where $f \in F$ denotes a specific field. The document language model (θ_d) is taken to be a weighted linear combination of the field language models (θ_{d_f}):

$$P(t|\theta_d) = \sum_{f \in F} \alpha_f P(t|\theta_{d_f}), \qquad (8)$$

where α_f is the weight associated with field f, such that $\sum_{f \in F} \alpha_f = 1$. The field-specific language models are estimated analogously to the unstructured

Field	Content
rdfs:label	Audi A4
rdfs:comment	The Audi A4 is a compact executive car produced since late 1994 by the German car manufacturer Audi, a subsidiary of the [...]
dbpprop:production	1994 2001 2005 2008
rdf:type	dbpedia-owl:MeanOfTransportation
	dbpedia-owl:Automobile
dbpedia-owl:manufacturer	dbpedia:Audi
dbpedia-owl:class	dbpedia:Compact_executive_car
owl:sameAs	freebase:Audi A4
is dbpedia-owl:predecessor of	dbpedia:Audi_A5
is dbpprop:similar of	dbpedia:Cadillac_BLS

Fig. 5. Excerpt from the fielded document representation of the entity *Audi A4*, based on its RDF description in DBpedia. URIs are shortened for convenience and are typeset in typewriter font. URLs in the content part are typically replaced by the name/label/title of the resource they point to [31, 32].

document model (cf. Eq. 5), the main differences being that term occurrences are restricted to the given field and a field-specific collection language model is used for smoothing:

$$P(t|\theta_{d_f}) = (1 - \lambda_f)P_{ML}(t|d_f) + \lambda_f P_{ML}(t|C_f), \tag{9}$$

where both components are maximum likelihood estimates:

$$P_{ML}(t|d_f) = \frac{n(t, d_f)}{|d_f|} \qquad P_{ML}(t|C_f) = \frac{\sum_d n(t, d_f)}{\sum_d |d_f|} \tag{10}$$

In Eq. 10 $n(t, d_f)$ denotes the number of occurrences of term t in field f of document d and $|d_f|$ stands for the length of the field. The smoothing parameter λ_f is set using Dirichlet smoothing.

Now that we have discussed the retrieval model, two main questions remain to be addressed: (i) How to organize document content into fields? and (ii) How to estimate the corresponding field weights? As we shall see, these two questions are not independent of each other; having a larger number of fields can make the setting of field weights quite challenging. We differentiate between two settings. In one case, fields may be seen as alternative (in a sense "interchangeable") descriptions of the same content. In the other case, fields capture distinct properties or aspects; here, fields are characterized by distinctive term distributions. Our fundamental assumption, common to both settings, is that the information contained in the different fields is complementary in nature and that is why we would benefit from combining these fields.

Fields as Alternative Document Representations. A typical application scenario is web document retrieval. Fields used here include title, headings, meta keywords and descriptions, anchor text, and body text. These are all descriptions of the same content and mainly differ in the number of words used (but not in the vocabulary). It is likely that many of the high probability terms according to the field language model (i.e., $P(t|\theta_{d_f})$) are shared among the different fields. Therefore, this approach rewards documents where the same query term appears in multiple fields.

In the absence of training data, field weights (α_f in Eq. 8) can be set uniformly (i.e., $\alpha_f = 1/|F|$, where $|F|$ is the total number of fields) or proportional to the field length (measured as the sum of field lengths of the given field type, i.e., $\alpha_f \propto \sum_d |d_f|$). An alternative solution is to set field weights proportional to their individual performance (that is, using only one particular field language model for ranking documents at a time) [33]. Obviously, this last method requires training queries with corresponding relevance assessments.

Fields Representing Distinct Aspects. Our use-case for illustrating this setting is entity retrieval, where documents describe a single type of entity, e.g., people or movies, and structured representations are readily available (for example in XML or RDF). For the sake of simplicity we assume that fields are not hierarchically organized. The underlying assumption here is that each query term has an implicit mapping to one or more fields (where "more" means at most a handful fields). Kim et al. [24] proposes a method, termed *probabilistic retrieval model for semi-structured data* (PRMS), that uses the distribution of words in the fields to provide clues for this mapping process. Under this approach the static field weights (α_f in Eq. 8) are replaced by a mapping probability $P(f|t)$:

$$P(t|\theta_d) = \sum_{f \in F} P(f|t)P(t|\theta_{d_f}). \tag{11}$$

The probability of mapping a (query) term t to a given document field f is estimated by applying Bayes' theorem and combining the prior field probability $P(f)$ and the probability of a term occurring in a given field $P(t|f)$:

$$P(f|t) = \frac{P(t|f)P(f)}{P(t)} = \frac{P(t|f)P(f)}{\sum_{f' \in F} P(t|f')P(f')}. \tag{12}$$

The prior probability of the term, $P(t)$, is further rewritten using the law of total probability (second step in Eq. 12); we write f' in the denominator when marginalizing over all possible fields so that to avoid confusion with the field f for which the mapping probability is being computed. In the end, we are left with two components to be estimated. The prior $P(f)$ is the probability of mapping the query term to field f before observing collection statistics; if could be set manually, for example, based on domain-specific background knowledge, or left to be uniform. The probability of a term given a field, $P(t|f)$ is conveniently estimated using the collection language model of that field, i.e., $P(t|f) = P_{ML}(t|C_f)$. This, we already have from earlier (see Eq. 10). Figure 6 shows the top fields and their mapping probabilities for an example query.

| t = "Meg" | | t = "Ryan" | | t = "war" | |
f	P(f|t)	f	P(f|t)	f	P(f|t)
cast	0.407	cast	0.601	genre	0.927
team	0.381	team	0.381	title	0.070
title	0.187	title	0.017	location	0.002

Fig. 6. Example mapping probabilities for the query *Meg Ryan war* when searching in the IMDB collection

Two key assumptions made in PRMS are that (i) the collection is homogeneous and (ii) each field has a distinctive distribution of terms. These conditions are met in our example where the collection is limited to entities of a single type; in heterogenous collections with multiple types of entity, PRMS cannot be applied successfully [12]. One possible remedy is to rank each entity type with a type-specific model (that considers only fields specific to that type) and then merge results [23]. Another option is to reduce the number of fields considered by grouping them together [10, 31].

4.3 Further Reading

It was observed quite early in studies of retrieval models that searching on multiple document representations (such as title and abstract or free text and manually assigned index terms) and combining these representations during retrieval was more effective than searching on a single representation [13, 18]. All established retrieval frameworks have been generalized to multi-field document retrieval, including BM25 [38] and Divergence From Randomness [36]. These models, as well as the ones we have discussed earlier in this section, combine evidence from multiple fields on the term level, inside the document representation. It is also possible to combine evidence on the query level; the idea there is to rank documents using individual representations (possibly using different retrieval techniques depending on the particular representation) and then combine these retrieval results to produce a final ranking. This technique is often referred to as *meta-search* or *data fusion* in the literature [1, 30]. Robertson et al. [38] argue that components that contribute to the document score should be combined across fields at an earlier stage, i.e., on the term level and not on the query level. In this section we limited ourselves to flat structures, that is, a set of fields, ignoring any (hierarchical) relationships that may exist between them. Both language modeling and BM25 have been extended to handle hierarchical structures for element level XML retrieval [29, 34]. It is also possible to incorporate hierarchical field structures for entity retrieval, but the benefits of that over flat structures are yet to be explored [31].

5   Modeling Queries

A keyword query is a very sparse representation of the user's underlying information need. Obtaining a more detailed specification, a process known as *query modeling,* has been a topic of active research from the very early years of IR [39]. The focus of our attention here is on queries that comprise not only a sequence of terms, but, optionally, additional components as well. It is paramount that we want to avoid the user having to use structured query languages. The non-keyword part that we aim for as extra input is (i) often highly application specific, (ii) typically collected through specialized user interfaces or query assistance services, and (iii) may or may not be provided by the user.[1] Such additional query components can entail, for example, (i) semantic annotations with entities or concepts, (ii) target types/categories, or (iii) examples of items (documents or entities) that the user deems relevant. This results in what we call a *keyword++* (or semistructured) query.

Previous benchmarking evaluation campaigns have presented several examples for scenarios that come with such enriched queries.[2] The TREC 2007 Enterprise track addresses a topic distillation task where users have to create overview pages on specific topics [3]. The additional information provided by the user consists of a small number of example documents; see Figure 7. The INEX 2007-2009 Entity Ranking track focuses on the retrieval of entities, where entities are represented by their corresponding Wikipedia article [14]. Keyword queries are complemented with target categories and/or a small number of example entities; see Figure 8. The TREC Entity track studies the related entity finding task: returning a ranked list of entities of a specified type that engage in a given relationship with a particular source entity [7]; see Figure 9.

Although this section is titled "modeling queries," in order to utilize this extra information, we will be required to make changes in the representation of documents as well, as we shall soon see.

5.1   Term-Based Modeling

The ranking of documents so far was based on (log) query likelihood, as defined in Eq. 4. We repeat this formula for convenience:

$$\log P(q|\theta_d) = \sum_{t \in q} n(t, q) \log P(t|\theta_d). \tag{13}$$

Throughout Section 4, our focus was on devising ways to improve the estimation of the document language model, $P(t|\theta_d)$. Next, we shift our attention to refining the representation of the query. Notice that this formula considers all query

---

[1] It is worth pointing out that the non-keyword components can also be obtained automatically; clearly this will not be of the same quality as if it was provided by the user explicitly, but can still improve retrieval performance. Importantly, estimating specific query components is a problem significantly easier than automatically translating an unstructured query into a structured one.

[2] The descriptions of information needs are called "topics" in TREC lingo. As can be seen in Figure 7 and 8, these also include narratives and/or extended descriptions of the information being sought. We do not use those fields here and consider only `<query>` in Figure 7 and `<title>` in Figure 8 as the keyword query.

```
<top>
    <num>CE-012</num>
    <query>cancer risk</query>
    <narr>
        Focus on genome damage and therefore cancer risk in humans.
    </narr>
    <page>CSIR0145-10349105</page>
    <page>CSIR0140-15970492</page>
    <page>CSIR0139-07037024</page>
    <page>CSIR0138-00801380</page>
</top>
```

Fig. 7. Example topic description from the TREC 2007 Enterprise track

terms with equal importance. What we would like, instead, is to be able to weigh individual terms differently. Therefore, we replace $n(t, q)$ with $P(t|\theta_q)$ and refer to it as the *query model*. Analogously to the document model, this is a probability distribution, i.e., $\sum_t P(t|\theta_q) = 1$. Substituting back to Eq. 13 we arrive at the following equation:

$$\log P(q|\theta_d) = \sum_{t \in q} P(t|\theta_q) \log P(t|\theta_d). \tag{14}$$

This generalized model equals to ranking based on negative Kullback-Leibler (KL) divergence between the query and document models,[3] also known as the *KL-divergence retrieval model* [25, 46]. The estimation of the document model θ_d is the same as with the query likelihood retrieval model, but the query model θ_q offers interesting opportunities for leveraging additional input and/or feedback information to improve retrieval accuracy.

In the baseline case, each query term receives equal weight:

$$P_{BL}(t|\theta_q) = \frac{n(t, q)}{|q|}, \tag{15}$$

where $|q|$ is the length of the query, measured in the number of terms. This is equivalent to the query likelihood scoring.

For improved query modeling, the basic idea is to interpolate the original (baseline) query model with an expanded query model $\hat{\theta}_q$:

$$P(t|\theta_q) = (1 - \alpha)P_{BL}(t|\theta_q) + \alpha P(t|\hat{\theta}_q), \tag{16}$$

where $\alpha \in [0, 1]$ is a parameter to control the importance of the expanded model. Using a mixture of the original and expanded query models ensures that we do not drift too far away from the original query. Figure 10 illustrates the idea with the original query shown on the left side and the expanded query (after mixing with the original query using Eq. 16) is on the right.

---

[3] Apart from a query-dependent constant, which does not affect the ranking.

```
<inex_topic topic_id="95" query_type="XER">
    <title>Tom Hanks movies where he plays a leading role.</title>
    <entities>
        <entity id="142417">Apollo 13</entity>
        <entity id="468293">Philadelphia</entity>
        <entity id="41528">Forrest Gump</entity>
        <entity id="158982">You've got mail</entity>
    </entities>
    <categories>
        <category id="101422">movies</category>
        <category id="81332">films</category>
    </categories>
    <description>
        This query should return the names of movies in which
        Tom Hanks played the leading role.
    </description>
    <narrative>
        Tom Hanks is a popular actor and the winner of many awards.
        This query should return his all the feature films in which he
        played the lead.
    </narrative>
</inex_topic>
```

Fig. 8. Example topic description from the INEX 2007 Entity Ranking track

```
<query>
    <num>22</num>
    <entity_name>
        Organization of Petroleum Exporting Countries (OPEC)
    </entity_name>
    <entity_homepage id="clueweb09-en0010-21-28880">
        http://www.opec.com/
    </entity_homepage>
    <target_entity>location</target_entity>
    <target_type_dbpedia>Country</target_type_dbpedia>
    <narrative>
        Find countries that are members of OPEC
        (the Organization of Petroleum Exporting Countries).
    </narrative>
</query>
```

Fig. 9. Example topic description from the TREC 2011 Entity track

t	$P_{BL}(t\|\theta_q)$	t	$P(t\|\theta_q)$
machine	0.5000	vision	0.2796
vision	0.5000	machine	0.2762
		image	0.0248
		vehicles	0.0224
		safe	0.0220
		cam	0.0214
		traffic	0.0178
		technology	0.0176
		camera	0.0173
		object	0.0147

Fig. 10. Baseline (left) and expanded (right) query models for the query *machine vision*; only the top 10 terms are shown

One possible route for leveraging example documents (denoted as E), provided by the user as additional input, is to use them for estimating the expanded query model. This can be done with the help of (pseudo) relevance feedback techniques. We illustrate it with two popular and effective models, called *relevance models*, proposed in [28]. The principal idea is to construct relevance models based on co-occurrences of the original query terms with other terms in the set of feedback documents. We use these relevance models as our expanded query model $\hat{\theta}_q$. Relevance model 1 (RM1) assumes full independence between the original query terms and the expansion terms:

$$P_{RM1}(t|\hat{\theta}_q) \approx \sum_{d \in E} P(d)P(t|\theta_d) \prod_{t' \in q} P(t'|\theta_d), \qquad (17)$$

where E is the set of example documents, and $P(t|\theta_d)$ is a smoothed document language model (cf. Eq. 5). Mind that t stands for a term in the expanded query model while $t' \in q$ denotes original query terms. For convenience, document priors are assumed to be uniform.

Relevance model 2 (RM2) tackles a different sampling strategy, where original query terms $t' \in q$ are still assumed to be independent of each other, but they are dependent on the expansion term t.

$$P_{RM2}(t|\hat{\theta}_q) \approx P(t) \prod_{t' \in q} \sum_{d \in E} P(t'|\theta_d)P(d|t), \qquad (18)$$

where $P(d|t)$ is computed as

$$P(d|t) = \frac{P(t|\theta_d)P(d)}{P(t)} = \frac{P(t|\theta_d)P(d)}{\sum_{d' \in E} P(t|\theta_{d'})P(d')}. \qquad (19)$$

In Eq. 19 the probability of a document given a term is first rewritten using Bayes' theorem, then the probability of the term in the denominator is marginalized over all example documents (denoted with d' to avoid confusion with d).

RM1 can be viewed as sampling of all query terms conditioned on t: a strong mutual independence assumption, compared to the pairwise independence assumptions made by RM2. Empirical evaluation has shown that RM2 is more robust, and performs slightly better that RM1 [4, 28].

The sampling of expansion terms does not have to be dependent on the original query. In a scenario where the user provides example documents, we can expect that these documents provide important aspects that are not covered by the keyword query. Thus, avoiding biasing the selection of expansion terms toward the original query can possibly lead to a more accurate representation of the underlying information need. The method introduced in [4] estimates the expanded query model as follows:

$$P_{EX}(t|\hat{\theta}_q) \approx \sum_{d \in E} P(t|\theta_d)P(d|E), \qquad (20)$$

where $P(d|E)$ is the importance of a given document given the set of example documents E. In the simplest case, this probability is distributed uniformly among the examples, i.e., $P(d|E) = 1/|E|$. Alternatively, it is also possible to bias towards documents that are more relevant given the original query, $P(d|E) \propto P(d|q)$, or just the opposite—reward documents that are the most dissimilar to the query, assuming, that these bring in aspects that are not well described by the keyword query, $P(d|E) \propto 1 - P(d|q)$.

A word on pragmatic considerations before we move forward. The expanded query models tend to be quite large, as they contain all terms that appear in the feedback documents (the set of examples E in our case). Most of these expansion terms have an extremely small probability assigned to them and have negligible impact on document ranking, yet they slow down computation considerably. Therefore, it is common practice to limit expansion terms to the set of top 10-30 words with the highest term probability ($P(t|\hat{\theta}_q)$) as it provides a good tradeoff between effectiveness and efficiency [4, 43].

5.2   Category-Based Modeling

Next, we consider scenarios where the move beyond term-based representations, both for documents and for queries. We assume that a category system exists as part of the data collection and documents are assigned to one or more categories; a prime example for such data set is Wikipedia. As an illustration, Figure 11 lists the Wikipedia categories assigned to the article about the movie *Saving Private Ryan*. Moreover, we assume that the user provides a small number of target categories, along with the keyword query, like it is shown in Figure 8. In reality, category systems tend to grow quite large and are hierarchically organized. This presents a number of challenges. First, the categorization itself is imperfect; there might be inconsistencies, missing category assignments, documents placed in too general or too specific categories, and so on. Second, relevant results are not necessarily assigned to the categories provided by the user (who may not be completely familiar with the category system). Therefore, simply filtering on the target categories is insufficient, more robust techniques are needed.

> 1998 films | English-language films | 1990s drama films | 1990s war films | Amblin Entertainment films | American war films | Best Drama Picture Golden Globe winners | DreamWorks films | Epic films | Films directed by Steven Spielberg | Films produced by Steven Spielberg | Films set in France | Films set in 1944 | Films shot in the Republic of Ireland | Films that won the Best Sound Mixing Academy Award | Films whose cinematographer won the Best Cinematography Academy Award | Films whose director won the Best Director Academy Award | Films whose director won the Best Director Golden Globe | Films whose editor won the Best Film Editing Academy Award | Operation Overlord films | Paramount Pictures films | War epic films | War films

Fig. 11. Wikipedia categories for the movie *Saving Private Ryan*

A standard way of using category information is to include a separate category similarity component in the overall ranking formula [6, 16, 22, 35]. A principled way realizing this idea is proposed in [6], where both documents and queries have a dual representation, one based on terms and one based categories. Formally, each document is represented as a pair, $d = (\theta_d^T, \theta_d^C)$, where θ_d^T is a probability distribution over terms and θ_d^C is a probability distribution over categories. Similarly, the query is also represented as a pair, $q = (\theta_q^T, \theta_q^C)$. The overall idea is illustrated in Figure 12, where the left and right sides symbolize the query and the document, respectively, where each have a term-based (top) and a category-based (bottom) representation, modeled as multinomial probability distributions. A word on notation before we continue: the type of representation, term-based or category-based, is indicated with T or C in the superscript; q and d in the subscript stand for query and document, respectively.

The probability of a document generating the query is estimated using a mixture of term-based and category-based components:

$$P(q|d) = \lambda_t \cdot P(\theta_q^T|\theta_d^T) + (1 - \lambda_t) \cdot P(\theta_q^C|\theta_d^C), \tag{21}$$

where λ_t is an interpolation parameter. Notice that the term-based component in Eq. 21 is essentially what we have worked on so far, and could be computed using Eq. 14. However, due to pragmatic reasons (see below) we need to include an additional transformation step. For the sake of space considerations, we detail only the term-based component. The category-based component is computed analogously (specifically, by replacing t with c and T with C in Eqs. 22, 23, and 24). We use KL divergence as the basis of distributional similarity:

$$KL(\theta_q^T||\theta_d^T) = \sum_t P(t|\theta_q^T) \cdot \log \frac{P(t|\theta_q^T)}{P(t|\theta_d^T)}. \tag{22}$$

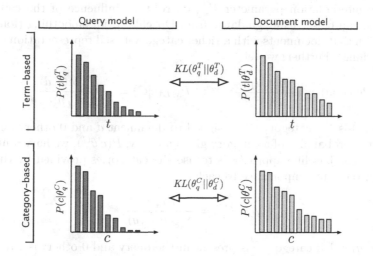

Fig. 12. A two-component model where both terms and categories are represented as probability distributions (top vs. bottom) for both queries and documents (left vs. right). KL divergence is used as the basis of distributional similarity.

Since KL divergence is a score (which is lower when two distributions are more similar), we turn it into a probability using Eq. 23:

$$P(\theta_q^T|\theta_d^T) = z^T \cdot \left(\max KL(\theta_q^T||\cdot) - KL(\theta_q^T||\theta_d^T) \right), \tag{23}$$

where $\max KL(\theta_q^T||\cdot)$ is the maximum KL divergence score observed for query q. Further, z^T is a normalization factor set as follows:

$$z^T = 1/\sum_d \max \left(KL(\theta_q^T||\cdot) - KL(\theta_q^T||\theta_d^T) \right). \tag{24}$$

Observe that Eq. 23 ranks documents in the same order as Eq. 14 does, albeit they differ in the actual values assigned. This does not make a difference when a single representation is used, but becomes an issue when term-based and category-based components need to be combined. Simply put, this transformation ensures that the probabilities are computationally tractable and "compatible;" the interested reader is referred to [6] for further details.

What remains to be defined, then, is the estimation of the ingredients for category-based similarity. Specifically, we need to define the probability of a category given a query, $P(c|\theta_q^C)$, and the probability of a category given a document, $P(c|\theta_d^C)$. We start with the latter. Similarly to the term-based representation, we need to employ smoothing on the document side to ensure that $P(c|\theta_d^C) > 0$ for all categories that might appear in the query. Analogously to the term-based case, we smooth the maximum likelihood estimate with a background model:

$$P(c|\theta_d^C) = (1 - \lambda^C)P_{ML}(c|d) + \lambda P_{ML}(c|C), \tag{25}$$

where the interpolation parameter λ^C controls the influence of the collection model, and can be set using guidance from Dirichlet prior smoothing (following the intuition that documents with a richer category-based representation require less smoothing). Further, we set

$$P_{ML}(c|d) = \frac{n(c, d)}{\sum_{c'} n(c', d)} \qquad P_{ML}(c|C) = \frac{\sum_d n(c, d)}{\sum_{c'} \sum_d n(c', d)}, \qquad (26)$$

where $n(c, d)$ is 1 if category c is assigned to document d and 0 otherwise.

As for the probability of a category given a query, $P(c|\theta_q^C)$, we have a number of options. The baseline approach is to use the categories provided by the user and assign the same importance to each:

$$P_{BL}(c|\theta_q^C) = \frac{n(c, q)}{\sum_{c'} n(c', q)}, \qquad (27)$$

where $n(c, q)$ is 1 if category c is present in the query and 0 otherwise. It is also possible to use the keyword query to obtain a ranking of categories (based on category labels or the contents of documents that belong to each category) and take the top-ranked categories (either with equal importance or with weights set proportional to the retrieval scores). This strategy has shown to be beneficial in expanding the typically small set of input categories provided by the user. It is worth pointing out that this method is applicable even when no input category information is given by the user at all.

A particularly nice feature of this framework is that it allows for category-based expansion analogously to the term-based case. Techniques introduced in Section 5.1 (blind relevance feedback and sampling from example documents) can be adopted in a straightforward way to categories. In fact, it has been shown that category-based feedback can be more beneficial than term-based feedback [6]. There exist further possibilities specific to categories. Most notably, hierarchical relationships between categories can also be utilized for expansion, for example, by considering parent and/or sub-categories up to a certain depth [15, 20, 42, 48].

5.3 Further Reading

Query expansion techniques mostly fall into two main categories: global and local. The idea of *global* analysis is to expand the query using global collection statistics based, for instance, on a co-occurrence analysis of the entire collection or using domain specific background knowledge [2]. *Local* approaches, on the other hand, typically use (known or assumed-to-be) relevant documents as examples from which expansion terms are selected [39, 41]; the methods we presented in Section 5.1 fall into this category. For a comprehensive overview on query expansion methods we refer the reader to [11]. Category-based modeling, discussed in Section 5.2, can be seen as a variant of *concept-based* information retrieval, where both documents and queries are represented using semantic concepts, instead of or in addition to keywords [17]. The TREC Entity track presents a scenario where the query seeks to find related entities ("Airlines that currently use Boeing 747 planes") and is annotated with the input entity ("Boeing 747") and with the target type ("Airline") [5]. Later editions of the track anchored these annotations in a knowledge base (DBpedia) [7]. Obtaining such semantic annotations for keyword queries automatically is a topic of active research, often involving methods at the intersection of information retrieval and databases [37, 40].

6 Summary

In this paper we have looked at various ways of utilizing structure for improving the ranking of document-based representations of objects or entities. The internal structure of documents can effectively be captured through the use of multiple document fields. Depending on the data source and application, these fields might be alternative descriptions of the same content or record different aspects of it; the two call for different field weight estimation methods. Structure, to a certain degree, can also be captured on the query side, even without the use of formal query languages. Users, for example, can provide target categories or a few example documents, if it is made sufficiently effortless for them through specialized interfaces or query assistance services. This extra information can then be used to obtain a richer representation of the underlying information need in the form of expanded query models. Finally, both documents and queries can be modeled beyond the term space. We have illustrated this using categories; this assumes a setting where documents are classified according to some category system and the user might supplement the keyword query with a small number of target categories. A particularly nice property of the proposed model is that query expansion techniques developed for the term-based representation can be adopted in a straightforward way to categories—this provides an effective solution to handle noisy category information.

References

[1] Aslam, J.A., Montague, M.: Models for metasearch. In: Proceedings of the 24th Annual International ACM SIGIR Conference on Research and Development in Information Retrieval (SIGIR 2001), pp. 276–284. ACM (2001)
[2] Bai, J., Nie, J.-Y.: Adapting information retrieval to query contexts. Inf. Process. Manage. 44(6), 1901–1922 (2008)
[3] Bailey, P., Craswell, N., de Vries, A.P., Soboroff, I.: Overview of the TREC 2007 enterprise track. In: The Sixteenth Text REtrieval Conference Proceedings (TREC 2007). NIST Special Publication 500-274 (2008)
[4] Balog, K., Weerkamp, W., de Rijke, M.: A few examples go a long way: constructing query models from elaborate query formulations. In: Proceedings of the 31st Annual International ACM SIGIR Conference on Research and Development in Information Retrieval (SIGIR 2008), pp. 371–378. ACM (2008)
[5] Balog, K., de Vries, A.P., Serdyukov, P., Thomas, P., Westerveld, T.: Overview of the TREC 2009 entity track. In: Proceedings of the Eighteenth Text REtrieval Conference (TREC 2009), NIST Special Publication 500-278 (February 2010)

[6] Balog, K., Bron, M., De Rijke, M.: Query modeling for entity search based on terms, categories, and examples. ACM Trans. Inf. Syst. 29(4), 22:1–22:31 (2011)

[7] Balog, K., Serdyukov, P., de Vries, A.P.: Overview of the TREC 2011 entity track. In: The Twentieth Text REtrieval Conference Proceedings (TREC 2011). NIST Special Publication 500-296 (February 2012)

[8] Bizer, C., Heath, T., Berners-Lee, T.: Linked data - the story so far. Int. J. Semantic Web Inf. Syst. 5(3), 1–22 (2009)

[9] Bizer, C., Lehmann, J., Kobilarov, G., Auer, S., Becker, C., Cyganiak, R., Hellmann, S.: Dbpedia - a crystallization point for the web of data. Web Semant. 7(3), 154–165 (2009)

[10] Blanco, R., Mika, P., Vigna, S.: Effective and efficient entity search in RDF data. In: Aroyo, L., Welty, C., Alani, H., Taylor, J., Bernstein, A., Kagal, L., Noy, N., Blomqvist, E. (eds.) ISWC 2011, Part I. LNCS, vol. 7031, pp. 83–97. Springer, Heidelberg (2011)

[11] Carpineto, C., Romano, G.: A survey of automatic query expansion in information retrieval. ACM Comput. Surv. 44(1), 1:1–1:50 (2012)

[12] Dalton, J., Huston, S.: Semantic entity retrieval using web queries over structured RDF data. In: Proceedings of the 3rd International Semantic Search Workshop, SEMSEARCH 2010 (2010)

[13] Das-Gupta, P., Katzer, J.: A study of the overlap among document representations. In: Proceedings of the 6th Annual International ACM SIGIR Conference on Research and Development in Information Retrieval (SIGIR 1983), pp. 106–114. ACM (1983)

[14] de Vries, A.P., Vercoustre, A.-M., Thom, J.A., Craswell, N., Lalmas, M.: Overview of the INEX 2007 entity ranking track. In: Fuhr, et al. (eds.) [19], pp. 245–251

[15] Demartini, G., Firan, C.S., Iofciu, T.: L3S at INEX 2007: Query expansion for entity ranking using a highly accurate ontology. In: Fuhr, et al. (eds.) [19], pp. 252–263

[16] Demartini, G., Firan, C.S., Iofciu, T., Krestel, R., Nejdl, W.: Why finding entities in Wikipedia is difficult, sometimes. Inf. Retr. 13(5), 534–567 (2010)

[17] Egozi, O., Markovitch, S., Gabrilovich, E.: Concept-based information retrieval using explicit semantic analysis. ACM Trans. Inf. Syst. 29(2), 8:1–8:34 (2011)

[18] Fisher, H.L., Elchesen, D.R.: Effectiveness of combining title words and index terms in machine retrieval searches. Nature 238, 109–110 (1972)

[19] Fuhr, N., Kamps, J., Lalmas, M., Trotman, A. (eds.): INEX 2007. LNCS, vol. 4862. Springer, Heidelberg (2008)

[20] Jämsen, J., Näppilä, T., Arvola, P.: Entity ranking based on category expansion. In: Fuhr, et al. (eds.) [19], pp. 264–278

[21] Kamps, J., Mishne, G., de Rijke, M.: Language models for searching in Web corpora. In: The Thirteenth Text REtrieval Conference Proceedings (TREC 2004). NIST Special Publication 500-261 (2005)

[22] Kaptein, R., Kamps, J.: Exploiting the category structure of Wikipedia for entity ranking. Artif. Intell. 194, 111–129 (2013)

[23] Kim, J., Croft, W.B.: Ranking using multiple document types in desktop search. In: Proceedings of the 33rd International ACM SIGIR Conference on Research and Development in Information Retrieval (SIGIR 2010), pp. 50–57. ACM (2010)

[24] Kim, J., Xue, X., Croft, W.B.: A probabilistic retrieval model for semistructured data. In: Boughanem, M., Berrut, C., Mothe, J., Soule-Dupuy, C. (eds.) ECIR 2009. LNCS, vol. 5478, pp. 228–239. Springer, Heidelberg (2009)

[25] Lafferty, J., Zhai, C.: Document language models, query models, and risk minimization for information retrieval. In: Proceedings of the 24th Annual International ACM SIGIR Conference on Research and Development in Information Retrieval (SIGIR 2001), pp. 111–119. ACM (2001)

[26] Lalmas, M., Baeza-Yates, R.: Structured text retrieval. In: Modern Information Retrieval - The Concepts and Technology Behind Search, 2nd edn. Pearson Education Ltd., Harlow (2011)

[27] Lavrenko, V.: A Generative Theory of Relevance. The Information Retrieval Series, vol. 26. Springer, Heidelberg (2008)

[28] Lavrenko, V., Croft, W.B.: Relevance based language models. In: Proceedings of the 24th Annual International ACM SIGIR Conference on Research and Development in Information Retrieval (SIGIR 2001), pp. 120–127. ACM (2001)

[29] Lu, W., Robertson, S., MacFarlane, A.: Field-weighted XML retrieval based on BM25. In: Fuhr, N., Lalmas, M., Malik, S., Kazai, G. (eds.) INEX 2005. LNCS, vol. 3977, pp. 161–171. Springer, Heidelberg (2006)

[30] Montague, M., Aslam, J.A.: Condorcet fusion for improved retrieval. In: Proceedings of the 11th International Conference on Information and Knowledge Management (CIKM 2002), pp. 538–548. ACM (2002)

[31] Neumayer, R., Balog, K., Nørvåg, K.: On the modeling of entities for ad-hoc entity search in the web of data. In: Baeza-Yates, R., de Vries, A.P., Zaragoza, H., Cambazoglu, B.B., Murdock, V., Lempel, R., Silvestri, F. (eds.) ECIR 2012. LNCS, vol. 7224, pp. 133–145. Springer, Heidelberg (2012)

[32] Neumayer, R., Balog, K., Nørvåg, K.: When simple is (more than) good enough: Effective semantic search with (almost) no semantics. In: Baeza-Yates, R., de Vries, A.P., Zaragoza, H., Cambazoglu, B.B., Murdock, V., Lempel, R., Silvestri, F. (eds.) ECIR 2012. LNCS, vol. 7224, pp. 540–543. Springer, Heidelberg (2012)

[33] Ogilvie, P., Callan, J.: Combining document representations for known-item search. In: Proceedings of the 26th Annual International ACM SIGIR Conference on Research and Development in Information Retrieval (SIGIR 2003), pp. 143–150. ACM (2003)

[34] Ogilvie, P., Callan, J.: Hierarchical language models for XML component retrieval. In: Fuhr, N., Lalmas, M., Malik, S., Szlávik, Z. (eds.) INEX 2004. LNCS, vol. 3493, pp. 224–237. Springer, Heidelberg (2005)

[35] Pehcevski, J., Thom, J.A., Vercoustre, A.-M., Naumovski, V.: Entity ranking in Wikipedia: utilising categories, links and topic difficulty prediction. Inf. Retr. 13(5), 568–600 (2010)

[36] Plachouras, V., Ounis, I.: Multinomial randomness models for retrieval with document fields. In: Amati, G., Carpineto, C., Romano, G. (eds.) ECIR 2007. LNCS, vol. 4425, pp. 28–39. Springer, Heidelberg (2007)

[37] Pound, J., Hudek, A.K., Ilyas, I.F., Weddell, G.: Interpreting keyword queries over web knowledge bases. In: Proceedings of the 21st ACM International Conference on Information and Knowledge Management (CIKM 2012), pp. 305–314. ACM (2012)

[38] Robertson, S., Zaragoza, H., Taylor, M.: Simple BM25 extension to multiple weighted fields. In: Proceedings of the 13th ACM International Conference on Information and Knowledge Management (CIKM 2004), pp. 42–49. ACM (2004)

[39] Rocchio, J.J.: Relevance feedback in information retrieval. In: Salton, G. (ed.) The SMART Retrieval System: Experiments in Automatic Document Processing, pp. 313–323. Prentice-Hall, Inc. (1971)

[40] Sawant, U., Chakrabarti, S.: Learning joint query interpretation and response ranking. In: Proceedings of the 22nd International Conference on World Wide Web (WWW 2013), pp. 1099–1110. International World Wide Web Conferences Steering Committee (2013)

[41] Tao, T., Zhai, C.: Regularized estimation of mixture models for robust pseudo-relevance feedback. In: Proceedings of the 29th Annual International ACM SIGIR Conference on Research and Development in Information Retrieval (SIGIR 2006), pp. 162–169. ACM (2006)

[42] Thom, J., Pehcevski, J., Vercoustre, A.-M.: Use of Wikipedia categories in entity ranking. In: The 12th Australasian Document Computing Symposium, ADCS 2007 (2007)

[43] Weerkamp, W., Balog, K., de Rijke, M.: Exploiting external collections for query expansion. ACM Trans. Web 6(4), 18:1–18:29 (2012)

[44] Westerveld, T., Vries, A., Jong, F.: Generative probabilistic models. In: Blanken, H.M., Blok, H.E., Feng, L., Vries, A.P. (eds.) Multimedia Retrieval. Data-Centric Systems and Applications, pp. 177–198. Springer, Heidelberg (2007)

[45] Zhai, C.: Statistical language models for information retrieval: a critical review. Found. Trends Inf. Retr. 2, 137–213 (2008)

[46] Zhai, C., Lafferty, J.: Model-based feedback in the language modeling approach to information retrieval. In: Proceedings of the 10th International Conference on Information and Knowledge Management (CIKM 2001), pp. 403–410. ACM (2001)

[47] Zhai, C., Lafferty, J.: A study of smoothing methods for language models applied to information retrieval. ACM Trans. Inf. Syst. 22, 179–214 (2004)

[48] Zhu, J., Song, D., Rüger, S.: Integrating document features for entity ranking. In: Fuhr, et al. (eds.) [19], pp. 336–347

Bridging Information Retrieval and Databases

Norbert Fuhr

University of Duisburg-Essen, Germany
norbert.fuhr@uni-due.de

Abstract. For bridging the gap between information retrieval (IR) and databases (DB), this article focuses on the logical view. We claim that IR should adopt three major concepts from DB, namely inference, vague predicates and expressive query languages. By regarding IR as uncertain inference, probabilistic versions of relational algebra and Datalog yield very powerful inference mechanisms for IR as well as allowing for more flexible systems. For dealing with various media and data types, vague predicates form a natural extension of text retrieval methods to attribute values, thus switching from propositional to predicate logic. A more expressive IR query language should support joins, be able to compute aggregated results, and allow for restructuring of the result objects.

1   Introduction

For several decades, information retrieval (IR) and databases (DB) have evolved as separate subfields of computer science (see e.g. the juxtaposition in [18, ch. 1]). However, in recent years, there have been increasing research activities to bridge the gap between these two areas and develop approaches integrating IR and DB features. There are various levels where such an integration can take place, namely at the physical, the logical or the conceptual level of information systems. In this article, we will focus on the logical level, mainly due to the fact that there is a nice theoretical framework that supports the integration of IR and DB at this level.

In the logical view on DB, the (retrieval) task of the system can be described as follows: given a query q, find objects o which imply the query, i. e. $o \rightarrow q$. On the other hand,, Rijsbergen defines IR as being based on uncertain inference where for a given query q, the IR system should compute the probability $P(d \rightarrow q)$ for each document d. By comparing the two definitions, we can see that IR can be regarded as a generalization of the DB approach here, since it replaces deterministic by uncertain inference.

Based on this interpretation, this article discusses how three major DB concepts can be adopted and extended in order to enhance current IR systems. In the next section, we will focus on inference, showing how probabilistic versions of relational algebra and Datalog increase the inferential capabilities of IR systems. Section 3 introduces vague predicates as a method for extending classical IR methods for dealing with attribute values and multimedia data. Query language expressiveness is discussed in Section 4, pointing out potential benefits

N. Ferro (Ed.): PROMISE Winter School 2013, LNCS 8173, pp. 97–115, 2014.

from more expressive IR query languages. Two further concepts are briefly addressed in Section 5, namely four-valued logic and the architecture of future IR systems. Section 6 concludes this contribution.

2 Inference

Following Rijsbergen's interpretation of IR as uncertain inference, this section will demonstrate the close connection between IR and the logical view on databases. For that, we start from relational algebra. As uniform notation, we will use Datalog (see e.g. [17], [3]).

First we show how document retrieval can be formulated in Datalog. For that, we assume that there is a predicate (a database relation) `docTerm(D,T)`, where each ground fact gives for a document D a term T the document is indexed with, e.g.:

`docTerm(d1,ir). docTerm(d2,ir).`
`docTerm(d1,db). docTerm(d2,oop).`

In our notation of Datalog formulas, constants start with lowercase letters and variables with capitals. A query now can be formulated as a logical formula involving the predicate `docTerm`, e.g.

`?- docTerm(D,ir)` searches for documents about IR, and

`?- docTerm(D,ir) & docTerm(D,db)` for documents both about IR and DB.

For demonstrating the close connection between relational algebra and IR, we also use the notation of database relations in tabular form. Our running example consists of the two relations shown in Figure 1. Now we discuss the five basic operations of relational algebra.

docTerm

DOCNO	TERM
1	ir
1	db
2	ir
3	db
3	oop
4	ir
4	ai
5	db
5	oop

author

DOCNO	NAME
1	smith
2	miller
3	johnson
4	firefly
4	bradford
5	bates

Fig. 1. Relations in our example database

Projection. As an example for projection, let us ask what the collection is about: `topic(T) :- docTerm(D,T)`, which results in the following four tuples:

`topic(ir). topic(db). topic(oop). topic(ai).`

Selection. If we want to know which documents are about IR, we would ask `aboutir(D) :- docTerm(D,ir)`, which returns the tuples `aboutir(1). aboutir(2). aboutir(4)`.

Join. This operation allows for the combination of two relations (which is an unusual concept in standard IR, where we mostly assume that all the necessary data is within one document or object). As an example, we want to know authors writing about IR:
`irauthor(A):- docTerm(D,ir) & author(D,A)`, resulting in the four tuples `irauthor(smith). irauthor(miller). irauthor(firefly). irauthor(bradford)`.

Union. If we want to know documents about IR or DB, this can be expressed via the union operator, which we map onto disjunction in Datalog:
`irordb(D) :- docTerm(D,ir). irordb(D) :- docTerm(D,db)`, giving us `irordb(1). irordb(2). irordb(3). irordb(4). irordb(5)`.

Difference. The last of the five basic relational algebra operators is (set) difference, which we can use e.g. for finding documents about IR, but not about DB:
`irnotdb(D) :- docTerm(D,ir) & not(docTerm(D,db))`, leading to the answer `irnotdb(2). irnotdb(4)`.

2.1 The Probabilistic Relational Model

Since IR is about *uncertain* inference, we have to add probabilities to the relational model [10,16], and switch from deterministic to probabilistic Datalog (pD) [8]. For that, let us assume, that we attach a probability value to each tuple, which gives a probability that this specific tuple belongs to the relation under consideration (see the example relation in Figure 2).

docTerm

β	DOCNO	TERM
0.9	1	IR
0.5	1	DB
0.6	2	IR
0.7	3	DB
0.8	3	OOP
0.9	4	IR
0.4	4	AI
0.8	5	DB
0.3	5	OOP

Fig. 2. Example probabilistic relation

Asking now for documents about DB via
`aboutdb(D) :- docTerm(D,db).` selects the following three tuples with their corresponding probabilistic weights:
`0.5 aboutdb(1). 0.7 aboutdb(3). 0.8 aboutdb(5).`
In contrast, when we ask for documents about both IR and DB
`aboutirdb(D) :- docTerm(D,ir) & docTerm(D,db),`
the weights of the tuples have to be combined. Assuming probabilistic independence (as is standard in most IR applications), we get
`0.45 aboutirdb(1).`

Extensional vs. intensional semantics. For more complex queries, however, we have to be careful in order to get the probabilities right. For illustrating this point, let us look at the following example:
`0.9 docterm(d1,ir). 0.5 docterm(d1,db). 0.7 link(d2,d1)`
`about(D,T) :- docTerm(D,T).`
`about(D,T) :- link(D,D1) & about(D1,T)`
`q(D) :- about(D,ir) & about(D,db).`
Obviously, the correct result cannot be computed in a straightforward way, like

$$P(q(d2)) =$$
$$= P(\texttt{about(d2,ir)}) \cdot P(\texttt{about(d2,db)})$$
$$= P(\texttt{link(d2,d1)}) \cdot P(\texttt{docterm(d1,ir)}) \cdot P(\texttt{link(d2,d1)}) \cdot P(\texttt{docterm(d1,db)})$$
$$= (0.7 \cdot 0.9) \cdot (0.7 \cdot 0.5).$$

The problem is that the probability associated with the link is multiplied twice into the result. This approach of combining the weights without paying attention to the associated probabilistic events is also called *extensional semantics*, where we suffer from "improper treatment of correlated sources of evidence" [13].

Instead, we have to use *intensional semantics*, where the weight of any derived fact is computed as a function of weights of underlying ground facts.

In [10] the concept of *event keys and event expressions* is introduced for handling intensional semantics. Here each tuple in a base relation of our database is associated with a unique identifier, a so-called event key, which denotes the corresponding probabilistic event (for didactic reasons, here we use event keys denoting the original tuple in abbreviated form), as in the following example

docterm

β	κ	DOC	TERM
0.9	dT(d1,ir)	d1	ir
0.5	dT(d1,db)	d1	db

link

β	κ	S	T
0.7	l(d2,d1)	d2	d1

Fig. 3. Probabilistic relations with event keys

For any derived fact, we now compute an event expression as Boolean combination of the underlying event keys, like e.g.

```
?- docTerm(D,ir) & docTerm(D,db).
```
resulting in
```
d1 [dT(d1,ir) & dT(d1,db)]                                    0.9 · 0.5 = 0.45
```
For the more complex query from above ?- about(D,ir) & about(D,db), we get
```
d1 [dT(d1,ir) & dT(d1,db)]                                    0.9 · 0.5 = 0.45
d2 [l(d2,d1) & dT(d1,ir) & l(d2,d1) & dT(d1,db)] 0.7 · 0.9 · 0.5 = 0.315
```

Recursion. Probabilistic Datalog can also deal with recursive rules, without running into problems. As an example, consider the probabilistic facts illustrated in Figure 4.

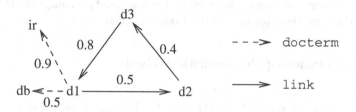

Fig. 4. An example for probabilistic rules with recursion

Using the same rules as before
```
about(D,T) :- docTerm(D,T).
about(D,T) :- link(D,D1) & about(D1,T).
```
the query ?- about(D,ir) would result in the following derived facts:
```
d1 [dT(d1,ir) | l(d1,d2) & l(d2,d3) & l(d3,d1) &
    dT(d1,ir) | ...]                                              0.900
d3 [l(d3,d1) & dT(d1,ir)]                                         0.720
d2 [l(d2,d3) & l(d3,d1) & dT(d1,ir)]                              0.288
```
Obviously, a naive evaluation algorithm would run into an infinite loop, as indicated in the event expression for d1. However, the underlying evaluation algorithm of probabilistic Datalog can handle these cases correctly [14] (by stopping when a fixpoint is reached).

Likewise, ?- about(D,ir) & about(D,db) would produce
```
d1 [dT(d1,ir) & dT(d1,db)]                                       0.450
d3 [l(d3,d1) & dT(d1,ir) & l(d3,d1) & dT(d1,db)]                 0.360
d2 [l(d2,d3) & l(d3,d1) & dT(d1,ir) & dT(d1,db)]                 0.144
```

Computation of probabilities for event expressions. Since event expressions can become rather complex, we need a method for computing the corresponding probability for any Boolean combination of event keys in a correct way. For that, we can apply the following method:

1. Transformation of the event expression into disjunctive normal form
2. Application of the inclusion-exclusion ('sieve') formula.

The latter is a generalization of the method for handling two conjuncts: $P(a \vee b) = P(a) + P(b) - P(a \wedge b)$. In the general case, where c_i denotes a conjunct of event keys (as a result of the first step), we have to compute the following alternating sum:

$$P(c_1 \vee \ldots \vee c_n) =$$
$$\sum_{i=1}^{n}(-1)^{i-1} \sum_{1 \leq j_1 < \ldots < j_i \leq n} P(c_{j_1} \wedge \ldots \wedge c_{j_i}).$$

Unfortunately, this formula has exponential complexity. However, there are methods for identifying the cases where extensional semantics computes the correct result [4], thus the sieve formula is used only when necessary.

2.2   Interpretation of Probabilistic Weights

The interpretation of the probabilities is based on a *possible worlds semantics*. Here we have a set of worlds $W = \{W_1, \ldots, W_n\}$, where each world W_j has a so-called probability of accessibility $P(W_j)$, such that $\sum_{i=1}^{n} P(W_i) = 1$. Each world contains a deterministic relational database. For computing the probability with which a formula (tuple) is true, we have to sum up the probabilities of those words in which the formula holds.

As a simple example, the probabilistic database containing the single tuple
`0.9 docTerm(d1,ir).`
has as possible interpretation
$P(W_1) = 0.9$: {`docTerm(d1,ir)`}
$P(W_2) = 0.1$: {}

When we have more than one tuple, then there are different possible interpretations. For the example

`0.6 docTerm(d1,ir). 0.5 docTerm(d1,db).`

there are, among others, the following interpretations:

I_1: $P(W_1) = 0.3$: {`docTerm(d1,ir)`}
    $P(W_2) = 0.3$: {`docTerm(d1,ir), docTerm(d1,db)`}
    $P(W_3) = 0.2$: {`docTerm(d1,db)`}
    $P(W_4) = 0.2$: {}
I_2: $P(W_1) = 0.5$: {`docTerm(d1,ir)`}
    $P(W_2) = 0.1$: {`docTerm(d1,ir), docTerm(d1,db)`}
    $P(W_3) = 0.4$: {`docTerm(d1,db)`}
I_3: $P(W_1) = 0.1$: {`docTerm(d1,ir)`}
    $P(W_2) = 0.5$: {`docTerm(d1,ir), docTerm(d1,db)`}
    $P(W_3) = 0.4$: {}

Here *probabilistic logic* would take a cautious approach and allow all these interpretations (and many others); by considering the extreme cases I_2 and I_3, we can infer that

$$P(\texttt{docTerm(d1, ir)}\&\texttt{docTerm(d1, db)}) \in [0.1, 0.5].$$

In contrast, probabilistic Datalog assumes that the underlying probabilistic events are all independent (unless specified otherwise), which is only true for interpretation I_1 here, and so we get a point estimate of 0.3 for the cooccurrence of the two events.

2.3   Extensions

Disjoint Events. In some IR applications, we need disjoint probabilistic events. As an example, assume that we are performing information extraction on a text talking about Paris, and we have no further clue which city is referred to here. We only have general knowledge that in 70% of all cases, Paris refers to the French capital, in 20% to the city in Texas and in 10% to Paris, Idaho. This knowledge could be mapped by the following relation of tuples with disjoint events; thus, in the corresponding interpretation, in each world, only one tuple belongs to the relation CiSt:

CiSt

β	City	State
0.7	Paris	France
0.2	Paris	Texas
0.1	Paris	Idaho

$P(W_1) = 0.7$: $\{\texttt{CiSt(paris, france)}\}$
$P(W_2) = 0.2$: $\{\texttt{CiSt(paris, texas)}\}$
$P(W_3) = 0.1$: $\{\texttt{CiSt(paris, idaho)}\}$

As a consequence, we have to consider the disjointness of events when computing the final probability from the event expression, like e.g. $P(\texttt{CiSt(paris, france)}$ & $\texttt{CiSt(paris, texas)}) = 0$

Relational Bayes. In some IR applications, the probabilistic weights are not given beforehand, they have to be derived from deterministic facts. Actually, all probabilistic indexing methods start from some deterministic facts (like e.g. tf·idf weighting). Thus it would be nice if we could formulate these weighting methods also as Datalog rules. The *Relational Bayes* described in [15] does exactly this job.

As a starting point, we regard an example similar to the previous one, where we now have a deterministic database of cities and their nationality observed in a text corpus.

nationality_and_city	
Nationality	City
"British"	"London"
"British"	"London"
"British"	"London"
"Scottish"	"London"
"French"	"London"
"German"	"Hamburg"
"German"	"Hamburg"
"Danish"	"Hamburg"
"British"	"Hamburg"
"German"	"Dortmund"
"German"	"Dortmund"
"Turkish"	"Dortmund"
"Scottish"	"Glasgow"

$\Longrightarrow$

nationality_city		
P(Nationality|City)	Nationality	City
0.600	"British"	"London"
0.200	"Scottish"	"London"
0.200	"French"	"London"
0.500	"German"	"Hamburg"
0.250	"Danish"	"Hamburg"
0.250	"British"	"Hamburg"
0.667	"German"	"Dortmund"
0.333	"Turkish"	"Dortmund"
1.000	"Scottish"	"Glasgow"

The mapping onto probabilities is performed by computing the conditional probabilities of nationalities conditioned on cities, which we express in probabilistic Datalog as follows:

```
1    # P(Nationality | City):
2    nationality_city  SUM(Nat, City) :-
3          nationality_and_city (Nat, City) | (City);
```

Here the conditioning operator | generates a uniform probabilistic distribution over all the tuples having the same value for the attribute we condition on (here: City), then the SUM operator groups by the attributes specified as argument (here: (Nat, City)), summing up the probabilities of tuples having the same values for these attributes.

As an application to IR, we can use this method for computing a simple form of tf weights, as shown in the following example:

term	
Term	DocId
sailing	doc1
boats	doc1
sailing	doc2
boats	doc2
sailing	doc2
east	doc3
coast	doc3
sailing	doc3
sailing	doc4
boats	doc5

p_t_d_space(Term, DocId) :- term(Term, DocId) | (DocId);		
$P(t\|d)$	Term	DocId
0.50	sailing	doc1
0.50	boats	doc1
0.33	sailing	doc2
0.33	boats	doc2
0.33	sailing	doc2
0.33	east	doc3
0.33	coast	doc3
0.33	sailing	doc3
1.00	sailing	doc4
1.00	boats	doc5

p_t_d SUM(Term, DocId) :- term(Term, DocId) | (DocId);		
$P(t\|d)$	Term	DocId
0.50	sailing	doc1
0.50	boats	doc1
0.67	sailing	doc2
0.33	boats	doc2
0.33	east	doc3
0.33	coast	doc3
0.33	sailing	doc3
1.00	sailing	doc4
1.00	boats	doc5

Probabilistic Rules. Another useful extension of probabilistic Datalog are probabilistic rules. We start with rules for deterministic facts, stating that 70% of all men like sports, but only 40% of all women:

```
0.7 likes-sports(X) :- man(X). 0.4 likes-sports(X) :- woman(X).
man(peter).
```
Knowing for certain that peter is a man, the corresponding interpretation is as follows:

$P(W_1) = 0.7$: {man(peter), likes-sports(peter)}
$P(W_2) = 0.3$: {man(peter)}

Things get more complex when we apply probabilistic rules on uncertain facts, e.g. when we don't know jo's gender:
```
# gender is disjoint on the first attribute
0.7 l-sports(X) :- gender(X,male).
0.4 l-sports(X) :- gender(X,female).
0.5 gender(X,male) :- human(X).
0.5 gender(X,female) :- human(X).
human(jo).
```
In probabilistic Datalog, the correct interpretation in this case is (see [8]):

$P(W_1) = 0.35$: {gender(jo,male), l-sports(jo)}
$P(W_2) = 0.15$: {gender(jo,male)}
$P(W_3) = 0.20$: {gender(jo,female), l-sports(jo)}
$P(W_4) = 0.30$: {gender(jo,female)}

Thus, for l-sports(jo), we have to sum the probabilities of the two worlds where this fact holds: $P(W_1) + P(W_3) = 0.55$

Another problem with probabilistic rules occurs when multiple rules derive the same fact, like in the following example:
```
sameauthor(D1,D2) :-
author(D1,X) & author(D2,X). 0.5 link(D1,D2) :- refer(D1,D2).
0.2 link(D1,D2) :- sameauthor(D1,D2).
```
In case we have two documents written by the same author and referring to each other, we might wonder about the probabilistic weight of link:
```
?? link(D1,D2) :- refer(D1,D2) & sameauthor(D1,D2).
```
The problem is that given $P(l|r)$ and $P(l|s)$, this does not yield enough information on how to compute $P(l|r \wedge s)$. Thus, this probability has to be specified explicitly, like in the following form:
```
0.7 link(D1,D2) :- refer(D1,D2) & sameauthor(D1,D2).
0.5 link(D1,D2) :- refer(D1,D2) & not(sameauthor(D1,D2)).
0.2 link(D1,D2) :- sameauthor(D1,D2) & not(refer(D1,D2)).
```

In fact, this form corresponds to *probabilistic inference networks* [13], where our rules define a so-called link matrix.

3   Vague Predicates

Vague Predicates play an important role when users are searching for objects with certain attributes (e.g. in online shops), but have only soft constraints on these facts, like e.g. searching for an LCD TV with high contrast and wide viewing angle, but for a reasonable price. Also, if the user does not know about standard sizes (e.g. asking for a 45 inch screen), this calls for a vague interpretation of this specification, instead of returning an empty answer set. In the following, we first discuss the underlying logical issue, and then present a solution that extends pD.

The Logical View on Vague Predicates. Current IR systems are based on proposition logic—a query term is present or absent in document, and thus either true or false (with a certain probability) in a document. Usually, similarity of values (e.g. similar terms) is not considered in standard text retrieval. On the other hand, multimedia IR deals with similarity already, like e.g. similarity of images, music or video (i. e. features thereof). In order to deal with these issues from a logical point of view, the transition from propositional to predicate logic becomes necessary.

In the previous sections of this article, we talked about (probabilistic) databases and Datalog, which are already based on predicate logic. So it seems quite natural to extend these formalisms to deal with similarity of values and vague predicates. The underlying ideas have been described in [9,8].

To illustrate these ideas, let us go back to the search for a 45 inch LCD TV. We assume that vague predicates are implemented as builtin predicates, e.g. in the form $\approx (X, Y)$. Then our query could be formulated as

`query(D):- category(D,tv) & type(D,lcd) & size(D,X) & ≈(X,45)`

For illustration purposes, here we represent the builtin predicate as a table shown below. With this interpretation, the system would be able to return the existing devices with sizes of 46 and 42 inches, although with a reduced certainty.

$$X \approx Y$$

β	...	0.7	0.8	0.9	1.0	0.9	0.8	...
X	...	42	43	44	45	46	47	...
Y	...	45	45	45	45	45	45	...

Vague Predicates in IR and Databases. There are many applications where the concept of vague predicates may be helpful. From a more formal point of view, we have various data types in a database, with a set of vague predicates for each data type. Here are some examples: When we have texts in various languages, then each language may be regarded as a specific data type, where language-specific stemming methods can be regarded as vague predicates. When we are searching for proper names (e.g. persons, companies or products) then phonetic similarity as well as spelling-tolerant search may be useful. For dates (e.g. "the email I received about a month ago"), a vague date condition might often be useful, as well as for amounts ("a TV set for up to 500 Euros"). Similar statements can be made for technical measurements ("at room temperature"), and the search for chemical formulas also involves certain concepts of similarity.

Overall, we see that vague criteria are very frequent in end-user querying of fact databases. However, as there is no appropriate support for them in SQL, this calls for the integration of IR methods.

Probabilistic Modeling of Vague Predicates. Once we want to use vague predicates, there is the problem of estimating the corresponding probabilistic weights. In the very beginning, one can define them in an ad-hoc way; but once we have a running system, we can use feedback data (e.g. clickthrough data) in order to derive better estimates. In [7], an approach based on machine learning has been proposed for this purpose. The basic idea is to construct a feature vector $x(q_i, d_i)$ from the query value q_i and document value d_i for each query-document pair; a simple feature could e.g. be the relative difference between q_i and d_i. Once we have collected enough training samples, we can apply some probabilistic classification method, like e.g. logistic regression. Figure 5 shows two examples of logistic functions, where the symmetric one could be used for vague equality, and the other one as a vague interpretation of 'greater than'.

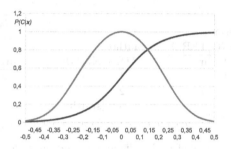

Fig. 5. Logistic functions

4   Expressiveness

The third major area where IR can benefit from DB concepts is expressiveness of the query language. Traditionally, IR has been focusing on the retrieval of relevant documents, where each document is regarded as a kind of independent, atomic unit. For this reason, there was hardly any need for an expressive query language. With the applications we are facing nowadays, however, there is a need for formulating more expressive queries. [1]

4.1   Retrieval Rules, Joins, Aggregations and Restructuring

In comparison to classical text retrieval as sketched above, pD already gives us a significant improvement in terms of expressiveness. Starting form logic rules like e.g. `about(D,T) :- docTerm(D,T)`, we are now able to consider document linking or anchor text (like in Web retrieval):
`about(D,T) :- link(D1,D),about(D1,T).`

---

[1] In many of today's IR applications, the required expressiveness is hard-coded in the application program; this approach corresponds to the very early days of DB development.

In case we have a thesaurus or an ontology, we can consider term hierarchy
`about(D,T) :- subconcept(T,T1) & about(D,T1).`
Also, it is possible to perform field-specific term weighting:
`0.9 docTerm(D,T) :- occurs(D,T,title).`
`0.5 docTerm(D,T) :- occurs(D,T,body).`
While these examples are just rules for methods provided by most of today's
IR systems, more database oriented queries can also be formulated in pD, es-
pecially when we want to consider relationships between documents and other
kinds of objects in the database. As shown above, joins allow for searching for
authors writing about certain topics, like e.g.
`irauthor(N):- about(D,ir) & author(D,N).`
We can also ask more complex queries, e.g. Smith's IR papers cited by Miller:
`?- author(D,smith) & about(D,ir) & author(D1,miller) & cites(D,D1).`

docTerm

β	DNO	TERM		author			irauths	
0.9	1	ir		DNO	NAME		1.7	smith
0.8	1	db		1	smith		0.6	miller
0.6	2	ir		2	miller			
0.8	3	ir		3	smith			
0.7	3	ai						

Fig. 6. Example of probabilistic aggregation with summing

Another important element of query expressiveness is *aggregation*. If we want
to know the names of the major IR authors, this could be formulated as
`irauthor(A):- docTerm(D,ir) & author(D,A).`
However, this form of aggregation through projection is not very meaningful,
since a person with a single paper certainly about IR would get the same weight
as another person with dozens of IR papers. Thus, we need some form of (probabilistic) counting, for which the relational Bayes mentioned above provides the
necessary functions. Figure 6 shows the evaluation of the query
`irauth(D,A):- docTerm(D,ir) & author(D,A).`
`irauths SUM(Name) :- irdbauth(Doc,Name) | (Name).`

4.2   Expressiveness in XML Retrieval

So far, we have hardly talked about document structure (only about links between documents). In many IR applications, document structure plays an important role, and the documents of a (sub)collection have a quite regular structure
(in contrast to Web documents). As XML is the most popular standard for representing document structure, here we discuss how we can exploit this structure for
increasing precision in retrieval. Figure 7 gives a survey over the possible views
on XML documents, which can also be regarded as a design space for XML IR
systems. Here we distinguish two dimensions, namely the *structure* and *content*

type. The former deals with the structural aspects of XML documents, starting from a simple view as a tree (nested) structure up to the database-oriented view as implemented in the XQuery language. The second dimension deals with the types of content we may find in XML documents. In most cases, we assume all content to be text only. However, markup of an element may indicate a specific data type (e. g. a date) or even complex object types. In the following, we describe each of the two design dimensions in more detail.

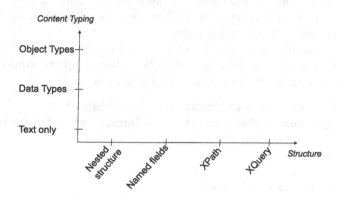

Fig. 7. Views on XML

XML Structure

Nested Structure. Whereas classical retrieval regards documents as atomic units, the XML markup of a document immediately implies a nested, tree-like structure. Following this view, a retrieval method should be able to retrieve subtrees (i. e. complete elements) instead of complete documents only. Typical query languages for this kind of retrieval provide no specific means for specifying structural constraints, in most cases they only allow for the specification of a set of terms. The corresponding retrieval method aims at performing a relevance-oriented selection of answer elements, i. e. the system should return the most specific relevant elements.

Named Fields. This view is somewhat orthogonal to the nested structure view: Here, we only regard the element names, without considering their structural relationships. Thus, a document can be seen as a set of named fields (sometimes also called a linear data model). Here we can refer to elements through field names only, whereas the context of an element is ignored (e. g., in a document, we may not be able to distinguish between the author of the document and that of a referenced paper). Another problem is that of false coordination: e. g., for a document with two authors from different institutions, our retrieval method may not be able to coordinate author names and affiliations correctly.

XPath. XPath provides full expressiveness for navigating through the document tree, by parent/child and ancestor/descendant relationships, whereas horizontal navigation is supported via operators like following/preceding, following-sibling and preceding-sibling; in addition, there are the attribute and the namespace axis. With these operators — in combination with the specification of element names — XPath allows for the selection of arbitrary elements.

XQuery. XQuery offers an even higher expressiveness than XPath, due to the fact that it was developed especially for database-like applications. Thus, in addition to XPath, it supports typical database operators like joins, aggregations and constructors for restructuring results.

As a simple example, assume a list of book titles with prices and publisher names stored in a file named 'bib.xml' ; then the following query would produce a list of publishers, each along with the average price of its books:

```
FOR $p IN distinct(document("bib.xml")//publisher)
LET $a := avg(document("bib.xml")//book[publisher = $p]/price)
RETURN
    <publisher>
        <name> {$p/text()} </name>
        <avgprice> {$$a} </avgprice>
    </publisher>
```

Here the FOR construct loops over all publishers, whereas the following LET retrieves all corresponding book prices and then computes their average. In the RETURN clause, the XML structure of the result is specified.

XML Content Typing. Now we regard the content dimension of XML retrieval.

Text. Most of today's XML retrieval systems assume that an XML document contains only text. In some sense, they still follow the traditional view of a document as a text block, which is now structured via XML tags.

Data Types. Different XML elements may contain different types of text, and this information could be exploited in retrieval. As discussed above, advanced IR system should support the notion of data types, where each such type is accompanied by a set of (vague) predicates.

Object Types. One can even go one step further and regard objects occurring in XML documents, like for example persons, locations or companies. Objects may have several attributes (of different data types), and queries may refer to any of these attributes. As an example, regard the following text excerpt from Wikipedia:

> Pablo Picasso (October 25, 1881 – April 8, 1973) was a Spanish painter and sculptor..... In Paris, Picasso entertained a distinguished coterie of

friends in the Montmartre and Montparnasse quarters, including André Breton, Guillaume Apollinaire, and writer Gertrude Stein.

If this text were marked up appropriately, a retrieval system should be able to answer queries like e. g. "To which other artists did Picasso have close relationships?" or "Where did he meet Gertrude Stein?". There is substantial work on named entity recognition methods, which allow for automatic markup of object types.

Overall, with data and object types, precision of XML retrieval can be increased.

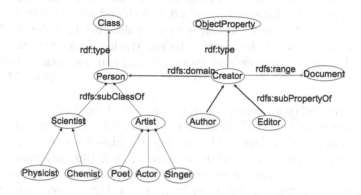

Fig. 8. OWL modeling

Towards Semantic Retrieval of XML Documents. In the discussion from above, we have not regarded the semantics of XML element names. In fact, some XML applications use rather cryptic element names. However, for new XML applications, the effort for using meaningful element names would be only marginal. Based on this information, the semantics of tag names could be exploited. In Figure 8, we have used OWL [12] for an example modelling of descriptions of artists and scientists (e. g. in Wikipedia). A first benefit would be the possibility to search for generalizations or specializations of concepts. (e. g. searching for artists would retrieve poets, actors and singers). In a similar way, also hierarchies on properties would be supported[2], and the domain and range of such properties can be considered

Readers familiar with XQuery and XPath Full Text [2] may have noticed that some of the features discussed here are already available in XQuery. However, weighting in XQuery is restricted to the text search part. Thus, probabilistic inference involving joins, rules or aggregations is missing.

---

[2] However, hierarchies of properties cannot be expressed in OWL.

5   Further Concepts

Here we want to point out two directions of ongoing research in the integration of IR and DB.

5.1   4-Valued (Probabilistic) Logics

In Section 2, we have demonstrated how we can enhance the inference capabilities of today's IR systems by using pD. Like in most logic-based approaches, this is only feasible if we have a consistent knowledge base. In IR, however, when dealing with large collections (from possibly heterogenous sources), it is inevitable that we introduce inconsistencies due to conflicting statements originating from different documents (e.g., there are many documents on the Web claiming that Barack Obama is a Muslim). Since we can derive anything from an inconsistent knowledge base, our standard logic-based approach is doomed to fail in such settings. The only way out is to use a different logical formalism, like e. g. four-valued logic [1]. In addition to the truth values *true* and *false*, there are also the values *unknown* and *inconsistent*. Then, for each statement, the probabilities for the four truth values add up to 1. In the Obama-Muslim example from above, a summarization over all relevant Web documents would yield a certain probability for *inconsistent*, besides a high probability for *false*.

Another benefit from 4-valued logic is that it allows for both open and closed world assumptions: Standard Datalog is based on the closed world assumption, i. e., if the system cannot infer a certain statement, then this statement is assumed to be *false*. For example, if we cannot derive `author(smith,doc123)`, then `smith` is not an author of the paper in question. For classical DB applications, this approach is very reasonable, assuming that a database is always complete and correct. On the other hand, for IR-oriented applications, a closed world assumption is often inappropriate. For example, if we are unable to infer `about(d123,ir)`, this does not mean that we are sure that this paper is not about IR. In fact, language models solve this problem by using a collection-based prior: if a term does not occur in a document, then a small default probability for the document being about the term is assumed (which is derived from the relative collection frequency of the term). From a logical point of view,[3] this situation should be modeled via an open world assumption, meaning that we cannot make a statement whether or not the document is about the term in question, represented as *unkown* in our four-valued logic. Further research will show if we can achieve reasonable benefits from an enhanced logical modeling.

4-valued probabilistic Datalog (with open and closed world assumptions) was introduced in [10], showing that the computational effort is roughly doubled in comparison to the two-valued case. In [11], this was extended towards an object-oriented logic, which allowed for the explicit modeling of contexts (e.g. documents) with accessibility probabilities. This idea was taken further in [6] for dealing with annotations, and in [5] for modeling summarization.

---

[3] Of course, the language model approach can be easily represented in pD, as shown in [15].

5.2 IR vs. DB Systems

Figure 9 shows a comparison between standard IR and DB systems. In the DB world, there is a clear separation between the DBMS and the application itself, while in the IR world, no such separation exists—the user interacts directly with the IR system. Besides the different architecture, this figure also highlights a major difference between IR- and DB-oriented research: In IR research, the pragmatic aspects of the application play an important role (which is, e.g., reflected in the central concept of relevance). On the other hand, in DB settings, all pragmatic aspects are delegated to the application component, which is mostly beyond the scope of DB research.

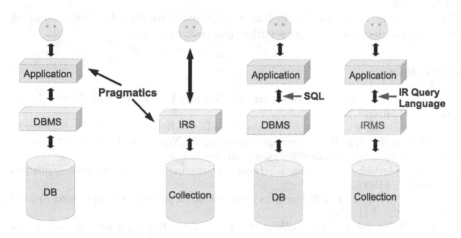

Fig. 9. Pragmatics in IR vs. DB   **Fig. 10.** Towards an IRMS

This figure might also stimulate another idea: Why should IR not switch to the DB-like architecture and introduce a separation between applications and IR management system? Given the broad variety of IR applications we are dealing with nowadays, building separate systems for each type of task is not very reasonable. Instead, it might be more effective to have a standardized IR management system (IRMS). On top this system, we can implement various applications (see Figure 10). Then of course, there is the question of the design of the interface between application and IRMS. In the DB world, SQL plays this role. In parallel, we would need an IR query language with comparable capabilities—the basic concepts of such a language have been described in this article.

6   Conclusion

In this article, we have focused on the logical view for bridging the gap between IR and DB. From this perspective, there are three major concepts that should become part of IR, namely inference, vague predicates and expressive query languages.

Concerning inference, the logical view interprets IR as being based on uncertain inference, which is a generalization of the traditional DB approach. We have seen that the probabilistic relational model supports the integration of IR and DB, while pD yields more powerful inference mechanism; especially, pD allows for formulating retrieval strategies as logical rules, thus making IR systems much more flexible than the current approaches.

For dealing with various media and data types, vague predicates form a natural extension of IR methods to attribute values, thus switching from propositional to predicate logic. The probabilistic weights of vague predicates can be learned from feedback data.

Finally, a more expressive query language would allow for joins, for computing aggregated results, and for restructuring the result objects.

References

1. Belnap, N.: A useful four-valued logic. In: Modern Uses of Multiple-Valued Logic. Reidel, Dordrecht (1977)
2. Case, P., Dyck, M., Holstege, M., Amer-Yahia, S., Botev, C., Buxton, S., Doerre, J., Melton, J., Rys, M., Shanmugasundaram, J.: Xquery and xpath full text 1.0 (2011), http://www.w3.org/TR/xpath-full-text-10/
3. Ceri, S., Gottlob, G., Tanca, L.: Logic Programming and Databases. Springer, Heidelberg (1990)
4. Dalvi, N.N., Suciu, D.: Efficient query evaluation on probabilistic databases. VLDB J. 16(4), 523–544 (2007)
5. Forst, J.F., Tombros, A., Roelleke, T.: Polis: A probabilistic logic for document summarisation. In: Proceedings of the 1st International Conference on Theory of Information Retrieval (ICTIR 2007) - Studies in Theory of Information Retrieval, pp. 201–212 (2007)
6. Frommholz, I., Fuhr, N.: Probabilistic, object-oriented logics for annotation-based retrieval in digital libraries. In: Nelson, M., Marshall, C., Marchionini, G. (eds.) Opening Information Horizons – Proc. of the 6th ACM/IEEE Joint Conference on Digital Libraries (JCDL 2006), pp. 55–64. ACM, New York (2006)
7. Fuhr, N.: A probabilistic framework for vague queries and imprecise information in databases. In: Proceedings of the 16th International Conference on Very Large Databases, Los Altos, California, pp. 696–707. Morgan Kaufman (1990)
8. Fuhr, N.: Probabilistic Datalog: Implementing logical information retrieval for advanced applications. Journal of the American Society for Information Science 51(2), 95–110 (2000)
9. Fuhr, N., Rölleke, T.: A probabilistic relational algebra for the integration of information retrieval and database systems. ACM Transactions on Information Systems 14(1), 32–66 (1997)
10. Fuhr, N., Rölleke, T.: HySpirit – a probabilistic inference engine for hypermedia retrieval in large databases. In: Schek, H.-J., Saltor, F., Ramos, I., Alonso, G. (eds.) EDBT 1998. LNCS, vol. 1377, pp. 24–38. Springer, Heidelberg (1998)
11. Lalmas, M., Roelleke, T., Fuhr, N.: Intelligent hypermedia retrieval. In: Szczepaniak, P.S., Segovia, F., Zadeh, L.A. (eds.) Intelligent Exploration of the Web, pp. 324–344. Springer, Heidelberg (2002)

12. McGuinness, D.L., van Harmelen, F.: OWL. Technical report, World Wide Web Consortium (2004), http://www.w3.org/TR/owl-features/
13. Pearl, J.: Probabilistic Reasoning in Intelligent Systems: Networks of Plausible Inference. Morgan Kaufman, San Mateo (1988)
14. Rölleke, T., Fuhr, N.: Probabilistic reasoning for large scale databases. In: Datenbanksysteme in Büro, Technik und Wissenschaft (BTW 1997), pp. 118–132. Springer, Heidelberg (1997)
15. Rölleke, T., Wu, H., Wang, J., Azzam, H.: Modelling retrieval models in a probabilistic relational algebra with a new operator: the relational Bayes. The International Journal on Very Large Data Bases (VLDB) 17(1), 5–37 (2007)
16. Suciu, D., Olteanu, D., Ré, C., Koch, C.: Probabilistic Databases. Synthesis Lectures on Data Management. Morgan & Claypool Publishers (2011)
17. Ullman, J.D.: Principles of Database and Knowledge-Base Systems, vol. I. Computer Science Press, Rockville (1988)
18. van Rijsbergen, C.J.: Information Retrieval, 2nd edn. Butterworths, London (1979)

Metrics, Statistics, Tests

Tetsuya Sakai

Waseda University, Japan
tetsuyasakai@acm.org

Abstract. This lecture is intended to serve as an introduction to Information Retrieval (IR) effectiveness metrics and their usage in IR experiments using test collections. Evaluation metrics are important because they are inexpensive tools for monitoring technological advances. This lecture covers a wide variety of IR metrics (except for those designed for XML retrieval, as there is a separature lecture dedicated to this topic) and discusses some methods for evaluating evaluation metrics. It also briefly covers computer-based statistical significance testing. The takeaways for IR experimenters are: (1) It is important to understand the properties of IR metrics and choose or design appropriate ones for the task at hand; (2) Computer-based statistical significance tests are simple and useful, although statistical significance does not necessarily imply practical significance, and statistical insignificance does not necessarily imply practical insignificance; and (3) Several methods exist for discussing which metrics are "good," although none of them is perfect.

1 Introduction

This lecture is intended to serve as an introduction to Information Retrieval (IR) effectiveness metrics and their usage in IR experiments using test collections. Evaluation metrics are important because they are inexpensive tools for monitoring technological advances. Forty years ago, Cooper [36,37] said: *"the best way to evaluate a retrieval system is, in principle at least, to elicit subjective estimates of the system's utility to its users, quantified in terms of the number of utiles (e.g. dollars) they would have been willing to give up in exchange for the privilege of using the system."* He also described this hypothetical evaluation scheme as follows: *"The system users in the sample are chosen at random from among the patrons as they enter the library and are about to make use of the retrieval system."* Now in the 21st Century, it is very difficult to find "the users in the library," observe them and ask them questions!

Sections 2 and 3 define and discuss "traditional" and "advanced" IR metrics, respectively. By traditional metrics, I mean those designed for evaluating a set of items or a ranked list of items based on relevance. By advanced metrics, I mean those designed for handling diversity, multi-query sessions, and IR systems that go beyond the ranked-list paradigm. (This lecture does not cover evaluation metrics specifically designed for XML retrieval, as there is a separate lecture dedicated to this topic.) Section 4 briefly describes computer-based statistical

N. Ferro (Ed.): PROMISE Winter School 2013, LNCS 8173, pp. 116–163, 2014.

significance tests that are useful for IR evaluation. Section 5 discusses tests for "evaluating evaluation metrics": one ultimate goal of IR researchers is to build systems that completely and efficiently satisfy the user's information needs, and we often regard evaluation metrics as crude indicators of user satisfaction or user performance. What are "good" metrics? Finally, Section 6 summarises this lecture.

A word of warning: in this lecture, I will present my personal views on IR effectiveness metrics and on methods for evaluating evaluation metrics. I discuss a lot of my own work because I know a lot about it. Hence I encourage the reader to go back to the original papers listed up in the references.

2   Traditional IR Metrics

Historically, IR was about *set retrieval*: should each document be retrieved or not? Section 2.1 describes some basic evaluation metrics for set retrieval, including the widely-used *recall, precision* and *F-measure* [68]. But with the advent of the digital information overload era, *ranked retrieval* has become the norm, so that the user can examine retrieved documents sequentially from the top and stop at her convenience. Section 2.2 describes a wide range of evaluation metrics for ranked retrieval, including *normalised Discounted Cumulative Gain* [49] (nDCG) which has been used widely not only in the IR research community but also for tuning commercial web search engines. These "traditional" set retrieval and ranked retrieval metrics require a gold standard (i.e. "right answers"): to be more specific, for each *search topic* (or *query*), a set of *relevant* documents is required. Note that "document" is a generic term that may refer to any *retrieval unit*: for example, it could be a web page, a textual passage, a multimedia file, a cluster of items and so on. Section 2.3 provides information for further reading.

2.1   Set Retrieval Metrics

Recall and Precision. Figure 1 is a Venn diagram that shows a set of relevant documents for a topic (D^*), a set of retrieved documents for that topic (D), and the intersection between the two ($D^* \cap D$). $D^* - D$ represents the documents that the retrieval system missed, while $D - D^*$ represents the nonrelevant documents retrieved. *Recall* (*Rec*) and *Precision* (*Prec*) directly reflect these properties, respectively: $Rec = |D^* \cap D|/|D^*|$, and $Prec = |D^* \cap D|/|D|$.

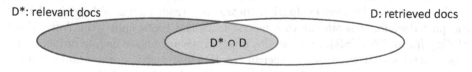

D*: relevant docs   D: retrieved docs

D* ∩ D

Fig. 1. Relevant/retrieved documents

E-measure. While it is clear that recall and precision have a trade-off relationship, we generally want both high recall and high precision. It would be useful to have a single, summary metric that incorporates this trade off. Let us first start with a basic version of *E-measure* [68], using Figure 1:

$$E\text{-}measure = \frac{|D^* \cup D| - |D^* \cap D|}{|D^*| + |D|} . \tag{1}$$

Using the aforementioned definitions of recall and precision, the above can alternatively be expressed as:

$$E\text{-}measure = 1 - \frac{1}{0.5\frac{1}{Prec} + 0.5\frac{1}{Rec}} . \tag{2}$$

But now it is clear that this version of E-measure assumes that recall and precision are equally important; let us generalise it by introducing a parameter α $(0 \leq \alpha \leq 1)$:

$$E\text{-}measure = 1 - \frac{1}{\alpha\frac{1}{Prec} + (1 - \alpha)\frac{1}{Rec}} . \tag{3}$$

Furthermore, by letting $\alpha = 1/(\beta^2 + 1)$, the generalised E-measure can be rewritten as:

$$E\text{-}measure = 1 - \frac{(\beta^2 + 1)PrecRec}{\beta^2 Prec + Rec} . \tag{4}$$

Here, the assumption is that the user attaches $\beta(\geq 0)$ times as much importance to recall as precision[1].

F-measure. *F-measure* [28], which is simply *one minus E-measure*, is much more widely used than E-measure, probably because we want the evaluation metric value to be large for an effective retrieval system:

$$F\text{-}measure = \frac{(\beta^2 + 1)PrecRec}{\beta^2 Prec + Rec} . \tag{5}$$

F-measure with $\beta = b$ is often expressed as F_b; note that F_1 is a harmonic mean of precision and recall.

2.2   Ranked Retrieval Metrics

nDCG. *Normalised Discounted Cumulative Gain* [49] (nDCG) has become one of the most widely-used evaluation metric for tradital ranked retrieval over the past decade. It is similar to a metric from the 1960s called the *Normalised Sliding Ratio* [67] (NSR), and handles *graded* relevance assessments unlike many other metrics that were used earlier in the IR community. For example, a topic may have some judged nonrelevant documents (relevance level 0), some partially

---

[1] $\frac{dE}{dRec} = \frac{dE}{dPrec}$ when $\frac{Prec}{Rec} = \beta$ [68].

relevant documents (relevance level 1) and highly relevant documents (relevance level 2). We decide in advance the *gain value* gv_x for each relevance level x: for example, we could simply let $gv_1 = 1$, $gv_2 = 2$, and $gv_3 = 3$, by assuming that the raw value of each relevant document is proportional to its relevance level. Also, it is common to let $gv_0 = 0$: a nonrelevant document is of no value.

For a given ranked list of documents, let $g(r) = gv_x$ if the relevance level of the document at rank r is x. In particular, let $g^*(r)$ denote the gain value at rank r of an *ideal list*[2], obtained by sorting all relevant documents in decreasing order of the relevance level. A few versions of nDCG exist, but the one described here [17] is probably the most widely-used:

$$nDCG = \frac{\sum_{r=1}^{l} g(r)/\log(r+1)}{\sum_{r=1}^{l} g^*(r)/\log(r+1)} \tag{6}$$

where l is the *measurement depth*, also known as the *document cutoff*. Note that the logarithm base b cancels out in the above definition: for convenience let us use $b = 2$ here. The key feature of nDCG is that the gain value of each retrieved relevant document is discounted based on its rank: for example, if we set the gain value of each highly relevant document to be 3, then for a highly relevant document at rank 1, its discounted gain is $3/\log(1+1) = 3$; but for a highly relevant document at rank 7, its discounted gain is $3/\log(1+7) = 1$.

The use of the *original* nDCG, which regards the logarithm base b as a *user patience parameter* [49], is not recommended. The problem is that discounting is not applied when $r \leq b$. For example, when $b = 10$, this version of nDCG cannot tell the difference between a system that returns a relevant document at rank 1 and one that returns a relevant document at rank 10. To address this, Järvelin *et al.* [50] have described yet another version of nDCG, which discounts the raw gain by $1 + \log_b r$ instead of $\log(1+r)$.

11-point Average Precision. This binary-relevance metric is a single-value summary of the *recall-precision curve* [108], but has been replaced in the early 1990s by (noninterpolated) *Average Precision*, which is described next. Although 11-point Average Precision is no longer popular, how to draw a recall-precision curve is perhaps still worth mentioning here.

Figure 2 shows how to compute *interpolated precision* for 11 recall points. In this example, the number of known relevant documents is five, and the system has managed to retrieve four of them. The recall ($Rec(r)$) and the precision ($Prec(r)$) at each rank r are shown on the left. For each recall point $i (\in \{0, 0.1, \ldots, 1\})$, interpolated precision is given by:

$$IP_i = \max_{r, Rec(r) \geq i} Prec(r) . \tag{7}$$

That is, for a given recall point i, the actual recall values that satisfy this level are first obtained, and then the highest precision value among these actual recall points is obtained.

---

[2] Pollock, who proposed NSR in 1968, called it the *master list* [67].

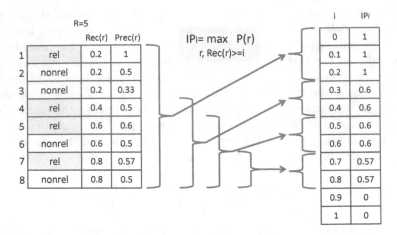

Fig. 2. Computing interpolated precision for the 11 recall points

The recall-precision curve is obtained by plotting the interpolated precision value for each i. Moreover, 11-point average precision is simply given by:

$$11pt\text{-}AP = \frac{\sum_{i \in \{0, 0.1, \ldots, 1\}} IP_i}{11} .\tag{8}$$

This averaging is not desirable for many IR applications, as the precisions at low recall points and those at high recall points are considered equally important.

Average Precision. *Average Precision* (AP) was one of the most widely-used evaluation metric for ranked retrieval during the 1990s, since it was introduced at the Second Text Retrieval Conference (TREC-2) [108]. Let R denote the number of known relevant documents for a topic. For a given ranked list of documents, let $I(r)$ be 0 if the document at rank r is nonrelevant, and 1 otherwise. Let $C(r) = \sum_{k=1}^{r} I(k)$: this is the number of relevant documents within top r. Hence the precision at r is given by $Prec(r) = C(r)/r$. Then AP is defined as:

$$AP = \frac{1}{R} \sum_r I(r) Prec(r) = \frac{1}{R} \sum_r I(r) \frac{C(r)}{r} .\tag{9}$$

One of the strengths of AP over 11-point average precision and other metrics is that it is *top heavy*: that is, it is sensitive to changes near the top ranks. For example, suppose that, through a system improvement, a relevant document has moved up by one rank from rank 2 to 1. Before this improvement, this document contributes a precision of 0.5 to AP; after the improvement, it contributes a precision of 1. In contrast, suppose a relevant document has moved from rank 100 to 99 (and that there is no other relevant document in the ranked list). This has little impact on AP, as the contributed precisions are $1/100 = 0.0100$ and $1/99 = 0.0101$, respectively.

Robertson [71] provided a user model for AP. There is a user population, and all users scan the ranked list from top to bottom, but different users stop scanning the list at different relevant documents (probably due to satisfaction). In AP, this probability distribution is assumed to be uniform across all relevant documents: that is, the probability that the user stops at each relevant document is $1/R$. Moreover, for each stopping point r, AP measures the *utility* of the top r documents in terms of precision $Prec(r)$. Hence, AP can be regarded as the *expected utility* for the user population.

The above formulation of AP and its user model assume that the document ranking is infinite, which may seem unrealistic. For those who want to use a small measurement depth l, the following variant of AP may be used:

$$AP = \frac{1}{\min(l, R)} \sum_r I(r) Prec(r) . \tag{10}$$

This ensures that the maximum possible AP is 1 even if $l < R$. Moreover, the user's stopping probability distribution can now be interpreted as either uniform over all relevant documents (if $l \geq R$) or uniform over the first l retrieved relevant documents (if $l < R$).

Unlike nDCG, AP cannot handle graded relevance. While the use of binary-relevance metrics such as AP is still common in the IR community, it should be noted that, with such metrics, it is impossible to design retrieval systems that can retrieve, say, highly relevant documents before marginally relevant ones. In light of this, several graded-relevance versions of AP have been proposed. One of them is called *Q-measure* [75,74] (or simply "Q"), which is discussed below. *Graded Average Precision* (GAP) [73] is a more recently-proposed alternative, which we shall omit in this paper as it is a little more complex than others. In contrast to Q which combines the ideas of nDCG and AP, GAP is based on a novel interpretation of graded relevance: more specifically, it assumes that the user has a binary notion of relevance, but that different users have different thresholds over the relevance levels. Sakai and Song [94] have compared Q and GAP in terms of *discriminative power* [77] (discussed in Section 5.1) and reported that Q outperformed GAP in some cases. In an earlier study, Sakai [80] compared Q with nDCG and Kishida's *generalised Average Precision* [57] (gAP), yet another graded-relevance version of AP, and demonstrated the advantage of Q's *user persistence parameter*, which gAP lacks.

Q-measure. *Q-measure* [75,74], a graded-relevance version of AP, replaces the precision $Prec(r)$ with the *blended ratio* $BR(r)$ which can handle graded relevance. Let $cg(r) = \sum_{k=1}^r g(k)$ and $cg^*(r) = \sum_{k=1}^r g^*(k)$: these are the (nondiscounted) *cumulative gains* [49] for the ranked list to be evaluated and for the ideal list, respectively. Then, for a given value of the *user persistence parameter* $\beta(\geq 0)$:

$$BR(r) = \frac{C(r) + \beta cg(r)}{r + \beta cg^*(r)} . \tag{11}$$

$BR(r)$ inherits the properties of $Prec(r) = C(r)/r$ and the *normalised Cumulative Gain* [49] $nCG(r) = cg(r)/cg^*(r)$. Moreover, in a binary-relevance evaluation environment (regardless of β), it is easy to prove that $BR(r) = Prec(r)$ holds if and only if $r \leq R$, while $BR(r) > Prec(r)$ holds if and only if $r > R$.

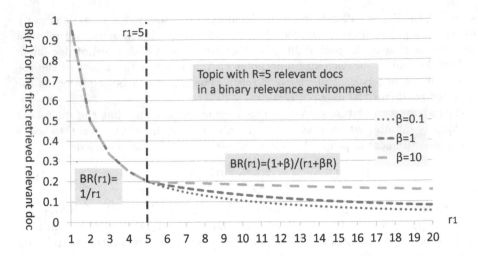

Fig. 3. Effect of β on $BR(r_1)$ in a binary relevance environment ($R = 5$)

Figure 3 illustrates the role of β for a topic with $R = 5$ relevant documents in a binary relevance environment. Here, the x axis represents r_1, the rank of the *first* relevant document found in the ranked list; the y axis represents the value of $BR(r_1)$. In a binary relevance environment, since $BR(r) = Prec(r)$ holds for $r \leq R$, note that $BR(r_1) = 1/r_1$ holds for $r_1 \leq R$. On the other hand, in a binary relevance environment, it is easy to show that $BR(r_1) = (1 + \beta)/(r_1 + \beta R)$ for $r_1 > R$. It can be observed from the figure that a large β represents a user who is very tolerant to relevant documents retrieved at low ranks; In practice, β is often set to 1, although this is an arbitrary choice.

Q can be defined as follows:

$$Q\text{-}measure = \frac{1}{R} \sum_r I(r)BR(r) = \frac{1}{R} \sum_r I(r) \frac{C(r) + \beta cg(r)}{r + \beta cg^*(r)} \tag{12}$$

or, for a given measurement depth l,

$$Q\text{-}measure = \frac{1}{\min(l, R)} \sum_r I(r)BR(r) . \tag{13}$$

Following Robertson's interpretation of AP [71], Q can be regarded as an evaluation metric which (a) assumes, just like AP, that the user's stopping probability distribution is uniform over all (or l) relevant documents; and (b) measures the utility at a given stopping rank in terms of the blended ratio [92]. Also, it is clear that Q reduces to AP when $\beta = 0$.

While Q is not as widely-used as nDCG, it has been used as one of the official metrics in the NTCIR Crosslingual IR (CLIR) task [58], Advanced Crosslingual Information Access (ACLIA) task [93] and the Geotemporal Information Retrieval (GeoTime) task [45].

Sakai and Robertson [92] have explored a few extensions of the above interpretation: they considered non-uniform stopping probability distributions, namely, a distribution based on relevant documents seen so far, and a distribution that takes the relevance levels into account. The family of these metrics is collectively known as *Normalised Cumulative Utility* (NCU).

R-precision, R-measure. *R-precision* [108] is a binary-relevance, early-TREC metric, defined for each topic with R relevant documents as $R\text{-}prec = Prec(R)$. That is, this is the precision (or equivalently, recall) at the measurement depth of R. Similarly, *R-measure* [75,74], a variant of Q, is defined as $R\text{-}measure = BR(R)$. These metrics can be regarded as a type of NCU where *all* users stop scanning the ranked list at rank R. Although R-measure leverages graded relevance, it gives a score of one to any system as long as the top R documents are all relevant, even if marginally relevant documents are ranked above the highly relevant ones.

RR. The basic assumption behind all of the above ranked retrieval metrics is that the user wants as many relevant documents as possible. While they may be suitable for *informational* search intents, there are also *navigational* search intents [14], which basically require just one document: in this case, we can assume that retrieving multiple relevant documents do not help the user.

Reciprocal Rank (RR) is a metric suitable for navigational intents. For a ranked list that does not contain a relevant document, we let $RR = 0$. Otherwise, let r_1 be the rank of the first relevant document in the ranked list: then $RR = 1/r_1$.

RR can also be seen as a member of the aforementioned NCU family: it is assumed that *all* users stop at rank r_1, and the utility at rank r_1 is measured by precision: $Prec(r_1) = C(r_1)/r_1 = 1/r_1$. Just like AP, it cannot handle graded relevance.

P$^+$. There are a few graded-relevance versions of RR: here, we discuss P$^+$ [76], which is a variant of Q and therefore a member of the NCU family. For a ranked list that does not contain a relevant document, we let $P^+ = 0$. Otherwise, let r_p be the rank of the document that is highest-ranked among the *most relevant* documents within the measurement depth l. For example, if a ranked list contains a marginally relevant document at rank 2, a highly relevant document at rank 4 and another highly relevant document at rank 6, then $r_p = 4$. (Whereas, note that $r_1 = 2$.) Then P$^+$ is defined as:

$$P^+ = \frac{1}{C(r_p)} \sum_{r=1}^{r_p} I(r) BR(r) . \tag{14}$$

Thus, P$^+$ is an NCU metric that (a) assumes that the user's stopping probability distribution is uniform over the top $C(r_p)$ relevant documents, i.e., all relevant documents at or above r_p; and (b) measures the utility at a given stopping rank in terms of the blended ratio just like Q.

Sakai [76] have discussed the advantages of P^+ over other graded-relevance versions of RR such as *Weighted Reciprocal Rank* (WRR) [44], *P-measure* (defined as $BR(r_p)$) and *O-measure* (defined as $BR(r_1)$). While P^+ itself is not a well-known metric, together with Q, it forms the basis of another metric for evaluating diversified search called $P+Q$, which we shall discuss in Section 3.1. Probably the most well-known graded-relevance metric that is suitable for navigational intents is *Expected Reciprocal Rank* [27] (ERR), which we shall discuss next.

ERR. Let $Pr(r)$ denote the probability that the user is satisfied at a document at rank r. ERR assumes that the user stops scanning the ranked list as soon as she is satisfied with a document, and that this satisfaction probability depends directly and solely on the relevance level of each document. For example, we can assume that $Pr(r) = 0$ if the document at r is nonrelevant; if we have marginally relevant, partially relevant and highly relevant documents (i.e. three relevance levels), we may let $Pr(r)$ be $(2^1 - 1)/2^3 = 1/8$, $(2^2 - 1)/2^3 = 3/8$ and $(2^3 - 1)/2^3 = 7/8$, respectively [27]. Under the *linear traversal* assumption (i.e. the user scans the list from top to bottom), the probability that the user is still unsatisfied at rank r is given by $dsat(r) = \prod_{k=1}^{r}(1 - Pr(k))$. ERR is then given by:

$$ERR = \sum_r dsat(r - 1)Pr(r)\frac{1}{r} .\tag{15}$$

ERR can also be regarded as an instance of NCU, which (a) assumes that the user's stopping probability over ranks is given by $dsat(r - 1)Pr(r)$, i.e. the probability that the user is dissatisfied with all documents between ranks 1 and $r - 1$ and finally satisfied at r; and (b) uses the RR at r to measure the utility. Note that RR is used rather than precision, since the document at r is considered to be the only useful one.

What distinguishes ERR from most of the other metrics discussed so far is its *diminishing return* property [26]: whenever a relevant document is found, the value of another relevant document found later in the list is discounted. For example, given the three-level probability setting as described above, the stopping probability for a highly relevant document at rank 2 would be $(1 - 0) * 7/8 = 0.8750$ if the document at rank 1 is nonrelevant; but it would be $(1 - 7/8) * 7/8 = 0.1094$ if the document at rank 1 is also highly relevant. The interpretation is that the second highly relevant document in the latter case is *redundant*, which aligns well with the definition of a navigational intent. This property is in contrast with other metrics such as nDCG and Q that discount the value of each relevant document based solely on its rank. Sakai and Robertson [92] have described another NCU metric that also possesses the diminishing return property: the stopping probability distribution of their metric is designed based on the assumption that "it is probably more likely that a user would stop after few relevant documents than after many."

Another interesting feature of ERR is that it does not have a recall component, unlike other graded-relevance metrics such as Q and nDCG: note that even though nDCG does not directly depend on R, the number of relevant documents, it can still be regarded as a *recall-dependent* metric as it relies on an ideal ranked list which requires enumeration of relevant documents[3]. ERR, on the other hand, does not rely on the notion of ideal list, and is not normalised.

RBP. *Rank-Biased Precision* [63] (RBP) is another recall-independent metric with a clear user model: like all other metrics discussed so far, the model assumes linear traversal, and furthermore assumes that, after the user examines rank r, she will either move on to rank $(r+1)$ with probability p or stop scanning the list with probability $1 - p$. The user behaves this way irrespective of the relevance of the documents, and p is a constant. This p can be regarded as a user persistence parameter: the higher p is, the more persistent she is.

RBP can handle graded relevance, with gain values $g(r) = gv_x$ set within the 0-1 range. It can be expressed as:

$$RBP = (1 - p) \sum_r p^{r-1} g(r) . \tag{16}$$

Note that RBP discounts the value of a relevant document based solely on the rank, just like other metrics such as nDCG and Q. Thus, unlike ERR, it does not possess the diminishing return property.

While Moffat and Zobel [63] have discussed the strengths of RBP such as its recall-independence, Sakai and Kando [89] have demonstrated a few of its shortcomings: for example, the maximum possible value of RBP varies widely depending on the parameter p^4; RBP has low *discriminative power* [77] (discussed in Section 5.1).

TBG. The metrics discussed so far treat a ranked list of documents as if they are just a list of document IDs with relevance levels. In modern IR contexts such as web search, however, the user often examines snippets (a.k.a. summaries) before reading the actual documents, and the document lengths vary. In light of this, Smucker and Clarke [104] have proposed to use the *time spent by the user* as the basis for discounting the value of a document instead the document rank.

While the general framework TBG proposes to accumulate the gains of relevant documents over *time*, the instantiation of TBG discussed by Smucker and Clarke [104] actually performs a *rank-based* gain accumulation as follows:

$$TBG = \sum_r g(r) \exp(-T(r)\frac{\ln 2}{h}) \tag{17}$$

where $T(r)$ is the *expected time to reach rank* r and h is the half-life for the time-based decay (i.e. discounting) function. This instantiation of TBG [104] is based

---

[3] Of course, we also have *Discounted Cumulative Gain* (DCG) [49], which is not normalised.

[4] In a binary relevance environment, the maximum RBP for a topic with R relevant documents is given by $(1 - p) \sum_{r=1}^{R} p^{r-1}$.

on binary relevance: the gain value $g(r)$ for every relevant document is estimated as the probability of click on a relevant summary times the probability of judging the actual document as relevant; that for every nonrelevant document is zero. As for $T(r)$, let T_S be the time to read any summary in seconds; let $L(r)$ be the length of the document at r in terms of the number of words; and let $Pr_{click}(r)$ be the probability of click at r, which depends on whether the document at r is relevant or nonrelevant. Then $T(r)$ is estimated as:

$$T(r) = \sum_{k=1}^{r-1}(T_S + Pr_{click}(k)T_D(k)) \tag{18}$$

where $T_D(r) = 0.018L(r) + 7.8$ is the estimated time to read the document at r.

As the summation over previous ranks in Eq. 18 shows, TBG relies on the linear traversal assumption. Moreover, as the formula for $T_D(r)$ shows, TBG further assumes that the document reading time grows linearly with the document length.

It is of note that TBG as defined above does not guarantee diminishing return, even though it discounts documents by taking relevance into account. Suppose we have a nonrelevant document at rank 1, and a relevant document at rank 2, and imagine that the nonrelevant document at rank 1, whose document length is 1000 words, is replaced with a new *relevant* document whose length is 10 words. Moreover, following the calibration results from Smucker and Clarke [104], let $Pr_{click}(r) = 0.64$ if the document at r is relevant and $Pr_{click}(r) = 0.39$ otherwise. Then, according to Eq. 18, the time to reach the relevant document at rank 2 *before* the replacement is $T(2) = T_S + 0.39 * (0.018 * 1000 + 7.8) = T_S + 10.062$, while the corresponding time *after* the replacement is $T(2) = T_S + 0.64 * (0.018 * 10 + 7.8) = T_S + 5.107$. Thus, by replacing a long nonrelevant document at rank 1 with a short relevant document, the time required to reach rank 2 has *decreased*, which means that the relevant document at 2 receives *more* weight according to the exponential decay function in Eq. 17. On the other hand, if the document length variance is relatively small, we can expect TBG to follow the diminishing return pattern most of the time.

Smucker and Clarke [102,103] have extended their TBG ideas in the context of stochastic simulation of user behaviours.

Prior to the proposal of TBG, Turpin *et al.* [105] and Yilmaz *et al.* [117] have also explored incorporating the snippet examination phase into IR evaluation. Several forms of time-based evaluation have also been proposed previously: for example, Dunlop [42] proposed a time-based evaluation method based on Cooper's *expected search length* [35].

U-measure. Sakai and Dou [85] recently proposed a general information access evaluation framework that can potentially handle not only ranked retrieval discussed here but also summaries, diversified search, multi-query sessions etc. that will be discussed in Section 3. Their *U-measure* framework is similar to TBG in that it takes document lengths into account, but unlike TBG (as instantiated by Smucker and Clarke [104]), it does not depend on the linear traversal assumption.

Figure 4 illustrates the construction of *trailtext*, which represents all the text the user has read during an information seeking process. This could be obtained

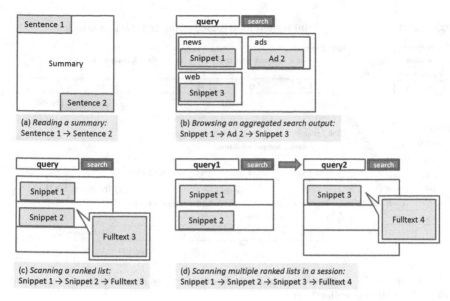

Fig. 4. Constructing trailtexts for various information access tasks

from direct user observation with eyetracking, or from user behaviour models with relevance assessments or click data. Since we are now discussing ranked retrieval, let us focus on Part (c) of this figure: here, the user scans a search result page, reads the first snippet, reads the second snippet and then visits the full text of the second document. The trailtext in this case is represented as a concatenation of these texts: "**Snippet 1 Snippet 2 Fulltext 3.**" The key idea of the U-measure framework is to define an evaluation metric over the trailtext rather than document ranks, so that any textual information seeking activities may be evaluated on a common ground.

Formally, a trailtext tt is a concatenation of n strings: $tt = s_1 s_2 \ldots s_n$. These strings may be documents, parts of documents, snippets, sentences, or any other fragments of text that have been read. We define the *offset position* of $s_k (1 \leq k \leq n)$ as $pos(s_k) = \sum_{j=1}^{k} |s_j|$ where the length of each string is measured in terms of the number of characters. Furthermore, we define the *position-based gain* as $g(pos(s_k)) = 0$ if s_k is considered nonrelevant and $g(pos(s_k)) = gv_x$ if its relevance level is considered to be x. Then U-measure is given by:

$$U\text{-}measure = \frac{1}{\mathcal{N}} \sum_{pos=1}^{|tt|} g(pos)D(pos) \tag{19}$$

where $\mathcal{N}$ is a normalisation factor, which is set to zero if normalisation is not required. Here, $D(pos)$ is a position-based decay function, which may be defined as:

$$D(pos) = \max(0, 1 - \frac{pos}{L}) \tag{20}$$

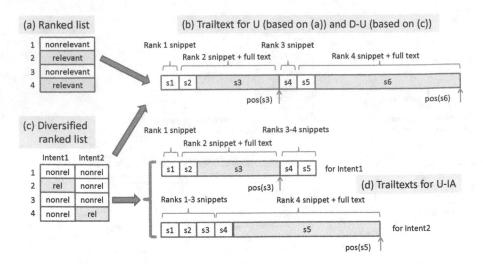

Fig. 5. Automatically constructing trailtexts from relevance assessments of traditional and diversified IR test collections

where $L(>0)$ is a parameter, which represents the amount of text read at which all relevant pieces of information become worthless for any user (set to $L = 132000$ by Sakai and Dou [85] based on web search session data). While an exponential decay function like the one used with TBG (Eq. 17) is also possible, the above simple linear function has been inherited from *S-measure* [91] which was proposed for summary evaluation. S-measure will be discussed in Section 3.3.

Figure 5 Part (a) shows a ranked list where the documents at ranks 2 and 4 are known to be relevant; Part (b) shows a possible trailtext for this list, under the linear traversal assumption. It is assumed that the four snippets plus the two relevant documents are read. In practice, it is assumed that only $F\%$ of every relevant document is read; $F = 20$ has been shown to be a reasonable choice [85].

Like ERR, U-measure possesses the diminishing return property. Suppose that, in Part (a), the nonrelevant document at rank 3 is replaced by a relevant document. Then, since it is now assumed that the document at rank 3 is also read, the trailtext shown in Part (b) will be longer, and the fourth document is pushed back towards the end of the trailtext. That is, the gain value for the fourth document has diminished.

Ranked Retrieval Metrics: Summary. Figure 6 provides a quick summary of the properties of the traditional ranked retrieval metrics. Some additional comments:

(a) The original AP cannot handle graded relevance, but a few graded-relevance versions exist (e.g. [57,73]). TBG as described by Smucker and Clarke [104] is binary-relevance-based.

(b) and (c) These properties are two sides of the same coin. nDCG, Q and P$^+$ depend on an ideal ranked list, which requires the enumeration of all

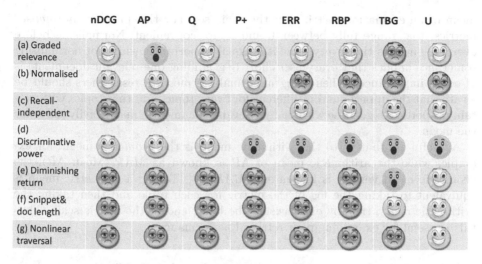

Fig. 6. Comparison of traditional ranked retrieval metrics

known relevant documents. AP and Q depend directly on the number of relevant documents. On the other hand, ERR, RBP, TBG and U are unnormalized (See the discussion on normalization below).

(d) nDCG, AP and Q are top-heavy metrics suitable for informational search intents, as they have been designed to consider many relevant documents. Hence, in terms of discriminative power (discussed in Section 5.1), they outperform other metrics such as P+ (See Sakai [76]), ERR (See Sakai and Song [94]), RBP (See Sakai and Kando [89]), TBG (See Smucker and Clarke [104] and Sakai and Dou [85]), and U (See Sakai and Dou [85]).

(e) ERR and U possess the diminishing return property, which is intuitive. TBG also shows this property unless the document lengths do not vary wildly. Diminishing return means that when a relevant document is found, the value of the next relevant document diminishes: this generally has a negative impact on discriminative power (See (d)).

(f) Besides TBG and U, a few other studies have considered the user's snippet reading behaviour (e.g. [105,117]). But only TBG and U consider the document length.

(g) The instantiation of TBG as described by Smucker and Clarke [104] depends on the time to reach rank r. This relies on the linear traversal assumption. Sakai and Dou [85] have demonstrated that U can quantify the difference between linear and nonlinear traversals in the context of click-based web search evaluation where click timestamps are available (See Section 3.2).

Normalisation and Averaging. Given a test collection with a topic set and relevance assessments for each topic, it is common to discuss the *arithmetic* mean of an evaluation metric over the topic set. For this purpose, *normalised* metrics, that range fully between 0 and 1, are convenient. Normalising before averaging implies that every topic is of equal importance, while not normalising sometimes implies that every user effort (e.g. finding one relevant document) is of equal importance. When using unnormalised metrics, researchers should be aware that the upperbound is different for every topic, and that topics with certain properties (e.g. those with many relevant documents) may heavily influence the mean.

A useful alternative to the arithmetic mean is the *geometric* mean: for example, while the arithmetic mean of AP is known as *MAP* (Mean AP), the geometric mean version is known as *GMAP* [70]. Taking a geometric mean is equivalent to taking the log of the metric for each topic and then taking the arithmetic mean, thereby emphasising the lower end of the metric scale. Thus this is useful for examining poor retrieval performance.

Condensed-list Metrics. Many modern large-scale test collections were built based on *pooling* [106,108], and therefore the relevance assessments are *incomplete* [16]: the target corpus probably contains more relevant documents that have never been assessed. Formally, let $\mathcal{D}$ denote the target corpus, and for a particular topic, let C_j denote the *contributions* (e.g. top-100 retrieved documents) from the j-th *contributor* to the test collection (e.g. a TREC participant). Then, the pool for this topic is given by $P = \bigcup_j C_j$, where $|P| \ll |\mathcal{D}|$, and the documents in $\mathcal{D} - P$ are never judged for this topic (See also Section 5.4). Moreover, the incomplete relevance assessments may also be *biased* towards particular types of relevant documents or towards particular types of retrieval systems. The incompleteness is a problem particularly when one wants to evaluate a system that did not contribute to the pools: the documents returned by such a system are either (I) judged relevant (possibly with relevance levels); (II) judged nonrelevant; or (III) unjudged. We do not know whether each unjudged document is relevant or not.

A standard practice in the IR community is to regard both documents of Types (II) and (III) as nonrelevant. However, a simple and useful alternative is to first create a *condensed list* from the raw ranked list by *removing all unjudged documents* from it, and then compute the evaluation metrics for the condensed list [79]. For example, if a raw ranked list contains an unjudged document at rank 1, a judged nonrelevant document at rank 2, and a judged relevant document at rank 3, the corresponding condensed list would have the judged nonrelevant document at rank 1 and the judged relevant document at rank 2. Thus condensing a ranked list *promotes* judged documents.

A condensed-list version of Metric M is referred to as M' [79]: in particular, AP' is also known as *Induced AP* [116]. Let r' denote the rank of a document in a condensed list. Then, from Eq. 9:

$$AP' = \frac{1}{R} \sum_{r'} I(r') \frac{C(r')}{r'} \ . \tag{21}$$

Buckley and Voorhees [16] designed a family of metrics known as *bpref* (binary preference) specifically for the purpose of conducting IR evaluation that is robust to incomplete relevance assessments. The basic idea is to evaluate systems based on their ability to prefer judged relevant documents over judged nonrelevant ones. However, Sakai [79] showed that bpref is equivalent to AP' except that it lacks the *top heaviness* property, and that some condensed-list metrics are in fact more robust to incompleteness than bpref. Subsequently, Sakai and Kando [89] generalised his experiments.

Let N denote the number of judged nonrelevant documents for a topic, and recall that R is the number of judged relevant documents. Using our notations, bpref can be expressed as:

$$bpref\_R = \frac{1}{R} \sum_{r'} I(r')(1 - \frac{\min(R, r' - C(r'))}{R}) \qquad (22)$$

if $R \leq N$, and

$$bpref\_N = \frac{1}{R} \sum_{r'} I(r')(1 - \frac{r' - C(r')}{N}) \qquad (23)$$

if $R \geq N$. Let us consider a case where $R = N = 500$, so that $bpref = bpref\_R = bpref\_N$, and recall our discussion of the top heaviness of AP. Thus, when a relevant document moves up from 2 to 1 in the condensed list, its contribution of precision to AP' changes from 0.5 to 1; whereas, when a relevant document moves up from 100 to 99, its contribution of precision to AP' increases from 0.0100 to 0.0101. The latter change is negligible and hence AP' is top heavy. In contrast, when a relevant document moves up from 2 to 1 in the condensed list, the contribution to bpref, $1 - (r' - C(r'))/N$, changes from $1 - (2 - 1)/500 = 0.9980$ to $1 - (1 - 1)/500 = 1$ and the difference is only 0.002; when a relevant document moves up from 100 to 99, the contribution to bpref changes from $1 - (100 - 1)/500 = 0.8020$ to $1 - (99 - 1)/500 = 0.8040$ and the difference is 0.002 again. It can be observed that this lack of top heaviness arises from the large constants R and N used as the denominator in Eqs. 22 and 23. Compare these with Eq. 21, which uses r' as the denominator.

Büttcher *et al.* [18] advocated the use of a metric called *RankEff* [2] for robust evaluation with incomplete and biased relevance assessments. However, Sakai [81] pointed out that RankEff is none other than bpref_N, whose limitation has already been discussed above. De Beer and Moens proposed graded-relevance versions of bpref called *rpref* [40]: one of them is similar to bpref_N and therefore suffers from the same problem; the other has a minor flaw, which can be fixed [79].

While condensed-list metrics handle incomplete relevance assessments more elegantly and robustly than bpref [79,89], they do not necessarily provide accurate evaluation results if the relevance assessments are biased. More specifically, Sakai [81] showed that, while standard metrics tend to underestimate *non-contributors* (i.e. systems that did not contribute to the pools), condensed-list metrics tend to overestimate them. This is because new systems return many unjudged documents: they are removed when the ranked list is condensed, which results in promotion of many relevant documents in the list.

2.3 Further Reading

Kekäläinen and Järvelin [56] have discussed graded-relevance versions of recall and precision called *generalised recall* and *generalised precision*. Several researchers have discussed appropriate decay functions for ranked retrieval evaluation [20,53,119].

Some ranked retrieval tasks require high recall. Patent search would be an example. Magdy and Jones [62] have recently proposed a recall-oriented evaluation metric specifically designed for patent search. In the context of patent invalidation search, Sakai [78] pointed out that *conditional relevance* [37] in a ranked list may be handled using an approach related to the condensed list: If Patent 1 at rank 1 and Patent 2 at rank 10 can invalidate a new patent application only if they are used together, then an evaluation metric that treats only Patent 2 in the ranked list as relevant may be useful.

On handling incompleteness and bias: in contrast to the simple condensed-list approach which can be used with any evaluation metric (See Section 2.2), there are also statistical approaches to estimating binary-relevance AP, such as *infAP* [116] and *statAP* [23]; Webber and Park [113] describe a *score adjustment* approach, which requires some new relevance assessments for the non-contributors.

Della Mea and Mizzaro's *Average Distance Measure* [41] is a metric that requires systems to estimate the absolute relevance score for each document, and is not a ranked retrieval metric per se. For ranked retrieval, it is not suitable as it lacks the top heaviness property [74].

The evaluation metrics discussed in this lecture assume per-document relevance assessments. An alternative would be to design evaluation metrics based on *preference judgments* [22]: is this document more relevant than another?

3 Advanced IR Metrics

Section 2 discussed set retrieval and ranked retrieval metrics: the evaluation target was a set or a ranked list of documents, where each document is either (graded) relevant or nonrelevant.

In this section, we discuss evaluation metrics for more diverse information access tasks. Section 3.1 discusses evaluation metrics for *diversified search*, which is especially important for web search where queries tend to be *ambiguous* and/or *underspecified* [32]. Section 3.2 discusses evaluation metrics for multi-query sessions (i.e. multiple ranked lists), and Section 3.3 discusses those for systems that generate a textual output in response to a query. Section 3.4 provides information for further reading.

3.1 Diversified Search Metrics

Given an ambiguous and/or underspecified query, diversified search aims at covering different search *intents* with a single, short list of retrieved documents. To evaluate diversified search, it is usually assumed that each topic has a set of known intents (or *subtopics*)[5]. In contrast to traditional IR evaluation where relevance assessments are obtained for each *topic*, in diversity evaluation, relevance assessments are obtained for each *intent*. Note that a document may be relevant to multiple intents of a given topic, with different degrees of relevance.

A diversified search test collection may consist of the following:

(a) A target corpus;
(b) A topic set $\{q\}$ that contains ambiguous or underspecified topics;
(c) A *topic type label* for each topic, e.g. "ambiguous", "underspecified (faceted)", etc. (*optional*);
(d) A set of intents $\{i\}$ for each topic;
(e) Intent probabilities $Pr(i|q)$ (*optional*);
(f) An *intent type label* for each intent, e.g. "informational", "navigational", etc. (*optional*); and
(g) (Graded) relevance assessments for each intent.

Subtopic Recall, or Intent Recall. *Subtopic recall* [118], also known as *intent recall* [94] (I-rec), is the proportion of intents covered by a search output. In the context of ranked retrieval, one way to express it would be as follows. Let $I_i(r)$ be 0 if the document at rank r is nonrelevant to Intent i, and 1 otherwise; let $isnew_i(r)$ be 1 if $I_i(k) = 0$ for $1 \leq k \leq r-1$, and 0 otherwise; and let $newint(r) = \sum_i isnew_i(r) I_i(r)$. This is the number of new intents covered at rank r. Then intent recall for ranked retrieval may be expressed as:

$$I\text{-}rec = \frac{\sum_r newint(r)}{|\{i\}|} . \tag{24}$$

This metric by itself is not sufficient for diversity evaluation as it is actually a set retrieval metric.

α-nDCG. α-*nDCG* [32] was probably the first metric to have considered the trade-off between relevance and diversity for ranked retrieval. It is an extension of nDCG: the key difference is that, prior to rank-based discounting, each document relevant to a particular intent is discounted based on the number of relevant documents already seen. Because *redundancy* within each intent is discouraged, the overall diversity of the ranked list is encouraged.

Let $C_i(r) = \sum_{k=1}^{r} I_i(k)$. α-nDCG is computed by replacing the standard gain values $g(r)$ in Eq. 6 with *novelty-biased* gains $ng(r)$:

$$ng(r) = \sum_i I_i(r)(1-\alpha)^{C_i(r-1)} \tag{25}$$

---

[5] "office" may be an *ambiguous* query, which may have intents such as "microsoft office" and "workplace"; "harry potter" may be an *underspecified* query, which may have intents such as "harry potter books", "harry potter films", "harry potter the character" and so on.

where α is a parameter that can be interpreted as the probability that the user judges a nonrelevant document to be relevant to intent i by mistake $(0 \leq \alpha < 1)$[6]. Unlike the standard nDCG, however, computing the ideal list based on $ng(r)$ and thereby obtaining the ideal novelty-biased gains $ng^*(r)$ is NP-complete, and a greedy approximation is required in practice.

It should be noted that α-nDCG cannot handle per-intent graded relevance. According to Eq. 25, the relevance level of a document (before discounting) is defined simply as the number of intents it covers[7]. For example, if $\alpha = 0.5$ (the setting used at the TREC diversity task [29]), a document relevant to only one intent will receive an $ng(r)$ of 1 if this is the first relevant one found for the intent, 0.5 if this is the second relevant one found, and 0.25 if this the third relevant one found, and so on. Also, the above version of α-nDCG does not consider the intent probabilities $Pr(i|q)$: Clarke et al. [30] extended the α-nDCG framework to incorporate them.

Leenanupub, Zuccon and Jose [59] proposed to set the parameter α of α-nDCG on a per-topic basis. Clarke, Kolla and Vechtomova [33] combined the ideas of RBP and α-nDCG and proposed another diversity metric called *Novelty- and Rank-Biased Precision* (NRBP).

Intent-Aware Metrics. Agrawal et al. [1] proposed the *intent-aware* (IA) approach to diversity evaluation. Let M_i be the value of a traditional IR metric computed for each intent i, using the per-intent relevance assessments for i. Then the IA version of this metric, denoted by M-IA, is simply defined as:

$$M\text{-}IA = \sum_i Pr(i|q)M_i \ . \tag{26}$$

More specifically, Agrawal et al. considered nDCG, AP and RR for M_i. Note that, to compute $nDCG\text{-}IA$, an ideal list needs to be created *for each intent* based on *per-intent* relevance assessments, so that $nDCG_i$ is computed prior to taking the expectation over the intents. The per-intent gain values $gv_{i,x}$ used for computing $nDCG_i$ are sometimes referred to as *local* gains, and the per-intent ideal list used as the denominator of $nDCG_i$ is sometimes referred to as *locally ideal* lists [94].

While IA metrics are simple to understand and to compute, they have several shortcomings. First, they do not range fully between 0 and 1: note, for example, that it is usually impossible for a system output to be locally ideal for every intent at the same time when computing nDCG-IA. Second, IA metrics generally tend to heavily reward relevance-oriented systems rather than diversity-oriented systems [30,94]. Third, they underperform other diversity metrics in terms of *discriminative power* [77] (discussed in Section 5.1).

---

[6] Whereas, it is assumed that the user never judges a relevant document to be non-relevant by mistake [32].

[7] To be more precise, α-nDCG defines the relevance level of a document as the number of *nuggets* it covers [32], but in practice, each intent (subtopic) is considered as a single nugget.

Perhaps the most useful (and the most popular) of the IA metrics is *ERR-IA*, the IA version of ERR [27]. A version of ERR-IA was used as the primary metric at the TREC Web Track Diversity Task [34]. As we discussed in Section 2.2, ERR has the diminishing return property, which, when used with the IA approach, serves as a mechanism for penalising redundancy for each intent i, just like the novelty-biased gain of α-nDCG does. Thus, unlike the other IA metrics, ERR-IA can reward diversity-oriented systems as it is supposed to. Clarke *et al.* [30] and Chapelle *et al.* [26] have independently shown that α-nDCG and ERR-IA can be formulated within a single framework.

D-measures. Sakai and Song [94] proposed the *D-measure* approach to diversity evaluation. Let *rel* be a random binary variable, which can either be 1 (relevant) or 0 (nonrelevant). According to the *Probability Ranking Principle* [69] (PRP), systems should rank the documents $\{d\}$ by $Pr(rel = 1|q, d)$. In the context of diversity evaluation where the query q has a set of intents $\{i\}$, we let $rel = 1$ for (q, d) if and only if there exists at least one intent i such that $rel = 1$ for (i, d). If we assume that the intents for query q are mutually exclusive, then the PRP reduces to ranking documents by $\sum_i Pr(i|q)Pr(rel = 1|i, d)$, where $Pr(rel = 1|i, d)$ is the probability that d is relevant to intent i. If we further assume that the local gain value $gv_{i,x}$ for each (i, d) pair is proportional to this probability, then the systems should rank documents by the *global gain*, given by $\sum_i Pr(i|q)gv_{i,x}$. The resultant list is called the *globally ideal* list. This can be understood as the requirement that documents highly relevant to many major intents should be ranked higher than those marginally relevant to few minor intents, which is intuitive.

Let $GG^*(r)$ denote the global gain value for the document at rank r in the globally ideal list. On the other hand, for a given diversified ranked list to be evaluated, let $g_i(r) = gv_{i,x}$ if the document at r is x-relevant to intent i, and let the global gain at r be defined as:

$$GG(r) = \sum_i Pr(i|q)g_i(r) . \tag{27}$$

By replacing the $g(r)$ of nDCG in Eq. 6 with $GG(r)$, *D-nDCG* can be defined as:

$$D\text{-}nDCG = \frac{\sum_{r=1}^{l} GG(r)/\log(r+1)}{\sum_{r=1}^{l} GG^*(r)/\log(r+1)} . \tag{28}$$

Similarly, based on the globally ideal list, other "D-measures" such as *D-Q* (a D- version of Q-measure) can be defined [94].

Note that while nDCG-IA requires multiple locally ideal lists, D-nDCG defines one globally ideal list, achieves the maximum value of 1 when the evaluated list is identical to the ideal list for ranks $[1, l]$. D-measures are "overall relevance" metrics that combine per-intent relevance assessments and intent probabilities.

At the NTCIR INTENT tasks [88], D-nDCG (overall relevance) was plotted against I-rec (pure diversity) for each participating system, which is useful for seeing which systems are relevance-oriented and which systems are diversity-oriented. Furthermore, to combine the two axes to provide a summary metric, the INTENT tasks also used $D\natural$-$nDCG$:

$$D\natural\text{-}nDCG = \gamma I\text{-}rec + (1 - \gamma)D\text{-}nDCG \tag{29}$$

where γ is a parameter ($0 \le \gamma \le 1$), simply set to 0.5 at NTCIR.

Sakai and Song [94,95] have demonstrated the advantages of the D-measure framework over α-nDCG and the IA metrics in terms of *discriminative power* [77] (discussed in Section 5.1) and the *concordance test* [82] (discussed in Section 5.3).

Sakai and Dou [85] have combined the idea of U-measure (See Section 2.2) with the above D-measure approach and with the IA approach to handle diversity evaluation. Figure 4(b)-(d) (See Section 2.2) illustrate how trailtexts can be constructed in the context of diversity evaluation: recall that U-measure can reflect the snippet/document reading behaviour of the user, and has the diminishing return property. Let s_k be a string (i.e. a snippet or part of full text), and let $pos(s_k)$ be the offset position of s_k within a trailtext. Then, using position-based local gain values $g_i(s_k)$ for each i, the position-based global gain can be defined as

$$g(pos(s_k)) = \sum_i Pr(i|q)g_i(pos(s_k)) . \tag{30}$$

Plugging in Eq. 30 to Eq. 19 gives D-U, the D-measure version of U-measure. Similarly, the IA version of U can be computed by first computing a "local" U-measure U_i for each intent, and then combining them across the intents:

$$U\text{-}IA = \sum_i Pr(i|q)U_i . \tag{31}$$

In fact, it can be shown analytically that D-U and U-IA behave similarly [85][8].

Intent-Type-Sensitive Metrics. All of the diversity metrics discussed above are *intent-type-agnostic*: they do not consider the informational/navigational intent type labels[9]. One could argue that, just as diversified search systems should try to allocate more space within the top search result page to popular intents (i.e. those with high $Pr(i|q)$ values), they should also try to allocate more space to the informational intents, while reserving one document slot for each popular navigational intent. Sakai's *intent-type-sensitive* diversity metrics do just that [82].

In the context of intent-type-sensitive diversity evaluation, we denote the sets of informational and navigational intents for query q as $\{i\}$ and $\{j\}$, respectively.

---

[8] In contrast, D-nDCG and nDCG-IA do *not* behave similarly, as normalisation is involved [94]: while D-nDCG normalises for the entire topic, nDCG-IA normalises per-intent (and is not normalised in its final form).

[9] For query "harry potter", "I want to know various facts about harry potter's characters" is probably an informational intent; "I want to visit `pottermore.com`" is probably navigational.

One simple idea for intent-type-sensitive evaluation would be to completely ignore "redundant" relevant documents for each navigational intent, by assuming that only the first relevant document found will be useful for that intent[10]. In accordance with this view, let us modify Eq. 27 as follows:

$$GG^{DIN}(r) = \sum_i Pr(i|q)g_i(r) + \sum_j isnew_j(r)Pr(j|q)g_j(r) \ . \tag{32}$$

That is, we "turn off" all "redundant relevant" documents for each navigational intent. Note that we do this only for the ranked list being evaluated: the globally ideal list remains unchanged. *DIN-nDCG* can now be defined as:

$$DIN\text{-}nDCG = \frac{\sum_{r=1}^{l} GG^{DIN}(r)/\log(r+1)}{\sum_{r=1}^{l} GG^*(r)/\log(r+1)} \ . \tag{33}$$

Since the modified global gain ignores some relevant documents for navigational intents, $GG^{DIN}(r) \leq GG(r)$ holds in general, and the maximum value of DIN-nDCG may be less than one if at least one navigational intent has multiple relevant documents. Clearly, DIN-nDCG is a generalisation of D-nDCG: if all of the intents for q are informational, it reduces to D-nDCG.

Another approach to intent-type-sensitive diversity evaluation is to borrow the IA approach, but to use two different metrics for handling the two intent types. More specifically, let us use Q-measure (Eq. 13) for each informational intent, and P^+ (Eq. 14) for each navigational intent: recall that the only difference between these two metrics is that while Q assumes a uniform stopping probability distribution over R (or l) relevant documents, P^+ assumes a uniform stopping probability distribution over the top r_p relevant documents. Then, our second intent-type-sensitive metric, $P+Q$, can be defined as:

$$P+Q = \sum_i Pr(i|q)Q_i + \sum_j Pr(j|q)P_i^+ \ . \tag{34}$$

Finally, Eqs. 33 or 34 may be combined with I-rec using a formula similar to Eq. 29: the resultant metrics are called DIN♯-nDCG and P+Q♯, respectively.

Diversity Metrics: Summary. Figure 7 provides a quick summary of the diversity metrics discussed above. Some additional comments:

(a) We have discussed Eq. 25: α-nDCG defines the graded relevance of a document as the number of intents it covers, and does not have a mechanism for directly handling per-intent graded relevance.

(b) The original α-nDCG [32] did not consider $Pr(i|q)$, but later it was incorporated [30].

---

[10] Even navigational intents generally have multiple relevant documents in diversity test collections that have been constructed at TREC and NTCIR.

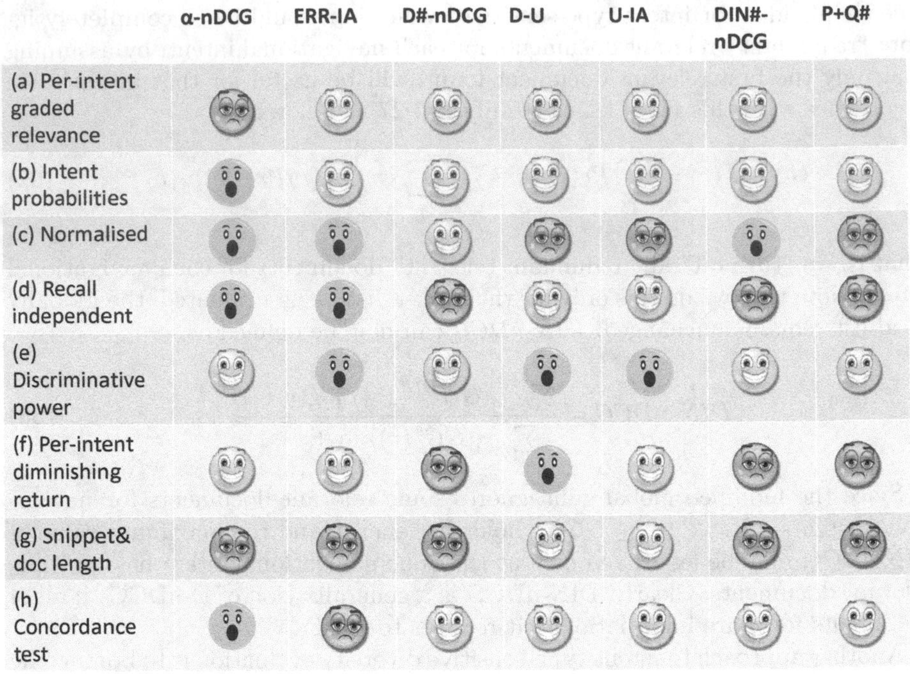

	α-nDCG	ERR-IA	D#-nDCG	D-U	U-IA	DIN#-nDCG	P+Q#
(a) Per-intent graded relevance							
(b) Intent probabilities							
(c) Normalised							
(d) Recall independent							
(e) Discriminative power							
(f) Per-intent diminishing return							
(g) Snippet& doc length							
(h) Concordance test							

Fig. 7. Comparison of diversity metrics

(c) and (d) Again, these are two sides of the same coin. α-nDCG requires an approximation of an ideal ranked list; there is a version of ERR-IA used at TREC that is normalised in a way similar to α-nDCG [30]. Normalisation generally implies the knowledge of all relevant documents, so the normalised metrics are recall-dependent. D(♯)-nDCG, DIN(♯)-nDCG and P+Q all require a globally ideal list which also implies the knowledge of all relevant documents. DIN(♯)-nDCG is "almost" normalised, but may not reach one if at least one navigational intent has multiple relevant documents.

(e) In terms of discriminative power, D(♯)-nDCG and α-nDCG outperform ERR-IA [94]; D(♯)-nDCG outperform D-U, U-IA and ERR-IA [85][11].

(f) α-nDCG, ERR-IA and U-IA possess the per-intent diminishing return property: for each intent, "redundant" relevant documents are penalised, so that diversity across intents is encouraged. D-U behaves similarly to U-IA, as the original U-measure already has the *per-topic* diminishing return property [85].

(g) To date, D-U and U-IA are the only diversity metrics that take the user's snippet and full text reading behaviour into account.

---

[11] These two studies [94,85] used a version of ERR-IA, which is an "IA version of normalised ERR."

(h) Let "$M_1 \gg M_2$" denote the relatioship: "M_1 outperforms M_2 in terms of the concordance test with some gold standard metrics." In terms of simultaneous concordance with I-rec and *effective precision*[12], DIN♯-nDCG $\gg$ D♯-nDCG $\gg$ P+Q♯ $\gg$ α-nDCG [82] while DIN-nDCG $\gg$ D-nDCG $\gg$ P+Q [96]; in terms of simultanesou concordance with I-rec and precision and *Precision for the Most Popular Intent* (PMP)[13], D♯-nDCG $\gg$ D-nDCG $\gg$ (a version of) ERR-IA [95]; In terms of simultaneous concordance with I-rec and precision, D♯-nDCG $\gg$ U-IA $\gg$ D-U $\gg$ D-nDCG $\gg$ α-nDCG $\gg$ ERR-IA [83][14].

It is worth noting that ERR-IA performs relatively poorly in terms of both discriminative power and the condordance test.

Chandar and Carterette [24] analysed α-nDCG, ERR-IA and the intent-aware version of AP using multi-way analysis of variance. Sakai, Dou and Clarke [86] have investigated the effect of the choice of intents on diversity evaluation with α-nDCG, ERR-IA and D(♯)-nDCG. Golbus, Aslam and Clarke [46] have combined the ideas of α-nDCG, IA metrics and D-measure and proposed a family of metrics called α♯-*IA measures*, which emphasise inherently difficult topics and subtopics. Brandt *et al.* [13] have proposed a dynamic tree-like presentation of diversified search results and discussed an evaluation method for it.

Sakai *et al.* [87] and Sakai [84] have experimented with condensed-list versions of D(♯)-nDCG and ERR-IA to investigate the possibility of evaluating *non-contributors* (See Section 2.2) with existing diversity test collections. The results suggest that condensed-list diversity metrics provide better estimates of the non-contributors' true performances than the raw-list metrics.

3.2   Session Metrics

In this section, we discuss evaluation metrics for multi-query sessions, which involve multiple ranked lists of documents.

Session DCG. Here, we define a *multi-query session* as a user's search activity involving at least one *query reformulation* (which could be done manually or possibly through a click on a query suggestion) and therefore multiple ranked lists of documents, but with an unchanging underlying information need. That is, there is a static set of (graded) relevant documents for this need.

In the above setting, the idea of nDCG can be extended as follows. First, arrange the m multiple ranked lists in chronological order, and concatenate the top l documents from the lists. (Alternatively, if the data contains click information, then each ranked list could first be truncated at the lowest click and

---

[12] Precision that ignores redundant relevant documents for navigational intents.

[13] Only documents that are relevant to the intent with the highest intent probability are considered relevant. This gold standard metric is meant to represent the diversity metrics's ability to emphasise important intents.

[14] This study [83] used the official ERR-IA performance values from TREC 2011.

then be concatenated [85].) Let **r** be the rank of a document in the concatenated list. (The list may contain duplicate documents: one possible approach to handling this is to simply keep only the first occurrence of each document in the list and remove all other duplicates, in a way similar to the construction of a condensed list [54].) The gain at **r**, i.e. $g(\mathbf{r})$, may be defined based on relevance assessments, clicks, or possibly both. Let $qnum(\mathbf{r})$ be a function that maps the document at **r** in the concatenated list to its query number: for example, if the document at **r** originally comes from the ranked list for the second query issued, then $qnum(\mathbf{r}) = 2$. Then a version of *session Discounted Cumulative Gain* [54] (sDCG) can be defined as:

$$sDCG = \sum_{\mathbf{r}} \frac{g(\mathbf{r})}{\log_4(qnum(\mathbf{r}) + 3) \log_2(\mathbf{r} + 1)} . \tag{35}$$

Thus the value of a relevant document is discouted not only by the rank in the concatenated list, but also by how many queries had to be issued in order to reach the document. In the original definition of sDCG [50], documents in later ranked lists could receive higher discounted gains than ones in the earlier lists, but the above formulation solves the problem.

The above sDCG is unnormalised: in a way similar to Eq. 6, it could be normalised based on a single ideal ranked list, which represents a situation where the user could obtain all relevant documents in decreasing order of relevance without ever reformulating a query. Note that in this case, duplicate relevant documents in the concatenated list obtained from the system shoud be removed: the same relevant documents should not be rewarded twice. (Järvelin *et al.*[50] describe a different normalisation scheme that involves concatenation of the top l documents from m ideal ranked lists, allowing duplicates.)

Click-based U. U-measure, which was discussed in Section 2.2, can handle the evaluation of multi-query sessions. If click data with timestamps are available, it can handle nonlinear traversals as well [85]. Figure 8 Parts (e) and (f) show how a trailtext may be constructed from clicks that involve two queries (i.e. two ranked lists), by assuming that clicked documents are relevant. Parts (g) and (h) show how a trailtext may be constructed from a nonlinear traversal: in this example, the click data shows that the document at rank 4 was clicked first, and then the one at rank 2 was clicked; here, we assume that the user read the four snippets first and then read (parts of) the two clicked documents. More generally, Figure 9 provides a pseudocode of a click-based version of U-measure, for a search engine whose average snippet length is 200 characters. Note that this is just a straightforward implementation of Eq. 19 from Section 2.2.

Kanoulas *et al.* [54] proposed more complex evaluation metrics for sessions, which consider multiple possible browsing paths over the multiple ranked lists. U-measure may also be extended along this line. Baskaya, Keskustalo and Järvelin [10] proposed an evaluation framework for sessions where the cost of various user actions such as query (re)formulations and clicking on "next page" are taken into account. This is in contrast to U-measure which assumes that the text that the

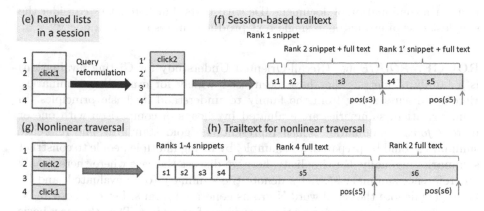

Fig. 8. Automatically constructing trailtexts from clicks or nonlinear traversals and sessions

```
snippetlen = 200;
g = 0.5; // gain of a clicked document: (2^l − 1)/2^H = (2^1 − 1)/2^1.
pos = 0; U = 0;
while read < querynumber, clickedrank, doclen > sorted by time
    if querynumber is new then initialise array snippetdone[];
    // stores whether or not snippet at rank r has already been read.
    for( r = 1; r ≤ clickedrank; r++)
        if snippetdone[r] == 0 then
            pos += snippetlen; //reads all snippets above a click.
            snippetdone[r] = 1;
        end if
    pos += F * doclen; // reads F% of clicked document.
    U += g * max(0, 1 − pos/L);
end while
return U;
```

Fig. 9. Algorithm for computing U-measure by reading a session data file, which consists of *querynumber*, *clickedrank* and *doclen* sorted by time

user has read is an adequate representation of the user effort. Azzopardi [9] viewed interactive IR applications as a stream of documents and proposed evaluation metrics such as "frequency of observing a relevant document."

3.3 Summarisation and QA Metrics

Query-focussed text summarisation and question answering are types of information access where the output provided by the system is *textual*, in contrast to the information access tasks previously discussed where the output was in essence a set of document IDs, a ranked list of document IDs or multiple ranked lists of document IDs (although TBG and U-measure consider snippets and document contents in addition). The textual output could be a single text, a ranked list of texts or a combination of document IDs with texts, but here let us consider the simplest case of evaluating a single text produced in response to a query.

ROUGE. *ROUGE* [60] (Recall-Oriented Understudy for Gisting Evaluation) is a family of metrics that have been used widely for evaluating summaries. Here we discuss a few from the family to understand its basic principles. In summarisation, summaries are evaluated by means of comparison with one or more *reference* summaries, which represent the gold standard. The reference summaries could be prepared, for example, by hiring multiple people to construct summaries manually. For simplicity, here we discuss the case where there is only one reference summary s^*. Let s denote the summary to be evaluated, and let $gram_N(s)$ denote the set of word N-grams generated from s. Let e denote an N-gram, and let $Count(e, s)$ denote the frequency of e within s. Then the most basic version of ROUGE, known as *ROUGE-N*, can be expressed as follows [60,64]:

$$ROUGE\text{-}N = \frac{\sum_{e \in gram_N(s) \cap gram_N(s^*)} \min(Count(e, s), Count(e, s^*))}{\sum_{e \in gram_N(s^*)} Count(e, s^*)} \tag{36}$$

It is clear that ROUGE-N is basically an N-gram recall measure: it was inspired by a machine translation evaluation metric called *BLEU*, which is based on N-gram precision [66].

Another version of ROUGE, called ROUGE-S, uses *skip bigrams* as the basic matching unit instead of N-grams, to allow more flexible matching between the system's summary and the reference summaries. For a given summary s, let $skip_2(s)$ denote the set of skip bigrams, that is, any word pair extracted from the text that preserves the word order, including bigrams[15]. Then ROUGE-S can be expressed as follows [60,64]:

$$Rec\text{-}S = \frac{\sum_{e \in skip_2(s) \cap skip_2(s^*)} \min(Count(e, s), Count(e, s^*))}{\sum_{e \in skip_2(s^*)} Count(e, s^*)} \tag{37}$$

$$Prec\text{-}S = \frac{\sum_{e \in skip_2(s) \cap skip_2(s^*)} \min(Count(e, s), Count(e, s^*))}{\sum_{e \in skip_2(s)} Count(e, s)} \tag{38}$$

$$ROUGE\text{-}S = \frac{(\beta^2 + 1)Prec\text{-}S\,Rec\text{-}S}{\beta^2 Prec\text{-}S + Rec\text{-}S} \tag{39}$$

It is clear that ROUGE-S is an F-measure (Eq. 5) based on skip bigrams. Lin [60] proposed a variant of ROUGE-S called *ROUGE-SU*, which uses unigrams in addition.

It can be observed that in summarisation evaluation, essentially IR metrics such as recall and F-measure are computed based on small textual units. (Manually constructed *semantic content units* [65] may be used instead of automatically

---

[15] In practice, a word distance constraint may be imposed in order to avoid pairs of words that are too far apart.

extracted units such as those mentioned above.) This is also true for *question answering* evaluation, where the small textual unit is referred to as *nuggets*: atomic pieces of information that address a certain aspect of the question [39].

Suppose that a set of gold-standard nuggets V^* is available for a question, and that we hired a group of assessors who independently labelled each nugget $v \in V^*$ as either *vital* or *okay* (i.e. non-vital). Then, using the vital labels as votes, a weight $w(v)$ can be assigned to each v. Furthermore, given a system's answer of length l (in characters, excluding white spaces), it can be manually compared with the nuggets from V^*, so that a set of *matched* nuggets $V(\subseteq V^*)$ is obtained. Let $allow = 100 * |V|$. Then the answer may be evaluated as follows [39]:

$$W\text{-}Rec = \frac{\sum_{v \in V} w(v)}{\sum_{v \in V^*} w(v)} \tag{40}$$

$$Prec_{allow} = 1 - \frac{\max(0, l - allow)}{l} \tag{41}$$

$$F\text{-}measure_{QA} = \frac{(\beta^2 + 1)Prec_{allow}W\text{-}Rec}{\beta^2 Prec_{allow} + W\text{-}Rec} \tag{42}$$

Note that $Prec_{allow} = 1$ if $l \leq allow$. Thus it is assumed that each matched nugget in V is entitled to use up 100 charaters. On the other hand, if $l > allow$, then the $(l - allow)$ characters in the answer is treated as noise.

Lin and Demner-Fushman [61] proposed an automatic unigram-matching method for replacing the aforementioned manual matching between the answer and the gold standard nuggets, and called their F-measure-based evaluation metric *POURPRE*. It should be noted that while automatic matching methods like ROUGE and POURPRE enable efficient evaluation for *extractive* systems, they may not be able to fully handle *abstractive* systems: for example, an intelligent summariser might *paraphrase* the information obtained from source documents, causing the automatic matching to fail.

S-measure, T-measure. Sakai, Kato and Song [91] defined a task related to muti-document summarisation and question answering called *one click access* and proposed an extension of nugget-based weighted recall (Eq. 40) called *S-measure*. Sakai and Kato [90] extended this framework and introduced a precision-like metric called *T-measure*, and an F-measure-like metric called $S\natural$.

Figure 10 illustrates the concept of one click access evaluation. One click assess systems are required to present important pieces of information first, and to minimise the amount of text the user has to read to obtain the information. If traditional nugget-based weighted recall is used, Outputs (a) and (b), which cover the same information, would receive exactly the same score. In contrast, S-measure prefers (b) over (a). On the other hand, T-measure imposes a length penalty and prefers (b) over (c). $S\natural$ reflects both of these properties, as shown below.

In the one click access evaluation framework, the basic evaluation unit is called the *iUnit*. Let V^* denote the set of gold-standard iUnits for a query, and

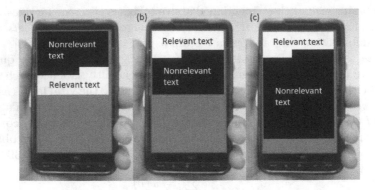

Fig. 10. Comparison of one click access systems

let $w(v)$ denote the weight assigned to an iUnit $v \in V^*$. Each iUnit n has a *vital string* $vs(v)$, which represents a minimal textual expression required in order to convey the information of the iUnit to the user [91]. For example, suppose that v represents a fact: "Paul McCartney was born on June 18, 1942." Then the vital string for v could possibly be defined as "born 6/18/1942." Thus the vital string defines how much minimal space the iUnit requires. For a given query, we first define a *Pseudo Minimal Output* (PMO) by sorting all $vs(v)$ where $v \in V^*$ by using $w(v)$ as the first key and $|vs(v)|$ as the second key and concatenating them. PMO approximates an ideal output that presents important and concise iUnits first. Let $pos^*(v)$ denote the *offset position* (end position in characters) of $vs(v)$ within the PMO.

Let $V (\subseteq V^*)$ be the set of iUnits identified within a system output. In one click access evaluation, a system output is manually compared with the gold-standard iUnits, and the *position* of each iUnit found within the system output is recorded. For each $v \in V$, let $pos(v)$ denote its offset position (end position in characters) within the system output. Then S-measure, a position-aware version of weighted recall (See Eq. 40), is defined as:

$$S\text{-}measure = \frac{\sum_{v \in V} w(v) \max(0, 1 - pos(v)/L)}{\sum_{v \in V^*} w(v) \max(0, 1 - pos^*(v)/L)} \qquad (43)$$

$$= \frac{\sum_{v \in V} w(v) \max(0, L - pos(v))}{\sum_{v \in V^*} w(v) \max(0, L - pos^*(v))} \qquad (44)$$

where L is a parameter representing how quickly the user's patience runs out [91]. For example, Sakai, Kato and Song [91] considered a Japanse one click access task with $L = 1000$: as the averege reading speed of Japanese text is known to be around 500 characters per minute, this task means that the user needs to gather information within two mintutes: after that, the value of any nugget becomes zero.

As S is only a position-aware version of recall, it gives the same score to Outputs (b) and (c). In order to introduce a length penalty to handle such cases, Sakai and Kato [90] introduced *T-measure*:

$$T\text{-}measure = \frac{\sum_{v \in V} |vs(v)|}{l} \tag{45}$$

where l is the system output length in characters. In contrast to the nugget precision used for question answering which uses an arbitrary allowance parameter (Eq. 41), T reflects the fact that different pieces of information require different amount of space. Finally, S♯ is a version of F-measure that is built on S and T:

$$S\sharp = \frac{(1 + \beta^2) T\flat S\flat}{\beta^2 T\flat + S\flat} \tag{46}$$

where $S\flat = \min(1, S\text{-}measure)$ and $T\flat = \min(1, T\text{-}measure)$ as the raw metrics are not theoretically bounded above by 1. These metrics have been used at the NTCIR One Click Access (1CLICK) task [55].

3.4 Further Reading

Recently, Arguello *et al.* [5] and Zhou *et al.* [120] have proposed evaluation methods for *aggregated search*, where not only web search results but also vertical search results (e.g. news, images, videos) need to be selectively presented. Here, the users' *vertical orientations* are take into accout: for example, for a given topic, some users might generally prefer images to textual web pages regardless of relevance. Zhou *et al.* [120] discuss the connection between diversity evaluation and aggregated search evaluation. So far, aggregated search in the research community has been considered to be the problem of arranging blocks of web search results and selected verticals on top of one another, although a more general and practical formulation would involve presentation in a two-dimensional space.

There are also information access tasks that are something of a mix between ranked retrieval and summarisation, and some evaluation methods have been proposed accordingly. Character-based bpref has been used for evaluating a ranked list of passages [4]; Yang and Lad [114] proposed a nugget-based evaluation method that models *utility* as *benefit* minus *cost of reading* for evaluating multiple ranked lists of passages for a standing information need. Character-based precision and recall have been used for evaluating XML passages [52]; Arvola, Kekäläinen and Junkkari [6] have proposed an evaluation method for an XML retrieval task where the user first sees a list of documents and then jumps to relevant passages of a document selected from that list. But as was mentioned earlier, XML retrieval evaluation is beyond the scope of this lecture.

The aforementioned U-measure [85] can potentially handle various information access tasks seamlessly by means of trailtext; it is easy to see that U (Eqs. 19 and 20) is a generalisation of an unnormalised version of S-measure (Eq. 43).

4   Computer-Based Significance Tests

4.1   Basics

As was mentioned earlier, evaluation metrics are typically computed over a set of topics (or search requests), and it is common to compare systems based on *Mean* AP (MAP), *Mean* nDCG etc. Significance test results or confidence intervals should accompany evaluation metric values: there are arguments against statistical significance testing (e.g. [48,51]), but reporting p-values is at least more informative than just saying "Our system's MAP was 0.333, while the baseline's MAP was 0.300." Is this difference likely to be substantial or due to chance?

Statistical significance testing starts with a *null hypothesis H_0*: in IR experiments, a typical null hypothesis would be that all systems that are being evaluated are equivalent. Then we try to compute and discuss the p-value: this is the *probability of the observed or even more extreme data, under H_0*. That is, "Assuming that the null hypothesis is true, how rare would this observation be?" Table 1 shows a contingency table that is used in significance testing: here, an arbitrary threshold called α is introduced. If the p-value is less than α, then what we have observed is something extremely rare, so we reject H_0: that is, we decide that the systems are probably *not* equivalent.

Table 1. Type I and Type II errors in significance testing

	Accept H_0	Reject H_0
H_0 is actually true (systems are actually equivalent)	correct conclusion (probability: $1 - \alpha$)	Type I error (probability: α)
H_0 is actually false (systems are actually different)	Type II error (probability: β)	correct conclusion (probability: $1 - \beta$)

The α is called the *significance level*, and is typically set to 0.05 (95% confidence level) or 0.01 (99% confidence level). However, note that this threshold directly affects our conlcusions: consider what happens when the p-value is 0.03. Thus, it is better to report the actual p-value instead of saying "the difference is significant at $\alpha = 0.05$." It is important to remember that statistical significance does not necessarily imply practical significance, and that statistical insignificance does not necessarily imply practical insignificance [47]. For example, Algorithm A may consistently and significantly outperform Algorithm B for any given topic, but each of the performance improvements may be too small for the user no notice; Algorithm A may have fail to significantly outperform Algorithm B, but your experiment may have used a small number of topics.

Classical significance tests may be used in IR experiments: when comparing two systems using a common topic set, for example, standard tests such as Student's t-test (a parametric test), Wilcoxon signed-rank test and the sign test (nonparametric tests) may be used[16]. In general, parametric tests rely on more assumptions but have higher *statistical power* ($1 - \beta$ in Table 1) [110]. But these tests can be found in any textbooks on statistics.

In this lecture, I will mention a few simple and useful significance testing methods that rely on computer power instead of assumptions on the underlying distributions (which often do not hold). Computer-based significance tests rely on fewer assumptions than classical tests, and are applicable to test statistics other than the mean. Here I quote Efron and Tibshirani who described the *bootstrap*, a very useful and versatile computer-based statistical framework [43]: "*The use of the bootstrap either relieves the analyst from having to do complex mathematical derivations, or in some instances provides an answer where no analytical answer can be obtained.*"

4.2 Paired Bootstrap Test

This section briefly describes the *paired bootstrap test* [43,77,100] which may be used instead of the t-test: suppose we have two systems X and Y that we want to compare using a test collection with n topics. Unlike the t-test, the bootstrap test does not require the normality assumption, and yet is as powerful.

For a topic set of size n, let $\mathbf{x} = (x_1, \ldots, x_n)$ and $\mathbf{y} = (y_1, \ldots, y_n)$ denote the per-topic performances as measured by some metric M. Thus the per-topic *differences* are given by $\mathbf{z} = (z_1, \ldots, z_n)$ where $z_i = x_i - y_i$. The *sample means*, defined as $\bar{x} = \sum_i x_i/n$ and $\bar{y} = \sum_i y_i/n$, are what are often reported in IR papers, e.g. MAP of X, MAP of Y, and so on. But what we really want to know is whether the *population means* of X and Y, which we denote by μ_X and μ_Y, are any different. Hence, let $\mu = \mu_X - \mu_Y$ and let us set up the following hypotheses for a two-tailed test:

$$H_0 : \mu = 0 \quad vs. \quad H_1 : \mu \neq 0. \tag{47}$$

Thus the null hypothesis H_0 says that the population means of X and Y are actually the same.

Just like classical significance tests, the bootstrap assumes that $\mathbf{z}$ is an independent and identically distributed sample drawn from an unknown distribution. Figure 11 shows how to obtain B *bootstrap samples* of the per-topic differences *that obey H_0*. For simplicity, let us assume that $n = 5$, $\mathbf{w} = (z_1 - \bar{z}, \ldots, z_5 - \bar{z}) = (0.2, 0.0, 0.1, 0.4, 0.0)$ and the b-th random sample of integers is $(1, 3, 1, 2, 4)$. Then, $\mathbf{w}^{*b} = (0.2, 0.1, 0.2, 0.0, 0.4)$.

---

[16] Some IR history: in the late 1970s, Van Rijsbergen wrote [68]: "*parametric tests are inappropriate because we do not know the form of the underlying distribution. [...] One obvious failure is that the observations are not drawn from normally distributed populations.*" He then wrote: "*the sign test [...] can be used conservatively.*" In the early 1990s, Hull wrote [47]: "*While the errors may not be normal, the t-test is relatively robust to many violations of normality. Only heavy skewness [...] or large outliers [...] will seriously compromise its validity.*"

```
w = (z₁ − z̄, ..., zₙ − z̄);
for b = 1 to B
    from a set of integers (1, ..., n),
    obtain a random sample of size n by sampling with replacement;
    for i = 1 to n
        j = i-th element of the sample of integers;
        wᵢ*ᵇ = j-th element of w;
    end for
end for
```

Fig. 11. Algorithm for creating B bootstrap samples $\mathbf{w}^{*b} = (w_1^{*b}, \ldots, w_n^{*b})$ for the Paired Test

Now let us consider the *studentized* statistic of $\mathbf{z}$:

$$t(\mathbf{z}) = \frac{\bar{z}}{\bar{\sigma}/\sqrt{n}} \tag{48}$$

where $\bar{z} = \sum_i z_i/n$, and $\bar{\sigma}$ is the standard deviation of $\mathbf{z}$, given by:

$$\bar{\sigma} = \sqrt{\sum_i (z_i - \bar{z})^2/(n-1)} \, . \tag{49}$$

Each bootstrap sample $\mathbf{w}^{*b}$ can be studentised in a similar way. Then, the p-value, or the *Achieved Significance Level* [43] (ASL), can be obtained as shown in Figure 12: this is simply the proportion of $t(\mathbf{w}^{*b})$ that are larger than $t(\mathbf{z})$. The p-value thus obtained should be reported together with the MAP values, etc.

```
count = 0;
for b = 1 to B
    if( |t(w*ᵇ)| ≥ |t(z)| ) then count++;
ASL = count/B;
```

Fig. 12. Algorithm for estimating the Achieved Significance Level based on the Paired Test

4.3 Unpaired Bootstrap Test

The bootstrap test described above was for a one-sample problem: we knew that x_i corresponds to y_i and we could discuss the per-topic performance differences z_i. More generally, however, there are times when we cannot assume that x_i corresponds to y_i. For example, suppose we have a set of AP values computed over a certain topic set, and another set of AP values computed over a *different* topic set. These topics may or may not differ in size. This section describes a simple bootstrap test that is applicable to such *two-sample* problems: are the two sets of performances substantially different?

Let $\mathbf{x} = (x_1, \ldots, x_n)$ and $\mathbf{y} = (y_1, \ldots, y_m)$ denote the per-topic performances as measured by some metric M, where m may or may not be equal to n. Then the observed difference between the two overall performances is given by $\hat{d} = M(\mathbf{x}) - M(\mathbf{y})$, where, for example, $M(\mathbf{x})$ denotes some summary statistic computed based on $\mathbf{x}$. But what we really want to know is whether the *true* difference d between X and Y is substantial. Hence our hypotheses for a two-tailed test would be:

$$H_0 : d = 0 \quad vs. \quad H_1 : d \neq 0. \tag{50}$$

As with classifcal significance tests, we assume that $\mathbf{x}$ and $\mathbf{y}$ are independently and identically distributed samples from unknown distributions F and G, respectively. Since we now need a distribution that obeys H_0, let us assume that $F = G$, that is, that the observed per-topic performances all come from the same distribution. Figure 13 shows how to obtain B bootstrap samples $\mathbf{x}^{*b}$ and $\mathbf{y}^{*b}$ that obey H_0. For simplicity, suppose that $\mathbf{x} = (0.1, 0.3)$, $\mathbf{y} = (0.2, 0.0, 0.0)$ and therefore that $\mathbf{v} = (0.1, 0.3, 0.2, 0.0, 0.0)$. If the b-th random sample of integers is $(1, 3, 1, 2, 4)$, then $\mathbf{x}^{*b} = (0.1, 0.2)$ and $\mathbf{y}^{*b} = (0.1, 0.3, 0.0)$. Thus, per-topic performance values are sampled with replacement without looking at whether they come from $\mathbf{x}$ or $\mathbf{y}$.

```
v = (x₁,…,xₙ,y₁,…,yₘ);
for b = 1 to B
    from a set of integers (1,…,n+m),
        obtain a random sample of size n+m by sampling with replacement;
    for i = 1 to n
        j = i-th element of the sample of integers;
        x*b_i = j-th element of v;
    end for
    for i = n+1 to n+m
        j = i-th element of the sample of integers;
        y*b_{i-n} = j-th element of v;
    end for
end for
```

Fig. 13. Algorithm for creating bootstrap samples $\mathbf{x}^{*b} = (x_1^{*b}, \ldots, x_n^{*b})$ and $\mathbf{y}^{*b} = (y_1^{*b}, \ldots, y_m^{*b})$ for the Unpaired Test

Figure 14 shows how to compute the ASL based on the unpaired bootstrap test. Note that the ASL is the proportion of the bootstrap-based overall differences that are larger than the observed difference.

Webber, Moffat and Zobel [109] have demonstrated that *score standardisation* is useful for making the evaluation metric values such as $\mathbf{x}$ and $\mathbf{y}$ comparable across different test collections.

```
count = 0;
for b = 1 to B
    if( |M(x*ᵇ) − M(y*ᵇ)| ≥ |d̂| ) then count++;
ASL = count/B;
```

Fig. 14. Algorithm for estimating the Achieved Significance Level based on the Unpaired Test

4.4 Randomised Tukey's HSD Test

When more than two systems are being evaluated in an experiment, then significance tests suitable for that purpose should be used instead of conducting a pairwise test such as the t-test or the bootstrap test one at a time. If a pairwise test with a significance level of α is conducted for k system pairs, then the *family-wise error rate* amounts to $1 - (1 - \alpha)^k$: this is the probability of detecting at least one significant difference for a pair of systems that are in fact equivalent. Carterette [21] describes a simple computer-based test suitable for multiple comparisons, which is a randomised version of the *Tukey's Honestly Significant Differences (HSD) test*. The main idea behind Tukey's HSD is that if the largest mean difference observed is not significant, then none of the other differences should be significant either; the k significance tests are conducted simultaneously.

For an experimental environment where we have n topics and m systems (where $k = m(m - 1)/2$), let $\mathbf{U}$ be an n-by-m matrix whose element (i, j) represents the performance of the j-th system for topic i according to some metric M. Figure 15 shows how to obtain the ASL for each run pair based on the randomised Tukey's HSD test. The outcome of this test will generally be more conservative than that of pairwise tests conducted independently, as the family-wise error rate is now bounded above by α.

4.5 Further Reading

For one-sample problems, Smucker, Allan and Carterette [101] reported that the paired bootstrap test, the randomisation test (a.k.a. permutation test) and the t-test have little practical difference. Nevertheless, they advocate the use of the randomisation test, partly because the test does not require the assumption that the IR test topics are a random sample from a population of topics. They also argue that the use of the Wilcoxon and sign tests should be discontinued.

Robertson and Kanoulas [72] recently proposed a new methodology for significance testing in IR experiments, which views a document collection of a test collection as a sample from some larger population of documents. Thus, they discuss the interaction between a sampling of topics and a separate sampling of documents. A related approach has been described earlier by Cormack and Lynam [38].

```
foreach pair of runs (X, Y)
    count(X, Y) = 0;
for b = 1 to B
    for i = 1 to n // i.e. for every topic (every row of U)
        i-th row of U*ᵇ = random permutation of the i-th row of U;
    max*ᵇ = maxⱼ ū*ᵇⱼ; min*ᵇ = minⱼ ū*ᵇⱼ where
            ū*ᵇⱼ is the mean of j-th column vector of U*ᵇ;
    foreach pair of runs (X, Y)
        if( max*ᵇ − min*ᵇ > |ū(X) − ū(Y)| where
            ū(·) is the mean of the column vector for a given run in U )
        then count(X, Y) + +;
end for
foreach pair of runs (X, Y)
    ASL(X, Y) = count(X, Y)/B;
```

Fig. 15. Algorithm for obtaining the Achieved Significance Level with the two-sided, randomised Tukey's HSD given a performance value matrix U whose rows represent topics and columns represent runs [21]

5   Testing IR Metrics

One ultimate goal of IR researchers is to build systems that completely and efficiently satisfy the user's information needs, and we often regard evaluation metrics as crude indicators of user satisfaction or performance. But what are "good" metrics? There is no perfect method that answers this question. In general, it is difficult to involve real users in determining which metrics are good: we are using metrics instead of directly asking the users because it is difficult to involve real users! Below, we discuss some (imperfect) methods that have been used to "evaluate" evaluating metrics.

5.1   Discriminative Power

Suppose that two systems X and Y are being compared with evaluation metrics M_1 and M_2. According to M_1, X outperforms Y and the p-value is 0.0001; according to M_2, X outperforms Y but the p-value is 0.3. If these two metrics are compared while the probability of Type I Error α (i.e. probability of concluding that two systems are different even though they are in fact equivalent) is held constant (e.g. $\alpha = 0.05$), M_1 provides a statistically significant result while M_2 does not. If this trend can be observed for different systems pairs, then one might prefer to use M_1 in IR experiments. This property of M_1 reflects its consistency or stability across the topics.

More specifically, suppose that m systems are being compared; this gives us $m(m − 1)/2$ system pairs. We can obtain a p-value for each of these pairs and for each metric, and draw *Achieved Significance Level (ASL) curves* [77] like the ones shown in Figure 16. Here, the y-axis represents the ASL (i.e. p-values), and the x-axis represents the system pairs sorted by ASL. Sakai [77] originally used

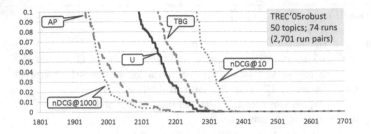

Fig. 16. ASL curves from Sakai and Dou [85]

the pairwise bootstrap test for producing ASL curves, but this example [85] uses the randomised version of the Tukey's HSD test. Metrics whose curves are close to the origin are the ones with high *discriminative power* [77,79]: they produce smaller p-values for many run pairs than other metrics do.

The discriminative power method may also be used for estimating the minimum performance delta required that gives a statistically significant result, given a topic set of size n [77]. With the randomised Tukey's HSD test, this can simply be estimated as the smallest value among the performance deltas that were actually found to be significant [82].

Discriminative power measures the consistency or stability of metrics based on significance testing[17]. It does *not* tell whether the metrics are measuring what we want to measure. Moreover, as was discussed earlier, statistical significance does not necessarily imply practical significance (while statistical insignificance does not necessarily imply practical insignificance). Despite this limitation, discriminative power is a moderately popular method for evaluating evaluation metrics(e.g. [30,46,53,59,73,104,111]).

Prior to the proposal of the discriminative power method, Buckley and Voorhees [15] and Voorhees and Buckley [107] proposed methods that are related to discriminative power. The "swap method" [107] splits the topic set of a given test collection in half, uses these two topic sets to evaluate systems independently, and asks how consistent the pairwise evaluation outcomes are. However, their methods do not consider statistical significance. Sanderson and Zobel [99] used the t-test for *filtering* run pairs before conducting the swap method. Unlike the discriminative power method, however, the swap method cannot directly estimate the performance delta between two systems that can be considered substantial for the *full* topic set: for example, if the topic set contains $n = 50$ topics, then it needs to be split into two sets of 25 topics [77]. A similar split-topic method was used by Zobel in the 1990s [121].

---

[17] We assumes that a metric is a function of some gold standard data and a system output – and nothing else. For example, something that *knows* that Output X is from Google and Output Y is Bing and uses this information to say that (say) "Y is better than X" for *any* query [97] is *not* a metric.

5.2   Rank Correlation

Rank correlation compares two rankings. Thus, to evaluate the sanity of an evaluation metric M, it is possible to produce a system ranking according to M, and compare it with another system ranking according to a "well-established" metric M^*. (Here, it is assumed that the two metrics rank the same set of systems.) This is also an imperfect method for evaluating evaluation metrics: we want new metrics to correlate relatively well with "established" metrics: an extremely low correlation would suggest that either previous IR research or the new metric is wrong; an extremely high correlation would suggest that it is not necessary to introduce the new metric.

Rank correlation statistics can be regarded as a special type of ranked retrieval metrics where the gold standard data also take the form of a ranked list. The most widely-used rank correlation statistic in the IR community is *Kendall's* τ. Let m be the size of the two ranked lists, so that there are $m(m-1)/2$ pairs of ranked items within each list. Let $conc$ denote the number of item pairs for which the two ranked lists are concordant (e.g. if Item X is ranked above Item Y in one list, Item X is also ranked above Item Y in the other list); similarly, let $disc$ denote the number of item pairs for which the two lists are discordant. Then τ is simply given by:

$$\tau = \frac{conc - disc}{m(m-1)/2} \, . \tag{51}$$

One of the problems with τ in the context of IR evaluation is that the swaps near the top of the ranks and those near the bottom of the ranks are treated equally, even though what happens near the top of the ranks is generally more important. Thus several researchers have proposed alternative rank correlation statistics that have the *top heaviness* property. Here, we describe a relatively widely-used variant of τ, known as τ_{ap} [115], which is easy to compute.

The raw τ_{ap} interprets one of the two ranked lists as the gold standard (i.e. correct ranking). Let $correct(r)$ denote the number of items above rank r in the evaluated list that are *correctly* ranked with respect to the item at rank r. For example, suppose that Item Y is at rank r in the evaluated list, and that Item X is ranked above it. If the gold-standard list also has X above Y, then Item Y contributes to $correct(r)$. Then τ_{ap} is given by:

$$\tau_{ap} = \frac{2}{m-1} \sum_{r=2}^{m} \left(\frac{correct(r)}{r-1} \right) - 1 \, . \tag{52}$$

While Kendall's τ is a monotonic function of the probability that a randomly chosen pair of ranked items is ordered concordantly, τ_{ap} is a monotonic function of the probability that a randomly chosen item and *one ranked above it* are ordered concordantly; unlike τ, the raw τ_{ap} is asymmetric. However, a symmetric version can easily be obtained by averaging two correlation values when each list is treated as the gold standard [115]. Both τ and τ_{ap} lie between -1 and 1.

Pollock [67], Carterette [19] and Webber, Moffat and Zobel [112] have also discussed top-heavy rank correlation statistics. Carterette's d_{rank} measure incorporates correlations among system pairs; *Rank-Biased Overlap* by Webber *et al.* is applicable even to any pair of system rankings of different lengths.

5.3 Predictive Power and Concordance Test

Probably the most natural way to evaluate evaluation metrics is to "ask the user." As was mentioned earlier, Cooper [36,37], in the early 1970s, described a hypothetical interviewing method for users who "*enter the library.*" However, it is clear that such a method is not feasible for most of today's IR systems such as web search engines.

Nevertheless, it is probably worthwhile to ask real people questions, and to check if evaluation metrics behave similarly to their judgments. Specifically, suppose a human participant is shown two outputs X and Y, and is asked to judge which is better. A collection of such *preference judgments* can be seen as the gold standard: if an evaluation metric agrees with the participant's preference between X and Y, then that is a correct prediction. This can be performed for many pairs of outputs, and possibly for many participants. The ability to predict the correct preference has been referred to as *predictive power* [98]. Sanderson *et al.* [98] investigated the predictive power of traditional IR and diversity IR metrics, although they had to evaluate the latter type of metrics by treating each intent of a topic as an independent topic. Hence it may be difficult for the predictive power method to evaluate the ability of a diversity metric to actually reward diversity. Zhou *et al.* [120] reported on a similar experiment for aggregated search evaluation metrics. These studies leveraged Amazon Mechanical Turk (AMT). Similarly, in the context of diversity evaluation, Chandar and Carterette [25] used AMT to investigate what kind of novel document the user would want to see right after seeing a document relevant to a particular intent. While it should be remembered that the "Turkers" are not real users with an information need, these types of inexpensive, human-in-the-loop evaluation of evaluation metrics are probably good complements to "user-free" evaluation methods such as discriminative power.

In the context of evaluating diversity IR metrics, Sakai [82] described the *concordance test*, a user-free version of the predictive power test. Because diversity IR metrics are complex, the concordance test tries to examine how "intuitive" they are, by using some "gold-standard" metrics instead of the preference judgments. For example, for diversified search, since we want both high diversity and high relevance, it is possible to regard *intent recall* or *precision* as a gold standard. Moreover, simultaneous agreement with both of these metrics may also be examined. Note that these gold-standard metrics themselves are not good enough for diversity evaluation: these merely represent the basic properties of the more complex diversity metrics that should be satisfied.

Figure 17 shows a simple algorithm for comparing two candidate metrics M_1 and M_2 given a gold standard metric M^*: concordance with multiple gold standards may be computed in a similar way. Here, for example, $M_1(q, X)$ denotes the value of metric M_1 computed for the output of system X obtained in response to topic q. Note that this algorithm focusses on the cases where M_1

```
Disagreements = 0;  Correct₁ = 0;  Correct₂ = 0;
foreach pair of runs (X, Y)
    foreach topic q
        ΔM₁ = M₁(q, X) − M₁(q, Y);
        ΔM₂ = M₂(q, X) − M₂(q, Y);
        ΔM* = M*(q, X) − M*(q, Y);
        if( ΔM₁ × ΔM₂ < 0 ) then // M₁ and M₂ strictly disagree
            Disagreements + +;
            if( ΔM₁ × ΔM* ≥ 0) ) then// M₁ is concordant with M*
                Conc₁ + +;
            if( ΔM₂ × ΔM* ≥ 0) ) then // M₂ is concordant with M*
                Conc₂ + +;
        end if
    end foreach
Conc(M₁|M₂, M*) = Conc₁/Disagreements;
Conc(M₂|M₁, M*) = Conc₂/Disagreements;
```

Fig. 17. Concordance test algorithm for a pair of metrics M_1 and M_2, given the gold-standard metric M^*

Table 2. Simultaneous concordance with intent recall and precision: TREC 2011 Web Track Diversity Task data; measurement depth $l = 10$ [83]. Statistically significant differences with the sign test are indicated by ‡ ($\alpha = 0.01$).

	D-nDCG	D-U	U-IA	ERR-IA	α-nDCG
D♯-nDCG	**48%**/0%‡	**47%**/38%‡	**45%**/39%†	**70%**/29%‡	**68%**/35%‡
	(415)	(771)	(745)	(1106)	(913)
D-nDCG	-	42%/**65%**‡	40%/**67%**‡	**66%**/40%‡	**58%**/48%‡
		(562)	(568)	(1044)	(974)
D-U	-	-	33%/**80%**‡	**66%**/40%‡	**62%**/45%‡
			(54)	(1472)	(1323)
U-IA	-	-	-	**67%**/38%‡	**63%**/43%‡
				(1463)	(1299)
ERR-IA	-	-	-	-	19%/**76%**‡
					(292)

and M_2 disagree with each other. While it is clear that this is also an imperfect method for evaluating metrics as it assumes that the gold-standard metrics represent the real users' preferences, it is useful to be able to quantify exactly how often the metrics satisfy the basic properties such as "preference for a more diversified output" or "preference for a more relevant output" [82,95].

Table 2 shows some examples of concordance test results, taken from Sakai [83]. Here, both intent recall and precision are used as the gold-standard metrics, and six diversity metrics are compared using the data from the TREC 2011 Diversity Task [31]. The α-nDCG and ERR-IA values are from the official TREC results computed by ndeval[18]; the D(♯)-nDCG values were computed using

---

[18] http://trec.nist.gov/data/web/11/ndeval.c

NTCIREVAL[19]; the D-U and U-IA values are from the Sakai and Dou [85][20]. This TREC data set contains 50 topics and 17 "Category A" runs [31], giving us $50 * 17 * 16/2 = 6800$ pairs of ranked lists. For example, the table shows the following information for D♯-nDCG versus ERR-IA:

- D♯-nDCG and ERR-IA disagree with each other for 1106 ranked list pairs out of 6800;
- Of the 1106 disagreements, D♯-nDCG is concordant with both intent recall and precision 70% of the time, while ERR-IA is concordant with them only 29% of the time.
- The difference between D♯-nDCG and ERR-IA is statistically significant at $\alpha = 0.01$ (though not shown in the table, D♯-nDCG wins 592 times, while ERR-IA wins only 130 times)[21].

It can be observed that, as was mentioned in Section 3.1, D♯-nDCG ≫ U-IA ≫ D-U ≫ D-nDCG ≫ α-nDCG ≫ ERR-IA holds, where "≫" means "statistically significantly better than" in terms of simultaneous concordance with I-rec and precision.

5.4   Leave-One-Out Test

The Leave-One-Out (LOO) test [106,121] is useful for testing the reusability of test collections that have been built based on pooling. It can also be used for comparing the robustness of evaluation metrics to incompleteness and system bias (e.g. [18,89,87]). Figure 18 shows how the LOO test works: the relevance assessments of a topic is a union of the *contributions* from each participating team (or *contributors*). Then a LOO relevance assessment set can be created by removing the *unique contributions* from one team (e.g. Team A). Then, if the runs from this team are evaluted based on the LOO set, it is similar to the situation where the original test collection is used for evaluating a *non-contributor*, i.e. a team that did not contribute to the pooling process.

Formally, let m be the number of contributors, and let C_j denote the contributions from the j-th team ($j = 1, \ldots, m$). Each team may submit multiple runs[22]. The pool for this topic is given by $P = \bigcup_j C_j$, and the set of unique contributions from the j-th team is given by $U_j = C_j - \bigcup_{j' \neq j} C_{j'}$. Then the LOO set for the j-th team is given by $LOO_j = \bigcup_{j' \neq j} C_{j'} = P - U_j$. If the evaluation outcome for the j-th team based on LOO_j is similar to that based on the original relevance assessments P, then the test collection with that particular evaluation metric may be considered more or less reusable: the evaluation environment can properly evaluate systems that did not contribute to the pool.

---

[19] http://research.nii.ac.jp/ntcir/tools/ntcireval-en.html

[20] http://research.microsoft.com/u/

[21] Thus D♯-nDCG wins 54% of the time, while ERR-IA wins 12% of the time: whereas, the concordance percentages shown in the table include cases where D♯-nDCG and ERR-IA are tied.

[22] The original method of Zobel [121] left out one *run* at a time, but leaving out the entire team is more realistic and more stringent.

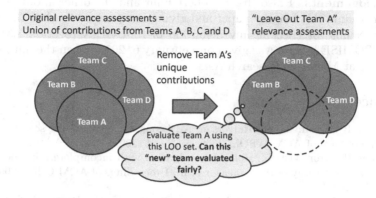

Fig. 18. Leaving out Team A

5.5 Further Reading

There are other ways to evaluate evaluation metrics or evaluation environments. For example, Aslam, Yilmaz and Pavlu [8] have examined the *informativeness* of evaluation metrics; Ashkan and Clarke [7] have extended this approach to diversity evaluation metrics. *Generalisability theory* has been used for testing the reliability of evaluation environments [11,23]. Before conducting experiments, it is always useful to discuss the theoretical properties of evaluation metrics: metrics may be studied or even designed using *measurement theory*, formal constraints and axioms ("axiometrics") [3,12]; just reformulating the definition of a known metric may reveal some of its (dis)advantages [79,81].

6 Summary

This lecture covered a wide variety of IR metrics and discussed some methods for evaluating evaluation metrics. It also briefly described computer-based statistical significance test methods that are useful for IR evaluation. The takeaways for IR experimenters are: (1) It is important to understand the properties of IR metrics and choose or design appropriate ones for the task at hand; (2) Computer-based statistical significance tests are simple and useful, although statistical significance does not necessarily imply practical significance, and statistical insignificance does not necessarily imply practical insignificance; and (3) Several methods exist for discussing which metrics are "good," although none of them is perfect.

Finally, the reader should be reminded that, to conduct good IR experiments, one should use a *competitive* baseline system (a statistically significant gain over an obsolete, fifty-year-old technique is unlikely to advance the state of the art), multiple evaluation metrics (to evaluate systems from several angles), and multiple test collections (to see how consistent and generalisable the results might be).

Acknowledgements. I also thank Nobert Fuhr and the other anonymous reviewer for reading this lengthy paper and giving me good feedback. I thank Dr. Hidetsugu Nanba for checking my definition of ROUGE-N (Section 3.3). The original PROMISE lecture was given on February 6, 2013, when the author was an employee at Microsoft Research Asia.

References

1. Agrawal, R., Sreenivas, G., Halverson, A., Leong, S.: Diversifying search results. In: Proceedings of ACM WSDM 2009, pp. 5–14 (2009)
2. Ahlgren, P., Grönqvist, L.: Retrieval evaluation with incomplete relevance data: A comparative study of three measures. In: Proceedings of ACM CIKM 2006, pp. 872–873 (2006)
3. Allan, J., Aslam, J., Azzopardi, L., Belkin, N., Borlund, P., Bruza, P., Callan, J., Carman, M., Clarke, C.L., Craswell, N., Croft, W.B., Culpepper, J.S., Diaz, F., Dumais, S., Ferro, N., Geva, S., Gonzalo, J., Hawking, D., Jarvelin, K., Jones, G., Jones, R., Kamps, J., Kando, N., Kanoulas, E., Karlgren, J., Kelly, D., Lease, M., Lin, J., Mizzaro, S., Moffat, A., Murdock, V., Oard, D.W., de Rijke, M., Sakai, T., Sanderson, M., Scholer, F., Si, L., Thom, J.A., Thomas, P., Trotman, A., Turpin, A., de Vries, A.P., Webber, W., Zhang, X., Zhang, Y.: Frontiers, challenges and opportunities for information retrieval: Report from SWIRL 2012. SIGIR Forum 46(1), 2–32 (2012)
4. Allan, J., Carterette, B., Lewis, J.: When will information retrieval be "good enough"? In: Proceedings of ACM SIGIR 2005, pp. 433–440 (2005)
5. Arguello, J., Diaz, F., Callan, J., Carterette, B.: A methodology for evaluating aggregated search results. In: Clough, P., Foley, C., Gurrin, C., Jones, G.J.F., Kraaij, W., Lee, H., Mudoch, V. (eds.) ECIR 2011. LNCS, vol. 6611, pp. 141–152. Springer, Heidelberg (2011)
6. Arvola, P., Kekäläinen, J., Junkkari, M.: Expected reading effort in focused retrieval evaluation. Information Retrieval 13(5), 460–484 (2010)
7. Ashkan, A., Clarke, C.L.: On the informativeness of cascade and intent-aware effectiveness measures. In: Proceedings of ACM SIGIR 2013, pp. 407–416 (2011)
8. Aslam, J.A., Yilmaz, E., Pavlu, V.: The maximum entropy method for analyzing retrieval measures. In: Proceedings of ACM SIGIR 2005, pp. 27–34 (2005)
9. Azzopardi, L.: Usage based effectiveness measures. In: Proceedings of ACM CIKM 2009, pp. 631–640 (2009)
10. Baskaya, F., Keskustalo, H., Järvelin, K.: Time drives interaction: Simulating sessions in diverse searching environments. In: Proceedings of ACM SIGIR 2012, pp. 105–114 (2012)
11. Bodoff, D., Li, P.: Test theory for assessing IR test collections. In: Proceedings of ACM SIGIR 2007, pp. 367–374 (2007)
12. Bollman, P., Cherniavsky, V.S.: Measurement-theoretical investigation of the MZ-metric. In: Proceedings of ACM SIGIR 1980, pp. 256–267 (1980)
13. Brandt, C., Joachims, T., Yue, Y., Bank, J.: Dynamic ranked retrieval. In: Proceedings of ACM WSDM 2011, pp. 247–256 (2011)
14. Broder, A.: A taxonomy of web search. SIGIR Forum 36(2) (2002)
15. Buckley, C., Voorhees, E.M.: Evaluating evaluation measure stability. In: Proceedings of ACM SIGIR 2000, pp. 33–40 (2000)
16. Buckley, C., Voorhees, E.M.: Retrieval evaluation with incomplete information. In: Proceedings of ACM SIGIR 2004, pp. 25–32 (2004)

17. Burges, C., Shaked, T., Renshaw, E., Lazier, A., Deeds, M., Hamilton, N., Hullender, G.: Learning to rank using gradient descent. In: Proceedings of ICML 2005, pp. 89–96 (2005)

18. Büttcher, S., Clarke, C.L., Yeung, P.C., Soboroff, I.: Reliable information retrieval evaluation with incomplete and biased judgements. In: Proceedings of ACM SIGIR 2007, pp. 63–70 (2007)

19. Carterette, B.: On rank correlation and the distance between rankings. In: Proceedings of ACM SIGIR 2009, pp. 436–443 (2009)

20. Carterette, B.: System effectiveness, user models, and user utility: A conceptual framework for investigation. In: Proceedings of ACM SIGIR 2011, pp. 903–912 (2011)

21. Carterette, B.: Multiple testing in statistical analysis of systems-based information retrieval experiments. ACM TOIS 30(1) (2012)

22. Carterette, B., Bennett, P.N., Chickering, D.M., Dumais, S.T.: Here or there: Preference judgments for relevance. In: Macdonald, C., Ounis, I., Plachouras, V., Ruthven, I., White, R.W. (eds.) ECIR 2008. LNCS, vol. 4956, pp. 16–27. Springer, Heidelberg (2008)

23. Carterette, B., Pavlu, V., Kanoulas, E., Aslam, J.A., Allan, J.: Evaluation over thousands of queries. In: Proceedings of ACM SIGIR 2008, pp. 651–658 (2008)

24. Chandar, P., Carterette, B.: Analysis of various evaluation measures for diversity. In: Proceedings of DDR 2011, pp. 21–28 (2011)

25. Chandar, P., Carterette, B.: What qualities do users prefer in diversity rankings? In: Proceedings of DDR 2012 (2012)

26. Chapelle, O., Ji, S., Liao, C., Velipasaoglu, E., Lai, L., Wu, S.L.: Intent-based diversification of web search results: Metrics and algorithms. Information Retrieval 14(6), 572–592 (2011)

27. Chapelle, O., Metzler, D., Zhang, Y., Grinspan, P.: Expected reciprocal rank for graded relevance. In: Proceedings of ACM CIKM 2009, pp. 621–630 (2009)

28. Chinchor, N.: MUC-4 evaluation metrics. In: Proceedings of MUC-4, pp. 22–29 (1992)

29. Clarke, C.L., Craswell, N., Soboroff, I.: Overview of the TREC 2009 web track. In: Proceedings of TREC 2009 (2009)

30. Clarke, C.L., Craswell, N., Soboroff, I., Ashkan, A.: A comparative analysis of cascade measures for novelty and diversity. In: Proceedings of ACM WSDM 2011, pp. 75–84 (2011)

31. Clarke, C.L., Craswell, N., Soboroff, I., Voorhees, E.: Overview of the TREC 2011 web track. In: Proceedings of TREC 2011 (2012)

32. Clarke, C.L., Kolla, M., Cormack, G.V., Vechtomova, O., Ashkan, A., Büttcher, S., MacKinnon, I.: Novelty and diversity in information retrieval evaluation. In: Proceedings of ACM SIGIR 2008, pp. 659–666 (2009)

33. Clarke, C.L.A., Kolla, M., Vechtomova, O.: An effectiveness measure for ambiguous and underspecified queries. In: Azzopardi, L., Kazai, G., Robertson, S., Rüger, S., Shokouhi, M., Song, D., Yilmaz, E. (eds.) ICTIR 2009. LNCS, vol. 5766, pp. 188–199. Springer, Heidelberg (2009)

34. Clarke, C.L., Craswell, N., Voorhees, E.: Overview of the TREC 2012 web track. In: Proceedings of TREC 2012 (2013)

35. Cooper, W.S.: Expected search length: A single measure of retrieval effectiveness based on the weak ordering action of retrieval systems. JASIS 19(1), 30–41 (1968)

36. Cooper, W.S.: On selecting a measure of retrieval effectiveness. JASIS 24(2), 87–100 (1973)

37. Cooper, W.S.: On selecting a measure of retrieval effectiveness: Part II. Implementation of the philosophy. JASIS 24(6), 413–424 (1973)
38. Cormack, G.V., Lynam, T.R.: Statistical precision of information retrieval evaluation. In: Proceedings of ACM SIGIR 2006 (2006)
39. Dang, H., Lin, J.: Different structures for evaluating answers to complex questions: Pyramids won't topple, and neither will human assessors. In: Proceedings of ACL 2007, pp. 768–775 (2007)
40. De Beer, J., Moens, M.F.: Rpref: A generalization of bpref towards graded relevance judgments. In: Proceedings of ACM SIGIR 2006, pp. 637–638 (2006)
41. Della Mea, V., Mizzaro, S.: Measuring retrieval effectiveness: A new proposal and a first experimental validation. JASIST 55(6), 503–543 (2004)
42. Dunlop, M.D.: Time, relevance and interaction modelling for information retrieval. In: Proceedings of ACM SIGIR 1997, pp. 206–213 (1997)
43. Efron, B., Tibshirani, R.J.: An Introduction to the Bootstrap. Chapman & Hall/CRC (1993)
44. Eguchi, K., Oyama, K., Ishida, E., Kando, N., Kuriyama, K.: Overview of the web retrieval task at the third NTCIR workshop. NII Technical Reports NII-2003-002E (2003)
45. Gey, F., Larson, R., Machado, J., Yoshioka, M.: NTCIR9-GeoTime overview - evaluating geographic and temporal search: Round 2. In: Proceedings of NTCIR-9, pp. 9–17 (2011)
46. Golbus, P.B., Aslam, J.A., Clarke, C.L.: Increasing evaluation sensitivity to diversity. Information Retrieval (2013)
47. Hull, D.: Using statistical testing in the evaluation of retrieval experiments. In: Proceedings of ACM SIGIR 1993. pp. 329–338 (1993)
48. Ioannidis, J.P.: Why most published research findings are false. PLoS Med. 2(8) (2005)
49. Järvelin, K., Kekäläinen, J.: Cumulated gain-based evaluation of IR techniques. ACM Transactions on Information Systems 20(4), 422–446 (2002)
50. Järvelin, K., Price, S.L., Delcambre, L.M.L., Nielsen, M.L.: Discounted cumulated gain based evaluation of multiple-query IR sessions. In: Macdonald, C., Ounis, I., Plachouras, V., Ruthven, I., White, R.W. (eds.) ECIR 2008. LNCS, vol. 4956, pp. 4–15. Springer, Heidelberg (2008)
51. Johnson, D.H.: The insignificance of statistical significance testing. The Journal of Wildlife Management 63(3), 763–772 (1999)
52. Kamps, J., Pehcevski, J., Kazai, G., Lalmas, M., Robertson, S.: INEX 2007 evaluation measures. In: Fuhr, N., Kamps, J., Lalmas, M., Trotman, A. (eds.) INEX 2007. LNCS, vol. 4862, pp. 24–33. Springer, Heidelberg (2008)
53. Kanoulas, E., Aslam, J.A.: Empirical justification of the gain and discount function for nDCG. In: ACM CIKM 2009, pp. 611–620 (2009)
54. Kanoulas, E., Carterette, B., Clough, P.D., Sanderson, M.: Evaluating multi-query sessions. In: Proceedings of ACM SIGIR 2011, pp. 1053–1062 (2011)
55. Kato, M.P., Sakai, T., Yamamoto, T., Iwata, M.: Report from the NTCIR-10 1CLICK-2 Japanese subtask: Baselines, upperbounds and evaluation robustness. In: Proceedings of ACM SIGIR 2013 (2013)
56. Kekäläinen, J., Järvelin, K.: Using graded relevance assessments in IR evaluation. JASIST 53(13), 1120–1129 (2002)
57. Kishida, K.: Property of average precision and its generalization: An examination of evaluation indicator for information retrieval. NII Technical Reports NII-2005-014E (2005)

58. Kishida, K., Chen, K.H., Lee, S., Kuriyama, K., Kando, N., Chen, H.H.: Overview of CLIR task at the sixth NTCIR workshop. In: Proceedings of NTCIR-6, pp. 1–19 (2007)
59. Leenanupab, T., Zuccon, G., Jose, J.M.: A comprehensive analysis of parameter settings for novelty-biased cumulative gain. In: Proceedings of ACM CIKM 2012, pp. 1950–1954 (2012)
60. Lin, C.Y.: ROUGE: A package for automatic evaluation of summaries. In: Proceedings of the ACL 2004 Workshop on Text Summarization Branches Out (2004)
61. Lin, J., Demner-Fushman, D.: Methods for automatically evaluating answers to complex questions. Information Retrieval 9(5), 565–587 (2006)
62. Magdy, W., Jones, G.J.: PRES: A score metric for evaluating recall-oriented information retrieval applications. In: Proceedings of ACM SIGIR 2010, pp. 611–618 (2010)
63. Moffat, A., Zobel, J.: Rank-biased precision for measurement of retrieval effectiveness. ACM TOIS 27(1) (2008)
64. Nanba, H., Hirao, T.: Automatic evaluation in text summarization (in Japanese). Transactions of the Japanese Society for Artificial Intelligence 22(1), 10–16 (2008)
65. Nenkova, A., Passonneau, R., McKeown, K.: The pyramid method: Incorporating human content selection variation in summarization evaluation. ACM Transactions on Speech and Language Processing 4(2), Article 4 (2007)
66. Papineni, K., Roukos, S., Ward, T., Zhu, W.J.: Bleu: a method for automatic evaluation of machine translation. IBM Research Report RC22176 (2001)
67. Pollock, S.M.: Measures for the comparison of information retrieval systems. American Documentation 19(4), 387–397 (1968)
68. Rijsbergen, C.J.V.: Information Retrieval, 2nd edn. Butterworths (1979)
69. Robertson, S.E.: The probability ranking principle in IR. Journal of Documentation 33, 130–137 (1977)
70. Robertson, S.E.: On GMAP: and other transformations. In: Proceedings of ACM CIKM 2006, pp. 78–83 (2006)
71. Robertson, S.E.: A new interpretation of average precision. In: Proceedings of ACM SIGIR 2008, pp. 689–690 (2008)
72. Robertson, S.E., Kanoulas, E.: On per-topic variance in IR evaluation. In: Proceedings of ACM SIGIR 2012, pp. 891–900 (2012)
73. Robertson, S.E., Kanoulas, E., Yilmaz, E.: Extending average precision to graded relevance judgments. In: Proceedings of ACM SIGIR 2010, pp. 603–610 (2010)
74. Sakai, T.: New performance metrics based on multigrade relevance: Their application to question answering. In: Proceedings of NTCIR-4 (Open Submission Session) (2004)
75. Sakai, T.: Ranking the NTCIR systems based on multigrade relevance. In: Myaeng, S.-H., Zhou, M., Wong, K.-F., Zhang, H.-J. (eds.) AIRS 2004. LNCS, vol. 3411, pp. 251–262. Springer, Heidelberg (2005)
76. Sakai, T.: Bootstrap-based comparisons of IR metrics for finding one relevant document. In: Ng, H.T., Leong, M.-K., Kan, M.-Y., Ji, D. (eds.) AIRS 2006. LNCS, vol. 4182, pp. 374–389. Springer, Heidelberg (2006)
77. Sakai, T.: Evaluating evaluation metrics based on the bootstrap. In: Proceedings of ACM SIGIR 2006, pp. 525–532 (2006)
78. Sakai, T.: For building better retrieval systems: Trends in information retrieval evaluation based on graded relevance (in Japanese). IPSJ Magazine 47(2), 147–158 (2006)
79. Sakai, T.: Alternatives to bpref. In: Proceedings of ACM SIGIR 2007, pp. 71–78 (2007)

80. Sakai, T.: On penalising late arrival of relevant documents in information retrieval evaluation with graded relevance. In: Proceedings of EVIA 2007, pp. 32–43 (2007)

81. Sakai, T.: Comparing metrics across TREC and NTCIR: The robustness to system bias. In: Proceedings of ACM CIKM 2008, pp. 581–590 (2008)

82. Sakai, T.: Evaluation with informational and navigational intents. In: Proceedings of WWW 2012, pp. 499–508 (2012)

83. Sakai, T.: How intuitive are diversified search metrics? Concordance test results for the diversity U-measures. IPSJ SIG Technical Report 2013-IFAT-111 (2013)

84. Sakai, T.: The unreusability of diversified test collections. In: Proceedings of EVIA 2013 (2013)

85. Sakai, T., Dou, Z.: Summaries, ranked retrieval and sessions: A unified framework for information access evaluation. In: Proceedings of ACM SIGIR 2013, pp. 473–482 (2013)

86. Sakai, T., Dou, Z., Clarke, C.L.: The impact of intent selection on diversified search evaluation. In: Proceedings of ACM SIGIR 2013 (2013)

87. Sakai, T., Dou, Z., Song, R., Kando, N.: The reusability of a diversified search test collection. In: Hou, Y., Nie, J.-Y., Sun, L., Wang, B., Zhang, P. (eds.) AIRS 2012. LNCS, vol. 7675, pp. 26–38. Springer, Heidelberg (2012)

88. Sakai, T., Dou, Z., Yamamoto, T., Liu, Y., Zhang, M., Kato, M.P., Song, R., Iwata, M.: Summary of the NTCIR-10 INTENT-2 task: Subtopic mining and search result diversification. In: Proceedings of ACM SIGIR 2013 (2013)

89. Sakai, T., Kando, N.: On information retrieval metrics designed for evaluation with incomplete relevance assessments. Information Retrieval 11, 447–470 (2008)

90. Sakai, T., Kato, M.P.: One click one revisited: Enhancing evaluation based on information units. In: Hou, Y., Nie, J.-Y., Sun, L., Wang, B., Zhang, P. (eds.) AIRS 2012. LNCS, vol. 7675, pp. 39–51. Springer, Heidelberg (2012)

91. Sakai, T., Kato, M.P., Song, Y.I.: Click the search button and be happy: Evaluating direct and immediate information access. In: Proceedings of ACM CIKM 2011, pp. 621–630 (2011)

92. Sakai, T., Robertson, S.: Modelling a user population for designing information retrieval metrics. In: Proceedings of EVIA 2008, pp. 30–41 (2008)

93. Sakai, T., Shima, H., Kando, N., Song, R., Lin, C.J., Mitamura, T., Sugimoto, M., Lee, C.W.: Overview of NTCIR-8 ACLIA IR4QA. In: Proceedings of NTCIR-8, pp. 63–93 (2010)

94. Sakai, T., Song, R.: Evaluating diversified search results using per-intent graded relevance. In: Proceedings of ACM SIGIR 2011 (2011)

95. Sakai, T., Song, R.: Diversified search evaluation: Lessons from the NTCIR-9 INTENT task. Information Retrieval (2013)

96. Sakai, T., Song, Y.I.: On evaluation environments for web search result diversification. In: Forum on Information Technology 2013 (2013)

97. Sanderson, M.: Test collection based evaluation of information retrieval systems. Foundations and Trends in Information Retrieval 4, 247–375 (2010)

98. Sanderson, M., Paramita, M.L., Clough, P., Kanoulas, E.: Do user preferences and evaluation measures line up? In: Proceedings of ACM SIGIR 2010, pp. 555–562 (2010)

99. Sanderson, M., Zobel, J.: Information retrieval system evaluation: Effort, sensitivity, and reliability. In: Proceedings of ACM SIGIR 2005, pp. 162–169 (2005)

100. Savoy, J.: Statistical inference in retrieval effectiveness evaluation. Information Processing and Management 33(4), 495–512 (1997)

101. Smucker, M.D., Allan, J., Carterette, B.: A comparison of statistical significance tests for information retrieval evaluation. In: Proceedings of ACM CIKM 2007, pp. 623–632 (2007)
102. Smucker, M.D., Clarke, C.L.A.: Modeling user variance in time-biased gain. In: Proceedings of ACM HCIR 2012 (2012)
103. Smucker, M.D., Clarke, C.L.A.: Stochastic simulation of time-biased gain. In: Proceedings of ACM CIKM 2012, pp. 2040–2044 (2012)
104. Smucker, M.D., Clarke, C.L.A.: Time-based calibration of effectiveness measures. In: Proceedings of ACM SIGIR 2012, pp. 95–104 (2012)
105. Turpin, A., Scholer, F., Järvelin, K., Wu, M., Culpepper, J.S.: Including summaries in system evaluation. In: Proceedings of ACM SIGIR 2009, pp. 508–515 (2009)
106. Voorhees, E.M.: The philosophy of information retrieval evaluation. In: Peters, C., Braschler, M., Gonzalo, J., Kluck, M. (eds.) CLEF 2001. LNCS, vol. 2406, pp. 355–370. Springer, Heidelberg (2002)
107. Voorhees, E.M., Buckley, C.: The effect of topic set size on retrieval experiment error. In: Proceedings of ACM SIGIR 2002, pp. 316–323 (2002)
108. Voorhees, E.M., Harman, D.K. (eds.): TREC: Experiment and Evaluation in Information Retrieval. The MIT Press (2005)
109. Webber, W., Moffat, A., Zobel, J.: Score standardization for inter-collection comparison of retrieval systems. In: Proceedings of ACM SIGIR 2008, pp. 51–58 (2008)
110. Webber, W., Moffat, A., Zobel, J.: Statistical power in retrieval experimentation. In: Proceedings of ACM CIKM 2008, pp. 571–580 (2008)
111. Webber, W., Moffat, A., Zobel, J.: The effect of pooling and evaluation depth on metric stability. In: Proceedings of EVIA 2010, pp. 7–15 (2010)
112. Webber, W., Moffat, A., Zobel, J.: A similarity measure for indefinite rankings. ACM TOIS 28(4) (2010)
113. Webber, W., Park, L.A.: Score adjustment for correction of pooling bias. In: Proceedings of ACM SIGIR 2009, pp. 444–451 (2009)
114. Yang, Y., Lad, A.: Modeling expected utility of multi-session information distillation. In: Azzopardi, L., Kazai, G., Robertson, S., Rüger, S., Shokouhi, M., Song, D., Yilmaz, E. (eds.) ICTIR 2009. LNCS, vol. 5766, pp. 164–175. Springer, Heidelberg (2009)
115. Yilmaz, E., Aslam, J., Robertson, S.: A new rank correlation coefficient for information retrieval. In: Proceedings of ACM SIGIR 2008, pp. 587–594 (2008)
116. Yilmaz, E., Aslam, J.A.: Estimating average precision with incomplete and imperfect judgments. In: ACM CIKM 2006 Proceedings, pp. 102–111 (2006)
117. Yilmaz, E., Shokouhi, M., Craswell, N., Robertson, S.: Expected browsing utility for web search evaluation. In: Proceedings of ACM CIKM 2010, pp. 1561–1564 (2010)
118. Zhai, C., Cohen, W.W., Lafferty, J.: Beyond independent relevance: Methods and evaluation metrics for subtopic retrieval. In: Proceedings of ACM SIGIR 2003, pp. 10–17 (2003)
119. Zhang, Y., Park, L.A.F., Moffat, A.: Click-based evidence for decaying weight distributions in search effectiveness metrics. Information Retrieval 13(1), 46–69 (2010)
120. Zhou, K., Cummins, R., Lalmas, M., Jose, J.M.: Evaluating aggregated search pages. In: Proceedings of ACM SIGIR 2012, pp. 115–124 (2012)
121. Zobel, J.: How reliable are the results of large-scale information retrieval experiments? In: Proceedings of ACM SIGIR 1998, pp. 307–314 (1998)

Semistructured Data Search Evaluation

Ralf Schenkel

Universität Passau, Germany
ralf.schenkel@uni-passau.de

Abstract. Semistructured data is of increasing importance in many application domains, but one of its core use cases is representing documents. Consequently, effectively retrieving information from semistructured documents is an important problem that has seen work from both the information retrieval (IR) and databases (DB) communities. Comparing the large number of retrieval models and systems is a non-trivial task for which established benchmark initiatives such as TREC with their focus on unstructured documents are not appropriate. This chapter gives an overview of semistructured data in general and the INEX initiative for the evaluation of XML retrieval, focusing on the most prominent Adhoc Search Track.

1 Introduction

Semistructured data such as XML and, more recently, RDF is of increasing importance in many application domains, but one of its core use cases is representing documents. Consequently, effectively retrieving information from semistructured documents is an important problem that has seen work from both the information retrieval (IR) and database (DB) communities. At the same time, access to semistructured data with IR-inspired methods such as keyword queries or imprecise, relaxed queries is also becoming more important in other domains where the amount of data and data formats is exploding. While a large number of proposals for retrieval models, scores, algorithms, and systems exist, comparing them in terms of quality of the retrieved results is a non-trivial task. Benchmark initiatives such as TREC have focused on unstructured documents and are therefore not well suited for evaluating semistructured retrieval approaches. A new benchmark initiative, INEX, was established in 2002, and has since then provided a large number of test collections for diverse retrieval tasks on semistructured data. This chapter gives an overview of semistructured data in general and the INEX initiative, focusing on the most prominent Adhoc Search Track.

The remainder of this chapter is structured as follows. In the following Section 2, we will introduce background on semistructured data and semistructured information retrieval. In Section 3, we will introduce the INEX benchmark initiative and give an overview of its tracks. The focus of Section 4 will be the INEX Adhoc track, which had been the main INEX track for ten years.

N. Ferro (Ed.): PROMISE Winter School 2013, LNCS 8173, pp. 164–181, 2014.

1.1 Further Reading

This chapter does not discuss individual approaches or systems for semi-structured information retrieval; we refer the interested reader to the INEX workshop proceedings, most of which have appeared in the Springer LNCS series or are available from the current INEX homepage[1]. A broader overview of XML retrieval methods can be found in [1].

Kazai et al. [19,23] report insights from the first year of INEX, and Lalmas and Tombros [25] provide an overview of the evaluation methodology developed in INEX from 2002 to 2006. As the discussion of the individual INEX track in this chapter is limited, we refer the interested reader again to the INEX workshop proceedings, or to the yearly summary article about INEX in SIGIR Forum (usually in the June issue). A large number of evaluation metrics have been designed for the various tracks and tasks at INEX, and this chapter can only discuss a small selection of them. Further discussion of evaluation metrics can be found, for example, in [3,15,16,22,21,29,31].

2 Semistructured Data

2.1 Background

In general, semistructured data combines structured information with unstructured text. For many years, the classic example of semistructured information has been documents in the extended markup language (XML), where documents are imposed a tree structure indicated by tags. Similarly, HTML documents combine structure (such as links, tables, lists, etc.) and textual information. More recently, the literature has considered relational databases (where the unstructured part is formed by the text in the tables' attributes) and semantic data; in the latter case, a common use case considers structured facts extracted from textual documents, and the source documents are used as source of unstructured information connected to the facts extracted from it.

In this chapter, we will focus on semistructured information represented as XML, since this is the dominant format used in benchmarks. We will now introduce some foundations of XML.

An XML document consists of a nested tree of *elements*, which can contain a mixture of other elements and text in its body. The boundaries of an element are denoted by a pair of opening and closing *tags* in square brackets (where the name of the tags denotes the name of the element, and the closing tag includes a trailing / before its name); each opening tag must be followed later by a closing tag, and any opening tags in the body of an element must be followed by the appropriate closing tag before the closing tag of the element. In addition to their content, elements may contain attributes, which are essentially key-value pairs. Figure 1 shows a simple example document with data from DBLP. The allowed nesting structure of elements and the allowed content of elements can be restricted by defining the schema of the document in languages such as XML Schema [13,30].

---

[1] http://inex.mmci.uni-saarland.de/

```
<article key="journals/cacm/Gentry10" mdate="2010-04-26">
  <author>Craig Gentry</author>
  <title>
    Computing arbitrary functions of encrypted data.
  </title>
  <pages>97-105</pages>
  <year>2010</year>
  <volume>53</volume>
  <journal>Commun. ACM</journal>
  <number>3</number>
  <ee>http://doi.acm.org/10.1145/1666420.1666444</ee>
  <url>db/journals/cacm/cacm53.html#Gentry10</url>
</article>
```

Fig. 1. Data-centric XML document from DBLP

XML documents are often classified into data-centric or document-centric documents. Data-centric documents have a very regular structure and contain no or very few elements with long textual information; often, the nesting of elements is limited such that an element contains either subelements or text, but not both (i.e., there is hardly any mixed content). Since such documents are often created automatically, documents from the same source often have a similar or even identical structure. The example document from Figure 1 is data-centric.

Document-centric documents, on the other hand, represent textual information with some added structure such as meta information about the document. Usually, the structure of the content (such as sections, paragraphs, titles, figures, etc.) and layout information (boldface, italics, etc.) are represented with nested XML tags. The elements of such documents therefore contain a lot of text with embedded tags; mixed content is predominant; the nesting structure of their elements is very irregular. Since the structure of two text documents can be very different, document-centric XML documents from the same source usually have a very different structure. Figure 2 shows (an excerpt of) a document-centric XML document from the INEX 2006 benchmark collection, based on Wikipedia content.

2.2   Semistructured Document Retrieval

Information retrieval has, for a long time, considered retrieving the best documents for an information need. With often huge semistructured documents (such as a complete database table or a complete book with structural annotations), this document-based retrieval is no longer sufficient. Instead, the goal of semistructured document retrieval has been to identify and retrieve the best fragments of documents that satisfy the information need. For database tables, this could be the values of one or a few attributes of one or more tables, or a few rows of a table. For XML documents, the natural choice is to retrieve

```
<article xmlns:xlink="http://www.w3.org/1999/xlink/">
  <header>
    <title>Wiki markup</title>
    <id>42</id>
    <categories> <category>Markup languages</category> </categories>
  </header>
  <body>
  <section><st>Introduction</st>
    <p><b>Wiki markup</b> is used in <link xlink:href="../Wi/Wikipedia.xml"
    xlink:type="simple">Wikipedia</link>.</p> It allows for a rather rich
    annotation of texts with structure such as tables and lists, links to
    other documents, and much more.
  </section>
  <section>
    <st>Language Components</st>
    <list>
    <entry>tables</entry>
    <entry>lists</entry>
...
```

Fig. 2. Document-centric XML document from the INEX Wikipedia 2006 collection

elements with their content. Recently, this has been extended to retrieving arbitrary passages of documents and considering the element structure only as hints; this is obviously related to passage retrieval in unstructured documents. To stress that retrieval results focus on the relevant fragments of a document, the term *focused retrieval* has been coined. The dominant query paradigm has been keyword-based queries, which provides a limited natural language expression of the information need, but does not allow to express explicit structural constraints; such queries are therefore often called *content-only* (CO). Relevance of results can be determined solely by the content of elements, it is not possible to specify constraints on the tag(s) of result elements. Many existing approaches take the length of elements into account and prefer medium-sized elements that include much information that satisfies the information need (so they are *exhaustive* on the topic of the query), but are also *specific* and do not contain off-topic material.

From a database perspective, on the other hand, query languages such as SQL (for relational data) and XQuery (for XML data) allow for a very fine-grained specification of structural constraints for queries, but their capabilities to specify IR-style information needs are very limited in their original form. Additionally, they do not come with a built-in ranking mechanism, but retrieve all rows (for SQL) or elements (for XQuery) that match the structural constraints of the query. Consequently, these languages have been extended to support keyword constraints, for example in the form of XPath and XQuery FullText [4]. The following example query from [4] retrieves all paragraphs where 'usability' appears within books books where 'software' appears and orders results by some score (that is implementation-specific); note that there are many options beyond those shown here for query expansion, weighting, Boolean constructs, etc.:

```
for $p score $s in
  //book[title contains text "software"]/para[. contains text "usability"]
    order by $s descending
  return $p
```

Queries that combine content and structural constraints are often called *content-and-structure* (CAS). Relevance can be determined by the degree to which a result matches the content and the structural constraints of the query, and the tag(s) of allowed result elements can be specified. Existing approaches often allow for partial matches of the structural constraints or even support relaxation, for example retrieving sections when the query asks for paragraphs; in the latter case, the structural constraints are considered as hints, not as restrictions.

Even though languages such as XQuery with its full-text extensions are very powerful, they are often too complex for users, who thus frequently specify queries that are syntactically or, worse, semantically wrong. Experiences within the INEX benchmark in 2003 show that this can also be a problem for expert users: Of the 30 queries specified by participants (aka computer scientists with IR experience), 19 or 63% were incorrect [27]. IR systems for XML retrieval therefore provide simpler query languages with restricted capabilities, but that allow for a more natural query specification. We will discuss NEXI, the query language of the INEX benchmark, in the following section.

3 The INEX Initiative

3.1 Overview

INEX, the INitiative for the Evaluation of XML retrieval, started in 2002 as an informal benchmark consortium. Since then, INEX has focused on various aspects of focused retrieval of document-centric XML documents, organized in various tracks. It has had more than 500 participating research groups and more than 100 track organizers. INEX provides a yearly competition for the participating systems, and an annual workshop to discuss the results, the setup of the benchmark, and possible future tracks. Until 2008, the workshops took place in Schloss Dagstuhl; after subsequent workshops in Brisbane (Australia), Vught (The Netherlands), and Saarbrücken (Germany), since 2012 INEX has been embedded as a lab in the CLEF campaign.

The INEX initiative has considered a number of search tasks over the years. The unifying research question common to all of them has been to identify tasks where focused retrieval yields better (i.e., more relevant) results than document retrieval, how this 'better' can be quantified in terms of quality metrics, and if (and how) the structure can be exploited to improve retrieval quality. A secondary (but nevertheless important) goal was to provide means to compare performance of different systems for the same task, both in terms of result quality and retrieval speed. Similar to other benchmark initiatives such as TREC or CLEF, the general principle of INEX has always been to generate public test collections that can be used outside the scope of the yearly campaign.

3.2   Overview of the INEX Tracks

INEX organizes its work in different tracks that focus on a specific aspect of focused retrieval, including collections, topic formulation, type of documents, interaction, and performance metrics. In this section we will shortly review the INEX tracks, referencing the latest track overview paper. The AdHoc track had been the main track for many years and can be seen as INEX' core track, so we will discuss it at length in the following section.

- The **Heterogeneous Track**[10] (2004-2006) considered the problems introduced by documents from different sources that are heterogeneous in their syntax, semantics and document genre.
- The **Relevance Feedback Track** [5] (2004-2005; 2010-2012) examined how focused relevance feedback on the element level could be exploited to improve retrieval quality. In its first two years, the track extended established evaluation procedures from document retrieval to the XML case. In the last three years, a new evaluation platform was developed where participants supplied their feedback approach as an executable that communicates with a supplied evaluation platform which provided topics and, for each result retrieved by the search module, relevance information.
- The **Natural Language Processing Track** (2004-2006) examined how queries could be evaluated that were given in natural language instead of a structured query language. In one of its tasks, the goal was to create an equivalent NEXI query for an information need specified in natural language.
- The **Interactive Track** [26] (2004-2010) examines user search behavior in a number of different semi-structured collections. While initially the IEEE and Wikipedia collections from the Adhoc track were used, later experiments focused on a collection consisting of book meta data taken from the online bookstore Amazon and the social cataloging application LibraryThing. User interactions were observed for a number of search task categories, including explorative and data-gathering tasks. Participants could use a system provided by the organizers that would collect statistics about the interactions; in addition, questionnaire-based feedback was collected, and participants experimented with advanced mechanisms such as eye trackers.
- The **Multimedia Track** [42] (2005-2007) focused on using the structure of XML documents to extract, relate, and combine the relevance of different multimedia fragments. In addition to the Wikipedia collection from the Adhoc Track, it used a collection of Wikipedia images and their meta information (such as brief descriptions and authors), providing classifications and features for each image. Topics included multimedia information needs such as finding similar images, and results for such topics were either images or XML fragments. The track moved to ImageCLEF in 2008 [41].
- The **XML Mining Track**[43] (2005-2010) aimed at identifying key problems and challenges of the field of mining semistructured documents, focusing on generic tasks such as classification and clustering.
- The **Use Case Track** (2006) aimed at identifying the potential users, scenarios and use-cases of XML retrieval systems.

- The **XML Entity Ranking Track** [6] (2007-2009) focused on typed search tasks that require retrieving lists of entities instead of plain documents or elements. The track considered the entity ranking and list completion subtasks, where in the latter, each topic includes a set of example entities, and for both tasks, one or more target types (i.e., Wikipedia categories) of the results is provided.
- The **Link The Wiki Track** [38] (2007-2010) considered the problem of automatically discovering inter-document links. In the first years, Wikipedia documents stripped from their links were used, with the already existing links as ground truth. Eventually, participants developed algorithms that detected more than 80% of the links. In the last year of the track, the Te Ara collection was used, an unlinked document collection with a different structure than Wikipedia, and the participating systems were much less effective.
- The **(Social) Book Search Track** [24] (2007-) initially aimed at investigating book-specific relevance ranking strategies, user-interface issues and user behavior, exploiting special features, such as back of book indexes provided by authors, and linking to associated meta data like catalog information from libraries [18]. More recently, the track also included user-generated content associated to books from LibraryThing and book meta data from Amazon. The Social Book Search task evaluates the value of professional meta data and user-generated content for book search. In the Prove It task, systems must find relevant book parts that confirm or refute a factual claim. A third task, Structure Extraction, runs as a competition at ICDAR 2013[2].
- The **Efficiency Track** (2008-2010) aimed at a joint evaluation of both the effectiveness and efficiency of XML retrieval systems, focusing on real data and real queries. Using the existing INEX Adhoc collections, the track considered complex queries such as expanded queries and queries with a deeply nested structure, provided both in NEXI and XPath Full Text. It turned out especially in 2010, the last year where the track ran, that the available collections are small enough to be indexed in main memory, achieving extremely fast response times while preserving excellent result quality.
- The **Question Answering Track** [33] (2009-2010) aimed to evaluate complex question-answering tasks where answers are short texts generated from the Wikipedia by extraction of relevant short passages and aggregation into a coherent summary. In such a task, Question-answering, XML/passage retrieval and automatic summarization are combined in order to get closer to real information needs. The track evolved into the Tweet Contextualization Track.
- The **Web Service Discovery Track** [36] (2010) investigated techniques for discovering Web services based on searching service descriptions provided in Web Services Description Language (WSDL). The main outcome of the track was a test collection that allows future comparative experiments.
- The **Data-Centric Track** [45] (2010-2011) considered focused retrieval within highly structured XML collections, using an XMLified version of the

---

[2] https://doucet.users.greyc.fr/StructureExtraction/2013/

Internet Movie Database IMDB as document collection. In addition to the standard adhoc task, the track introduced a faceted search task where facet-value should be recommended to guide the user through a large set of query results. The track has evolved into the Linked Data Track.

– The **Snippet Retrieval Track** [37] (2011-) aims at providing a common forum for the evaluation of the effectiveness of snippets, i.e., a text fragment provided to help the user decide whether or not the result is relevant, and to investigate how best to generate informative snippets for search results.

– The **Tweet Contextualization Track** [34] (2011-), as an immediate off-spring of the Question Answering Track, considers contextualizing tweets using a recent cleaned dump of the Wikipedia. This means that a system must provide some context, which are fragments from Wikipedia pages, about the subject of a tweet.

– The **Linked Data Track** [44] (2012-) aims at investigating retrieval techniques over a combination of textual and highly structured data, where rich textual contents from Wikipedia articles serve as the basis for retrieval and ranking, while additional RDF properties carry key information about semantic relations among entities that cannot be captured by keywords alone. In addition to the Adhoc and Faceted tasks taken over from the Data Centric track, its Jeopardy track provides complex queries in SPARQL and natural language that should return entities (in the form of Wikipedia pages or URIs) as results.

4   INEX AdHoc Track

As mentioned before, the Adhoc Track [2] has been the main track at INEX over many years, and some of the major insights within INEX have been made in this track. We will now discuss this track in detail, starting with its document collections over the different tasks, topic development, assessment of results, and metrics uses to evaluate result quality.

4.1   Document Collections

The AdHoc track used different collections of structured text documents represented as XML. The different collections varied in the richness of their element structure, their topical diversity, and their size.

IEEE articles (2002-2005). In the first year of INEX, it was difficult to find an XML collection that was both interesting and had rich structure. Eventually, a collection of 12,227 XML articles from IEEE journals could be obtained with permission from IEEE, which was extended to 16,000 articles in 2005. Since that collection was derived from an SGML version, its element structure was limited to meta information about the article and information about document structure such as sections, paragraphs, lists, figures, and citations. As an additional complication, the tags were not self-explaining, making it challenging to invent useful queries that exploit the structure. Figure 3 shows the skeleton of such an article, with its clear separation into front matter (fm, including article title and author name), body (bdy, including the actual article content), and bottom matter (bm, including the bibliography).

```
<article>
  <fm>
    <ti>IEEE Transactions on ...</ti>
    <atl>Construction of ...</atl>
    <au>
      <fnm>John</fnm>
      <snm>Smith</snm>
      <aff>University of ...</aff>
    </au>
  </fm>
  <bdy>
    <sec>
      <st>...</st>
      <ss1>...</ss1>
      <ss1>...</ss1>
    </sec>
  </bdy>
  <bm>
    <bib>
      <bb>
        <au>...</au><ti>...</ti>
      </bb>
    </bib>
  </bm>
</article>
```

Fig. 3. Structure of INEX IEEE article

Wikipedia articles with simple XML markup (2006-2008). As the topical focus of the IEEE collection was rather narrow (namely scientific articles about computer science), finding reasonable topic and, even more, assessing the quality of a result was difficult. Starting from 2006, a broader collection was used that was derived from Wikipedia; for details, see [7]. Figure 2 shows a skeleton of an article from that collection. At its core, the collection had a very similar structure to the IEEE collection, so finding useful structured queries was still difficult. However, as the collection was now much more diverse in topic, finding good topics and assessing results was much easier now.

Wikipedia articles with simple XML markup and semantic annotations (2009-2011). As a final enrichment on the structural side, the new collection in 2009 introduced semantic markup. Based on Wikipedia and providing a similar article structure as the previous collection, articles and outgoing links were now annotated with categories from YAGO, enabling to formulate semantically rich queries such as 'articles about musicians where a war is mentioned'.

Details on the collection can be found in [35]. Figure 4 shows an excerpt of the article on the band 'Queen', which is annotated as a group and as an artist (as tags right after the top-level tag `article`). Additionally, the outgoing link to 'United Kingdom' is annotated as country, with the meaning that the target of this link belongs to the category country. Additional rich semantic tags were derived from infoboxes in Wikipedia (such as the `infobox_band` element in the example), which often provide useful information together with a meaningful tag (such as `band_name` in the example).

```
<article>
  <group confidence="1.0" wordnetid="26729"
        source="categories">
    <artist confidence="0.75" wordnetid="9187509">
      <header>
        <title>Queen (band)</title>
        <id>42010</id>
        ...
      <Infobox_band>
        <band_name>Queen</band_name>
        <years_active>1971 - Present</years_active>
        <status>Active</status>
        <country confidence="1.0" wordnetid="8023668">
          <link xlink:href="../Un/United+Kingdom.xml"
                xlink:type="simple">
          United Kingdom
          </link>
        </country>
      </Infobox_band>
  ...
```

Fig. 4. Structure of an INEX Wikipedia article with semantic markup

4.2 Topics

The INEX Adhoc Track compares system performance with a set of topics, where each topic specifies an information need. As most other INEX tracks and unlike TREC, the topics are proposed by participants, who also assess the retrieved results for 'their' topics for relevance (see later); topics are therefore very diverse in nature. Each topic includes a natural-language explanation of the underlying information need (the so-called *narrative*) and a number of other representations that are used by the participating systems to compute results for the topic.

Over the years, the Adhoc track has used a number of different topic types that vary in the structural hints they provide. *Content-only* (CO) topics provide only a keyword-style query, possibly with phrases and negative terms that should not appear in results; this query representation would be used by structure-oblivious systems that consider only the text of elements, not their tags or their nesting. *Content-and-Structure* (CAS) topics provide a structured query that include both structural and content conditions. In the early years of the track, the query specification was rather adhoc and did not use any established query language; Figure 5 shows an early CAS topic. Here, the `title` element provides both the anticipated tag of result elements (in the `te` tag, in the example results should have tag `article`) and conditions for so-called `support elements`, i.e., conditions on descending elements of the result element. In the example, the first such constraint specifies that there should be a section in the body of the document (`ce`) that is 'about' *non-monotonic reasoning* (`cw`), which is not considered a strict, DB-style constraint, but a hint towards relevant results. Similarly, it is possible to specify that an element should not be about something (such as 'calendar'), that an element's value should be from a numeric range (such as '1999-2000'), or that the complete result element should be about something (such as 'belief revision' in the example).

```
<INEX-Topic topic-id="09" query-type="CAS" ct-no="048">
  <Title>
    <te>article</te>
    <cw>non-monotonic reasoning</cw> <ce>bdy/sec</ce>
    <cw>1999 2000</cw> <ce>hdr//yr</ce>
    <cw>-calendar</cw> <ce>tig/atl</ce>
    <cw>belief revision</cw>
  </Title>
  <Description>
    Retrieve all articles from the years 1999-2000 that deal with
    works on nonmonotonic reasoning. Do not retrieve articles that
    are calendar/call for papers.
  </Description>
  <Narrative>
    Retrieve all articles from the years 1999-2000 that deal with
    works on nonmonotonic reasoning. Do not retrieve articles that
    are calendar/call for papers.
  </Narrative>
  <Keywords>
    non-monotonic reasoning belief revision
  </Keywords>
</INEX-Topic>
```

Fig. 5. Example for INEX CAS topic

In later years, topics included both content-only and content-and-structure query specifications, allowing to compare the effectiveness of the two query types (so-called *CO+S* topics). At the same time, the nonstandard format for CAS topics was changed, replacing the target and support elements with a query in the novel NEXI query language. NEXI [40] (for Narrowed Extended XPath I) is a subset of XPath that was extended by IR-style content conditions. The restriction was necessary as it turned out that full-fledged XPath queries were error-prone and, at the same time, not required to specify most reasonable structured queries on the existing collections. NEXI allows only the following two templates for structural queries: //A[B] (i.e., retrieve elements with tag A that satisfy condition B) and //A[B]//C[D] (i.e., retrieve elements with tag C that satisfy condition D and that are descendents of elements with tag A that satisfy condition B). Instead of a tag name, the wild card *can be used to match any element, and a disjunction of tag names is possible (going beyond XPath). Each condition is of the form about(path,text), where path is an XPath path with only the descendants-or-self or self axes, and text is a content condition; the intended semantics is that the element pointed to by path should satisfy the content condition in text. In addition to content conditions, it is possible to compare element values to numerical constants.

```
//article[(.//fm//yr = 2000 OR .//fm//yr = 1999)
        AND about(., "intelligent transportation")]
//sec[about(., automation +vehicle)]
```

Fig. 6. Example NEXI query

Figure 6 shows an example NEXI query, which asks for sections about 'automation vehicle' within articles about 'intelligent transportation' from the years 1999 or 2000.

Even though INEX has been a benchmark with an IR focus, many participants were from the DB community, so the exact semantics of especially CAS queries was heavily debated. In a DB interpretation, the CAS (or NEXI) query was a strict specification that each relevant result element must satisfy. In an IR interpretation, the query was merely a hint how relevant results could look like, and a relevant element had neither to match the requested target element nor satisfy any of the constraints on support elements. For the example query in Figure 6, the DB interpretation (also known as *SCAS* for strict CAS) would therefore allow only sec elements to be relevant, whereas the IR interpretation (also known as *VCAS* for vague CAS) also allowed elements with tag article or paragraph (or any others) to be relevant.

4.3   Tasks

The Adhoc track considered a number of tasks, each corresponding roughly to a use case. In the *Thorough task*, a participating system should find all (or, actually, the 1500 most) relevant elements in the collection and rank them by estimated relevance. Since the results will contain a lot of overlapping elements, the computed result list for a topic will not be immediately useful for a human user, so this task is seen as a system-oriented task that compares 'raw performance' of the systems.

As a more user-oriented task, the *Focused task* aims at finding all relevant information without any overlapping results, again ranked by estimated relevance. This means that if an article element was returned as a result, a contained section must not be returned since it contains the same textual information that is already contained in the already retrieved article element. While it is trivial to convert a result list from the Thorough track into one for the Focused track by removing any subsequent descendant of any element already retrieved, it is not clear that this yields the best possible result; for example, retrieving two section elements of a document could be 'better' than retrieving the full article, which may contain additional non-relevant material. We will soon discuss evaluation metrics for this task.

The *Relevant-in-context* task considers how a specific way how results should be presented to a user. Since a list of (unrelated) elements may not be easy to digest, in this task, systems should first retrieve the best *documents* for a topic, and then, within each document, retrieve the best non-overlapping *elements*. It is therefore a combination of a standard document retrieval task with an intra-document focused task. A resulting document could be shown to a user with the content of the relevant document highlighted, making it easy to find relevant material. As a natural companion task, the *Best-in-context* task asked for the best element in a (possibly long) document to start reading when information regarding a topic is wanted. In a search application, the user would be directly pointed at this position when a result document is shown.

4.4   Assessments

For each topic and each task, a system retrieves a list of result elements (thorough and focused), a list of elements grouped by document and ordered by estimated document relevance (relevant-in-context), or a list of entry elements (best-in-context). To quantify the quality of these results, it is first necessary to assess if each of these results is truly relevant, which must be done by human assessors. At INEX (and unlike TREC), the participating groups and not external experts perform the assessment. Since it is impossible to assess each and every result element retrieved by any system (or even every element in the whole collection), INEX follows the usual TREC-style pooling of results: From the submitted results for a topic, the top result documents from each group are added to the pool in a round-robin fashion until the size of the pool is reached, which is usually between 500 and 750, and the retrieved elements (and possibly other elements in these documents) were then assessed for their relevance.

Since the relevance of an element depends on the relevance of its ancestor and descendant elements, INEX has considered a number of complex ways to express how relevant an element is. Initially, each element was assessed for its exhaustivity and specificity regarding the topic. Here, *exhaustivity* (E) describes the extent to which the document component discusses the topic of request, and *specificity* (S) describes the extent to which the document component focuses on the topic of request. Both of these dimensions were measured on a four-point scale, ranging from 0 (not exhaustive/not specific) to 4 (very exhaustive/very specific). During the assessment procedure, the assessor had to give, for each element in the pool, its exhaustivity and specificity. As this required a very careful inspection of each element in isolation, the assessment procedure was very time-consuming, and the assessment of a single pool could easily take a week. As an additional complication, the exhaustiveness of an element could not be lower than the exhaustiveness of any of its descendants, since it contains all the content of its descendants; it could also not be more specific than any of its descendants. This led to many inconsistent assessments, even though obvious errors were caught already during assessment (such as decreasing exhaustivity when moving to parent elements).

A major milestone for improving assessment quality was the introduction of highlighting relevant text. Instead of considering each element of a document in isolation, the assessor now had to read the document once (without considering element boundaries) and highlight any text relevant to the original topic (as given in the narrative). As the same time, the relevance of an element was solely determined by its specificity, which was derived from the fraction of the element's content that was highlighted. This changed drastically reduced the work for assessing a result pool to a few hours per topic (on average one minute per document, and much quicker for documents that were obviously off-topic). As another consequence, assessments were now much more consistent across elements of the same document.

The various assessment methods are analyzed and compared in detail by Piwowarski et al. [32]. Even with the new assessment tool, the effort to collect enough assessments is still non-negligible. People have attempted to reduce assessment effort by reducing pool size [28] or carefully selecting documents to assess [8]. This is especially important when assessments are done using a crowdsourcing platform such as Amazon Mechanical Turk or Crowdflower, which has been done for a number of INEX tracks [20,44].

4.5   Evaluation Metrics

A core building block of any test collection are metrics to evaluate the quality of results retrieved for a specific task. INEX initially adopted established metrics from the document IR world, considering elements instead of documents. This first required to map the two-level relevance measure (exhaustivity and specificity) to a single numerical value between 0 and 1 that expresses the user-determined level of relevance of an element; this procedure is called *quantization* at INEX. Quantizations that were used until INEX 2002 included *strict* where an element was considered relevant (1) if and only if it was assigned the maximal values for both exhaustiveness and specificity; *generalized* where a graded relevance value was assigned; and other quantizations that put more focus on either specificity or exhaustiveness.

Given such a quantization, it is possible to apply any document-level relevance measure that can deal with non-binary relevance judgements. In its first years, INEX applied a recall-based evaluation for the Thorough task and considered average precision of results at 101 recall points (from 0.0 to 1.0), using the mean over all topics as the overall performance measure.

$$P(rel|retr)(x) := \frac{x \cdot n}{x \cdot n + esl_{x \cdot n}}$$

where x is a recall point $0, 0.01, \ldots, 1$ (i.e., point in the run where fraction x of relevant elements are found), n is the number of relevant elements for this topic in the collection, and $esl_{x \times n}$ is the expected search length (number of non-relevant elements at recall x, which needs special considerations if the ranking includes ties).

A number of other metrics were proposed for the Thorough task. We will now consider the xCG (extended cumulative gain) metric [21] introduced for INEX 2006. This compares the results retrieved by a system to an ideal result list formed by all relevant elements for a topic ordered in descending order of their quantization Q. Given a result list, the extended cumulated gain (xCG) at rank i can the be computed as follows

$$xCG[i] := \sum_{j=1}^{i} xG[i]$$

$$xG[i] := Q(result(i))$$

Similarly, the extended cumulative gain xCI of the ideal result list can be computed. The normalized xCG of the result list at rank i is then the ratio of its xCG value to that of the ideal result list:

$$nxCG[i] := \frac{xCG[i]}{xCI[i]}$$

Both metrics discussed so far were used in the Thorough task and can therefore not deal with overlapping results, i.e., elements in the result list where one is a descendant of the other. If a result list first includes a complete article, retrieving a section or paragraph from that same article later will not be useful for the user since it does not retrieve new information. However, the metrics we considered so far required that any element containing relevant content must be retrieved, irrespective of any overlap. More advanced metrics that focus on the focused retrieval task aim at eliminating this disadvantage (see, for example, [22]).

Around 2007, some years after the insight that overlap must be considered explicitly, another major insight was made: Allowing only elements as results is too restrictive since element boundaries are arbitrary and relevant content (aka highlighted text) often appears independently of element boundaries. As a natural consequence, the tasks were changed to retrieve text passages instead of elements, using the XML structure of the document only as a hint for the result granularity.

The evaluation metrics for the 2007 Focused task were therefore based on the retrieved relevant text, not the retrieved elements. For a result p, let $size(p)$ denote the number of characters in p and $rsize(p)$ the number of yet unseen relevant characters in p. The rank-based measures precision P and recall R can be defined as follows in this context:

$$P[r] := \frac{\sum_{i=1}^{r} rsize(p_i)}{\sum_{i=1}^{r} size(p)}$$

$$R[r] := \frac{\sum_{i=1}^{r} rsize(p_i)}{TRel(q)}$$

where $TRel(q)$ is the number of relevant characters for q.

Since 2007, the main evaluation metric for the Focused task has been interpolated precision [17].

5 Conclusions

The INEX initiative has improved the state-of-the-art of evaluating semistructured retrieval since its beginning in 2002. It brought a rich collection of test collections to use, with a variety of document collections and a large number of tracks making use of them. The Adhoc track, the main track at INEX for ten years, has led to a good understanding how to evaluate adhoc search tasks on document-centric XML. The track brought two main insights: First, the advantage of structured queries over content-only queries depends on both the collection and the information need, and the improvement of result quality—if any—is often not very big [39]. Second, focused retrieval (aka retrieving elements or other fragments of documents) is often not better than document (aka article-level) retrieval. Both insights were surprising, but are backed by a large number of independent experiments by different groups with different retrieval approaches.

INEX has mostly focused on document-centric XML and barely touched data-centric documents, with the recent data-centric track, and is currently actively expanding towards other semistructured data formats such as RDF. Defining good benchmarks for such collections is still largely unexplored. Consequently, even though a large body of work exist that consider keyword-based retrieval from data-centric XML, relational tables, or RDF collections, there is no established standard for evaluating their result quality, making it impossible to compare different approaches. This is a wide area where initiatives such as INEX, but also other upcoming initiatives such as the Semantic Search Challenge[3] or QALD[4] are urgently needed to provide a solid ground for system comparisons.

References

1. Amer-Yahia, S., Lalmas, M.: XML search: languages, INEX and scoring. SIGMOD Record 35(4), 16–23 (2006)
2. Arvola, P., Geva, S., Kamps, J., Schenkel, R., Trotman, A., Vainio, J.: Overview of the INEX 2010 ad hoc track. In: Geva, et al. (eds.) [14], pp. 1–32 (2010)
3. Arvola, P., Kekäläinen, J., Junkkari, M.: Expected reading effort in focused retrieval evaluation. Inf. Retr. 13(5), 460–484 (2010)
4. Case, P., Dyck, M., Holstege, M., Amer-Yahia, S., Botev, C., Buxton, S., Doerre, J., Melton, J., Rys, M., Shanmugasundaram, J.: XQuery and XPath full text 1.0 (2011), http://www.w3.org/TR/xpath-full-text-10/

---

[3] http://semsearch.yahoo.com/

[4] http://greententacle.techfak.uni-bielefeld.de/~cunger/qald/

5. Chappell, T., Geva, S.: Overview of the INEX 2012 relevance feedback track. In: Forner, et al. (eds.) [9] (2012)
6. Demartini, G., Iofciu, T., de Vries, A.P.: Overview of the INEX 2009 entity ranking track. In: Geva, S., Kamps, J., Trotman, A. (eds.) INEX 2009. LNCS, vol. 6203, pp. 254–264. Springer, Heidelberg (2010)
7. Denoyer, L., Gallinari, P.: The Wikipedia XML corpus. In: Fuhr, et al. (eds.) [12], pp. 12–19
8. Fetahu, B., Schenkel, R.: Retrieval evaluation on focused tasks. In: Hersh, W.R., Callan, J., Maarek, Y., Sanderson, M. (eds.) SIGIR, pp. 1135–1136. ACM (2012)
9. Forner, P., Karlgren, J., Womser-Hacker, C. (eds.): CLEF 2012 Evaluation Labs and Workshop, Online Working Notes, Rome, Italy September 17-20 (2012)
10. Frommholz, I., Larson, R.R.: The heterogeneous collection track at INEX 2006. In: Fuhr, et al. (eds.) [12], pp. 312–317
11. Fuhr, N., Kamps, J., Lalmas, M., Trotman, A. (eds.): INEX 2007. LNCS, vol. 4862. Springer, Heidelberg (2008)
12. Fuhr, N., Lalmas, M., Trotman, A. (eds.): INEX 2006. LNCS, vol. 4518. Springer, Heidelberg (2007)
13. (Sandy) Gao, S., Sperberg-McQueen, C.M., Thompson, H.S.: W3C XML schema definition language (XSD) 1.1 part 1: Structures (2012), http://www.w3.org/TR/xmlschema11-1/
14. Geva, S., Kamps, J., Schenkel, R., Trotman, A. (eds.): INEX 2010. LNCS, vol. 6932. Springer, Heidelberg (2011)
15. Gövert, N., Fuhr, N., Lalmas, M., Kazai, G.: Evaluating the effectiveness of content-oriented XML retrieval methods. Inf. Retr. 9(6), 699–722 (2006)
16. Kamps, J., Lalmas, M., Larsen, B.: Evaluation in context. In: Agosti, M., Borbinha, J., Kapidakis, S., Papatheodorou, C., Tsakonas, G. (eds.) ECDL 2009. LNCS, vol. 5714, pp. 339–351. Springer, Heidelberg (2009)
17. Kamps, J., Pehcevski, J., Kazai, G., Lalmas, M., Robertson, S.: INEX 2007 evaluation measures. In: Fuhr, et al. (eds.) [11], pp. 24–33 (2007)
18. Kazai, G., Doucet, A.: Overview of the INEX 2007 book search track (Book-Search'07). In: Fuhr, et al., [11], pp. 148–161
19. Kazai, G., Gövert, N., Lalmas, M., Fuhr, N.: The INEX evaluation initiative. In: Blanken, H.M., Grabs, T., Schek, H.-J., Schenkel, R., Weikum, G. (eds.) Intelligent Search on XML Data. LNCS, vol. 2818, pp. 279–293. Springer, Heidelberg (2003)
20. Kazai, G., Kamps, J., Koolen, M., Milic-Frayling, N.: Crowdsourcing for book search evaluation: impact of hit design on comparative system ranking. In: Ma, W.-Y., Nie, J.-Y., Baeza-Yates, R.A., Chua, T.-S., Bruce Croft, W. (eds.) SIGIR, pp. 205–214. ACM (2011)
21. Kazai, G., Lalmas, M.: extended cumulated gain measures for the evaluation of content-oriented XML retrieval. ACM Trans. Inf. Syst. 24(4), 503–542 (2006)
22. Kazai, G., Lalmas, M., de Vries, A.P.: The overlap problem in content-oriented XML retrieval evaluation. In: Sanderson, M., Järvelin, K., Allan, J., Bruza, P. (eds.) SIGIR, pp. 72–79. ACM (2004)
23. Kazai, G., Lalmas, M., Fuhr, N., Gövert, N.: A report on the first year of the INitiative for the Evaluation of XML retrieval. JASIST 55(6), 551–556 (2004)
24. Koolen, M., Kazai, G., Kamps, J., Preminger, M., Doucet, A., Landoni, M.: Overview of the INEX 2012 social book search track. In: Forner, et al. (eds.) [9]
25. Lalmas, M., Tombros, A.: Evaluating XML retrieval effectiveness at INEX. SIGIR Forum 41(1), 40–57 (2007)

26. Nordlie, R., Pharo, N.: Seven years of INEX interactive retrieval experiments – lessons and challenges. In: Catarci, T., Forner, P., Hiemstra, D., Peñas, A., Santucci, G. (eds.) CLEF 2012. LNCS, vol. 7488, pp. 13–23. Springer, Heidelberg (2012)
27. O'Keefe, R.A., Trotman, A.: The simplest query language that could possibly work. In: Proceedings of the 2nd INEX Workshop, pp. 167–174 (2003)
28. Pal, S., Mitra, M., Kamps, J.: Evaluation effort, reliability and reusability in XML retrieval. JASIST 62(2), 375–394 (2011)
29. Pehcevski, J., Piwowarski, B.: Evaluation metrics for structured text retrieval. In: Liu, L., Tamer Özsu, M. (eds.) Encyclopedia of Database Systems, pp. 1015–1024. Springer US (2009)
30. Peterson, D., (Sandy) Gao, S., Malhotra, A., Sperberg-McQueen, C.M., Henry, S. Thompson. W3C XML schema definition language (XSD) 1.1 part 2: Datatypes (2012), http://www.w3.org/TR/xmlschema11-2/
31. Piwowarski, B.: EPRUM metrics and INEX 2005. In: Fuhr, N., Lalmas, M., Malik, S., Kazai, G. (eds.) INEX 2005. LNCS, vol. 3977, pp. 30–42. Springer, Heidelberg (2006)
32. Piwowarski, B., Trotman, A., Lalmas, M.: Sound and complete relevance assessment for XML retrieval. ACM Trans. Inf. Syst. 27(1) (2008)
33. SanJuan, E., Bellot, P., Moriceau, V., Tannier, X.: Overview of the INEX 2010 question answering track (QA@INEX). In: Geva et al. (eds.)[14,] pp. 269–281 (2010)
34. SanJuan, E., Moriceau, V., Tannier, X., Bellot, P., Mothe, J.: Overview of the INEX 2012 tweet contextualization track. In: Forner, et al. (eds.) [9]
35. Schenkel, R., Suchanek, F.M., Kasneci, G.: YAWN: A semantically annotated Wikipedia XML corpus. In: Kemper, A., Schöning, H., Rose, T., Jarke, M., Seidl, T., Quix, C., Brochhaus, C. (eds.) BTW. LNI, vol. 103, pp. 277–291. GI (2007)
36. Thom, J.A., Wu, C.: Overview of the INEX 2010 web service discovery track. In: Geva, et al. (eds.) [14], pp. 332–335
37. Trappett, M., Geva, S., Trotman, A., Scholer, F., Sanderson, M.: Overview of the INEX 2012 snippet retrieval track. In: Forner, et al. (eds.) [9]
38. Trotman, A., Alexander, D., Geva, S.: Overview of the INEX 2010 link the wiki track. In: Geva, et al. (eds.) [14], pp. 241–249
39. Trotman, A., Lalmas, M.: Why structural hints in queries do not help XML-retrieval. In: Efthimiadis, E.N., Dumais, S.T., Hawking, D., Järvelin, K. (eds.) SIGIR, pp. 711–712. ACM (2006)
40. Trotman, A., Sigurbjörnsson, B.: Narrowed Extended XPath I (NEXI). In: Fuhr, N., Lalmas, M., Malik, S., Szlávik, Z. (eds.) INEX 2004. LNCS, vol. 3493, pp. 16–40. Springer, Heidelberg (2005)
41. Tsikrika, T., Kludas, J.: Overview of the WikipediaMM Task at ImageCLEF 2008. In: Peters, C., et al. (eds.) CLEF 2008. LNCS, vol. 5706, pp. 539–550. Springer, Heidelberg (2009)
42. Tsikrika, T., Westerveld, T.: The INEX 2007 multimedia track. In: Fuhr, et al. (eds.) [11], pp. 440–453
43. De Vries, C.M., Nayak, R., Kutty, S., Geva, S., Tagarelli, A.: Overview of the INEX 2010 XML mining track: Clustering and classification of XML documents. In: Geva, et al. (eds.) [14], pp. 363–376
44. Wang, Q., Kamps, J., Camps, G.R., Marx, M., Schuth, A., Theobald, M., Gurajada, S., Mishra, A.: Overview of the INEX 2012 linked data track. In: Forner, et al. (eds.) [9]
45. Wang, Q., Ramírez, G., Marx, M., Theobald, M., Kamps, J.: Overview of the INEX 2011 data-centric track. In: Geva, S., Kamps, J., Schenkel, R. (eds.) INEX 2011. LNCS, vol. 7424, pp. 118–137. Springer, Heidelberg (2012)

Evaluation with Respect to Usefulness
Some Perspectives from Industry

Omar Alonso

Microsoft Corp.
1065 La Avenida, Mountain View, California, USA
omar.alonso@microsoft.com

Abstract. Commercial web search engines are used by millions of users across the globe on a daily basis to assist their information needs. A user enters a query in the search box and expects the search engine to return relevant search results. Evaluating the quality of search results is a very important aspect in the development and maintenance of those systems. In this paper we describe some of the current approaches for assessing quality in an industrial setting.

1 Introduction

Search engines are one of the most widely used systems on the web. The interface for a commercial search engine like Bing or Google is very simple. The user enters a few keywords in the input box and the system returns a search engine result page (SERP) that contains a list of web pages ranked by relevance. The user then clicks the web link that looks most relevant.

From the user's perspective, providing relevant results for any query is an indication of a good service. The user expects the system to interpret the best way possible those input keywords and return the right information back. A search engine that provides high value is the one that offers relevant results with minimum user interaction possible.

Behind the scenes of a search engine, quite a bit of research and development is being spent to make sure that the quality of the search results is always high. Technically, this requires studying and analyzing queries, documents, user interface changes, relevance assessments, and ranking functions.

Relevance is hard to evaluate due to its multidimensional and dynamic nature. In the context of information retrieval (IR), the commonly called Cranfield paradigm is considered to be the "standard" for evaluation ([5], [15]). Cranfield assumes relevance assessments (also called labels or judgments) are provided by experts on the topic. Given a query, the expert judges assess the relevance of a document on a binary or ternary scale. The performance of the retrieval system is then compared against the set of labels produced by the judges.

With the advent of the web, it is now possible to collect user activity data which can be very useful for evaluation purposes. The pre-web Cranfiedl style is still valid and depending on the domain, it may require some modifications.

N. Ferro (Ed.): PROMISE Winter School 2013, LNCS 8173, pp. 182–191, 2014.

Having access to user data and also the ability to require explicit feedback from users is a good combination for conducting relevance evaluation. We identify two types of IR evaluation: *offline* and *online*.

Offline evaluation consists on asking users to explicitly evaluate a system. Offline evaluation has a number of problems. It is expensive and slow to collect and maintain relevance assessments while, at the same time, judges may not agree on the labels. In Section 3, we will see that it is possible to lower the cost and increase the speed using a new approach.

Online evaluation uses data from real users about their interaction with the system. Users have a goal and they work to satisfy an information need. The main challenge is to detect when users are satisfied with the search results.

We intentionally left out the topics of search user interfaces and interactive retrieval. The books by Hearst [6] and Kelly [8] respectively provide in-depth content on the subjects.

This paper is organized as follows. In the next section we describe the types of evaluations that can be done when vast amounts of user data are available, which is the case of a commercial search engine. In Section 3, we examine a new approach based on crowdsourcing for collecting relevance assessments that is useful when there are budget constraints. In Section 4 we illustrate the case of social annotations in search, a feature that requires new evaluation strategies. We finalize by presenting the conclusions.

2   Online Retrieval Evaluation

On a single day, a search engine receives millions of search queries and collects millions of clicks by users. This data called *behavioral* or *online data* consists on queries (timestamp, IP address, etc.), click on results (order, dwell time, etc.), query reformulations, and mouse movement (selection, hover, etc.). This data reflects the behavior of users when they search for information. Using this new information source to understand user intent, activity, and evaluate retrieval performance is a very attractive proposition.

Using online data to enhance search engines is an active area of research that coverages many aspects. Joachims was one of the first to propose experiments that generate unbiased feedback about the quality of two search results [7]. A large scale validation of different techniques with real word data from commercial search engines is presented in [3]. The tutorial by Radlinski and Hofmann provides an excellent introduction to the topic [13].

2.1   Experimental Setup

We assume that we have a new ranking mechanisms and we are interested in comparing its performance against an existing one. We also assume that we do have logging infrastructure to capture and store all the user behavior possible. There are a number of challenges when creating such infrastructure as follows. While we would like to capture user data, we don't want to obstruct the user's task by degrading the performance and usability of the system. User privacy is an important consideration regarding what to store.

The typical examination that we would like to test is very similar to tasting experiments. For example, if the same query is sent to two different search engines A and B, which one performs better? This type of experiments need to be blind so we can capture the correct behavior. With respect to implementation, the user interface has to hide all evidence to avoid any user bias and, at the same time, should have a low usability impact.

In our setup, after the query is sent to both A and B, the returned ranking is mixed. The combined ranking is presented to the user and the links selected (ranked positions) are stored as user data.

2.2 Interleaving

Interleaving algorithms merge two rankings A and B into a single ranking called I, which is presented to the user. When the user clicks on a document in I, the system attributes the selection to A, B, or both. The goal of the technique is to produce a fair attribution with respect to biases in user behavior. By observing the collected data, we can determine user preference for the ranks. There are two main methods for interleaving: *balanced* and *team-draft*.

Balanced Interleaving. The method ensures that any top k results in I always contain the top k_a results from A and the top k_b results from B, where k_a and k_b differ by at most 1. Balanced interleaving means that the ranking I is constructed in a balanced way.

Team-Draft. Following a sports analogy for assigning teams for a match, each document represents a player and the rankings A and B are the preference orders of the two captains. In each round, the captains select their most prefer player that is sill available, add the player to the team and append the player to I. At each round, which captain selects is decided at random.

2.3 Summary

Having access to user data is a huge advantage to understand users better, their needs, and preferences. When developing and implementing ranking algorithms, interleaving techniques are extremely useful for eliciting preference feedback.

However, we need a production system in place and users that perform queries to collect such data. Let's imagine that we have a novel IR technique but we don't have access to click data and we don't have the budget to hire editors. What can we do? How can we test new ideas? How can we assess relevance and evaluate our new idea?

3   The Rise of Crowdsourcing in IR

Crowdsourcing has been adopted by the information retrieval community as a feasible strategy to evaluate retrieval quality and to collect labeled data for machine learning and test collections. While it is possible to use crowdsourcing effectively, implementing this type of new evaluations requires attention and using an ad-hoc approach can led to disastrous results.

Summarizing the state of the art in crowdsourcing is out of the scope for this paper. As further reading, the special issue on crowdsourcing and information retrieval edited by Lease and Yilmaz covers a number of research directions [10]. Alonso and Mizzaro conducted the first study on TREC relevance assessment using a specific crowdsourcing platform [1]. The tutorial on search evaluation and algorithmic search contains a review of the current findings and sheds some light into solutions that integrate crowdsourcing in novel ways [9]. TREC now runs a crowdsourcing task that investigates approaches for gathering high quality judgments [14]. In the rest of this section we present an overview on how to setup evaluation experiments that use crowdsourcing and the potential problems that may arise.

We define *crowdsourcing* as the activity to outsource a task to an undefined, generally large group of people via an open call. This is, as noted by other researchers, similar to the application of open source principles being Wikipedia the most famous example. The concept of *human computation* is centric to any crowdsourcing effort. Human computation is a computation that is performed by a human. An example of human computation is reCAPTCHA, the user-dialogue system that asks users to enter words seen in distorted text images.

3.1 Benefits

Speed and cost are probably the most attractive characteristics for using crowdsourcing in IR. Recruiting human subjects to evaluate the performance of a search system is a slow and expensive process. With crowdsourcing, a single person can run many different experiments at a fraction of the cost.

An advantage of crowdsourcing platforms is that there is no need to setup infrastructure. In contrast to a typical laboratory setting where dedicated machinery is available, crowdsourcing is a cloud-based approach that allows anyone to create an experiment and, at the same time, anyone can perform such task from anywhere on the planet.

In the case of IR, it is very easy to prototype and test new experiments. This agile process allows engineers to introduce experimentation early on in the product life cycle. In other words, implement a component and experiment as you go. For new ideas, this can be very helpful to get early feedback in terms of quality.

However, crowdsourcing is not the panacea so it is important to adjust expectations and use a systematic approach for conducting such experiments. Work quality control along with worker reliability are areas that the experimenter designer needs to keep a closer eye in practice. Crowdsourcing is another data point for data analysis and it should be complementary to other experiments.

Relevance evaluation in an industrial setting is an on-going activity. We can think of search quality evaluation as a *continuous* exercise where different measurement activities are carried on daily.

3.2 Methodological Considerations

While we do not advocate for a specific methodology, it is important to have at least a procedure to develop experiments. There are many characteristics of an experiment that may hurt the outcome. We may want to consider a procedure that takes an incremental approach that allows the designer to measure, evaluate and adjust at each step.

1. Prototype. Implement the experimental design and test the task using an internal team with a small data set. The goal here is to test if the experiment works. Many iterations are expected until the team believes that the experiment is ready.
2. Early stage. Once the prototype is ready, the next step is to test the task with a small data set in a crowdsourcing platform. The goal of this step is to test if the validity of the experiment with the crowd and use the results for calibration purposes and to adjust quality control mechanisms.
3. Repeatable production. If the experiment design works by producing reliable data in the previous step, the final step is to run the tasks continuously by partitioned the data and enhancements with respect to quality control.

Once a procedure is in place, there are a number of aspects that the experimenter designer has to take into account as a whole. As we are about to see, a lot of the implementation work on crowdsourcing solutions requires a multidisciplinary approach when designing experiments.

Asking Questions. Asking the right questions is no trivial matter. The instructions are key for the experiment. Workers may not be IR experts so we should not assume the same understanding in terms of terminology and task familiarity. Showing examples of what is expected helps workers to perform the job better. Having a technical writer that can take a specification provided by the experimenter and translate it into clear and plain English is highly desirable.

User Interface Design. In comparison to in-house editors that work on a specific setting, workers in a crowdsourcing platform have several tasks to choose from. The experiment should be self-contained, with the content well presented along with simple instructions that are clear about the task that needs to be completed. The choice of good fonts, colors, readable text, and layout helps workers on the task. It is recommended that the designer asks for feedback in the form of an open-ended question on the experiment.

Work Quality. Measuring and predicting worker quality is probably one of the most active research topics in crowdsourcing. We outline when to assess work quality and how to measure it. Ideally, we should assess work quality as often as possible. Table 1 shows at what time quality check points for inspection need to be placed. There are different techniques at each check point that have different purposes.

Table 1. When and how to place quality controls

When	How	Purpose
Beforehand	Qualification tests	Screening, selection, recruiting, and training
During	Check at random how workers are performing the task	Calibrate, reward (or penalize), weight
After	Compute accuracy, inter-rater agreement	Filter, calibrate, weight, and retain skilled workers

The most common strategy to measure work quality is to compare the results against a correct answer, usually known as gold set or ground truth. However, there are many scenarios where such correct and trusted data set is not available. Instead, we need to compare performance against other workers working on the same task. Table 2 summarizes the main points.

Table 2. Comparing worker's performance and potential issues

Comparison	How	Issues	Cost vs. benefit
Workers vs experts	Gold set (also known as honey pots, verifiable answers, or trap questions)	Assumes a known answer.	Need to produce known answers, percentage of work spent re-producing them
Workers vs other workers	Consensus, redundant labeling	Difficult to produce a known answer	Percentage of work that is redundant

Inter-Rater Agreement. Measuring the inter-agreement between judges and agreement between judges and the gold set is a good practice to evaluate the reliability of the labels produced by workers. There are a number of statistics which can be used to determine inter-rater reliability. Different statistics are appropriate for different types of measurement. The most used statistics for measuring agreement are Cohen's kappa (2 raters), Fleiss' kappa (n number of raters), and Krippendorff's alpha (n number of raters with missing values). Artstein and Poesio present a detailed discussion on inter-rater agreements [2].

3.3 Summary

There is published research and evidence from the field that show that crowd-sourcing in IR works. Crowdsourcing tasks have a fast turnaround, they are easy to experiment and require a few dollars to test. That said, we have to design the experiments carefully and examine a number of factors before we can consider the task ready for production purposes. In particular, guidelines, task usability, work quality, worker performance, and user feedback.

Now, say that we have a new source and a new idea. How to study relevance in a new domain? How can we evaluate new sources and relevance?

4   Social Relevance

Very recently, social networks such as Twitter and Facebook have become the primary source for consuming information on the Internet. One of the main differentiators of this type of content from traditional information sources available on the web is the fact that these social networks surface individuals' perspectives. The size of a post (a tweet or Facebook update) is smaller than a document or web page and other user activities such a "like" or "re-tweet" signals the importance of the selected content.

The integration of social data into a search engine is an active area of innovation in industry with *social annotation* as an example of such feature. That is, the annotation of web links with information from a social network has been implemented by Bing and Google ([12], [11], and [4]). Social annotations provide a potential number of benefits to the user as follows:

- Discovery of socially vetted recommendations
- Personalized search results
- Connecting to the lives of their friends
- Result diversity
- Emotionally connecting with an otherwise impersonal search engine

There is very little understanding whether these social features are useful or not. Some questions that need to be addressed: are such endorsements from friends more relevant to the user than from acquaintances or coworkers? Are expert opinions or those from friends who live in the vicinity of the restaurant more valuable? Do annotations on irrelevant results amplify their negative perception?

The value of social features for relevance is still an open problem. In this section, we describe how it is possible to evaluate social annotations and the type of experiments that can be constructed. The approach presented is generic enough and it doesn't rely on a specific social network.

4.1   Taxonomy of Social Relevance

We define a social annotation as a tuple, $\{q, u, c, v\}$, consisting of a query q, content u, a social network connection c and the connections interest valence v in the content (e.g., `like`, `dislike`, or `share`).

We are interested in detecting the cues that influence the perceived utility of a social annotation. For that, we provide three main aspects: query, social connection, and content. Query aspects contain query intent and query class. Social connections include circle, affinity, expertise, geographical distance, and interest valence. Finally, content aspects are similar to any traditional query-document relevance assessment task. Figure 1 shows the proposed taxonomy for social relevance.

With a taxonomy in place the next step is to produce an experiment that contains different types of social annotations and assess the value of them.

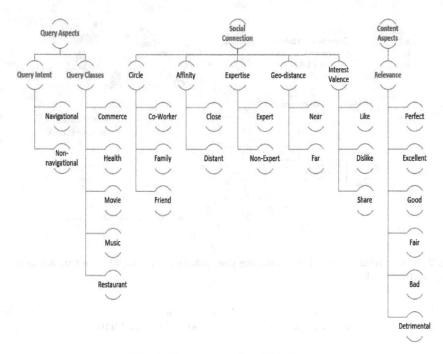

Fig. 1. Taxonomy of social relevance

4.2   Simulation and Experiment Construction

Conducting experiments that require social data present a number of challenges. Deploying experiments over the actual social networks of the participants is preferable, however several problems arise that make this infeasible, most notably privacy concerns. Simulating a social network to gather assessments carries its own risks. Firstly, we expect peoples personal social networks to vary in terms of attribute value distributions as well as diversity distribution. Secondly, the degree of an individual in their social network is significantly larger than the twelve in our virtual network, and also varies significantly

In order not to bias the social annotations to the specific social networks of workers, we simulated a new social network for our judges. We used this network to create the connections c and interest valences v for a set of random queries. The simulated social network consists of twelve connections spanning the social circles and affinities.

Like any evaluation experiment, we sample the search engine logs for queries and social annotations. A social annotation generator takes as input the original annotation (web page title, url, and snippet; no any personal information) in conjunction with the many characteristics of the simulated social network. The generator is template-based so it is also possible to produce different types of user interface treatments. Once the data is ready, the final step is to assess the value of the query-social annotation pair using a graded scale. Figure 2 shows

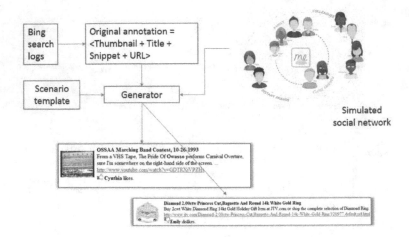

Fig. 2. Experimental setup for evaluating the quality of the social annotations using a simulated network

the process for generating social annotations and how they are presented to the judges. We collect assessments using a crowdsourcing platform.

4.3   Summary

Social features are rapidly evolving in search scenarios. Evaluating the value of social is a challenging problem that requires potential new metrics and creative ways of constructing experiments. We presented a taxonomy of aspects that influence the perceived utility of social annotations in a web search scenario, drawn from the query, social connection, and content relevance. Via a user study that requires a simulated social network, we took a first step at quantifying the utility of social annotations and gained insights on the complex interplay between the social relevance aspects.

5   Concluding Remarks

In this paper we outlined, at a very high level, three approaches for relevance evaluation. The first one, online evaluation, takes advantage of the wealth of click through data available in a search engine for improve retrieval performance. The second, crowdsourcing-based evaluation, is an attractive alternative for lowering the cost of assessment at scale and feasible when there is no online user data available. The third one, a combination of user data, simulation and crowdsourcing, looks prominent when we need to test relevance as usefulness.

There are still many open problems and challenges in retrieval evaluation, in particular with the inclusion of new social data sources as part of search engines.

References

1. Alonso, O., Mizzaro, S.: Using Crowdsourcing for TREC Relevance Assessment. Information Processing and Management 48(6), 1053–1066 (2012)
2. Artstein, R., Poesio, M.: Inter-coder Agreement for Computational Linguistics. Journal of Computational Linguistics 34(4), 555–596 (2008)
3. Chapelle, O., Joachims, T., Radlinski, F., Yue, Y.: Large-scale Validation and Analysis of Interleaved Search Evaluation. ACM Trans. Inf. Syst. 30(1), 6 (2012)
4. Fernquist, J., Chi, E.: Perception and Understanding of Social Annotations in Web Search. In: Proc. of WWW (2013)
5. Harman, D.: Information Retrieval Evaluation. Morgan & Claypool (2011)
6. Hearst, M.: Search User Interfaces. Cambridge University Press (2009)
7. Joachims, J.: Evaluating Retrieval Performance Using Clickthrough Data. In: Text Mining, pp. 79–96 (2003)
8. Kelly, D.: Methods for Evaluating Interactive Information Retrieval Systems With Users. Foundations and Trends in Information Retrieval 3(1-2), 1–224 (2009)
9. Lease, M., Alonso, O.: Crowdsourcing for Search Evaluation and Social-algorithmic Search. In: Proc. of SIGIR (2012)
10. Lease, M., Yilmaz, E.: Crowdsourcing for Information Retrieval: Introduction to the Special Issue. Information Retrieval 16(2) (2013)
11. Muralidharan, A., Gyngyi, Z., Chi, E.: Social Annotations in Web Search. In: Proc. of CHI (2012)
12. Pantel, P., Gamon, M., Alonso, O., Haas, K.: Social Annotations: Utility and Prediction Modeling. In: Proc. of SIGIR (2012)
13. Radlinski, F., Hofmann, K.: Practical Online Retrieval Evaluation. In: Serdyukov, P., Braslavski, P., Kuznetsov, S.O., Kamps, J., Rüger, S., Agichtein, E., Segalovich, I., Yilmaz, E. (eds.) ECIR 2013. LNCS, vol. 7814, pp. 878–881. Springer, Heidelberg (2013)
14. Smucker, M., Kazai, G., Lease, M.: Overview of the TREC 2012 Crowdsourcing Track. In: TREC 2012 (2012)
15. Voorhees, E., Harman, D.: TREC Experiment and Evaluation in Information Retrieval. MIT Press (2005)

Black Box Evaluation for Operational Information Retrieval Applications

Martin Braschler, Melanie Imhof, and Stefan Rietberger

Zurich University of Applied Sciences, Winterthur, Switzerland
{bram,imhf,riet}@zhaw.ch

Abstract. The black box application evaluation methodology described in this tutorial is applicable to a broad range of operational information retrieval (IR) applications. Contrary to popular, traditional IR evaluation approaches that are limited to measure the IR system performance on a test collection, the black box evaluation methodology considers an IR application in its entirety: the underlying system, the corresponding document collection, and its configuration/application layer. A comprehensive set of quality criteria is used to estimate the user's perception of the application. Scores are assigned as a weighted average of results from tests that evaluate individual aspects. The methodology was validated in a small evaluation campaign. An analysis of this campaign shows a correlation between the testers' perception of the applications and the evaluation scores. Moreover, functional weaknesses of the tested IR applications can be identified and then systematically targeted.

Keywords: information retrieval, application evaluation, black box, user perception.

1 Introduction

This tutorial paper explores a method to evaluate the quality of operational information retrieval (IR) applications. For the purpose of this paper, we define an IR application to consist of an IR system, a specific document collection (document base), a business application layer (including front-end), and a configuration set.

Traditionally, IR evaluation has concentrated on measuring the retrieval effectiveness of IR systems. The ranked list retrieved by an IR system is compared to the relevance of each document in a fixed test collection with respect to a query. However, such measurement ignores several important aspects of entire IR applications as defined above, which we expect to (sometimes strongly) affect the user's perception of (and, thus, satisfaction with) the application. For example, the user will not value a high retrieval effectiveness if the responsiveness of the IR system is too low.

The methodology presented herein employs a black box approach. It aims at practitioners, who conduct the evaluation "in the wild"; i.e. on an operational system. We have further explored how to adapt the methodology to different application domains, such as cultural heritage, search for innovation and medical image retrieval.

N. Ferro (Ed.): PROMISE Winter School 2013, LNCS 8173, pp. 192–207, 2014.

Substantial parts of the methodology have been developed as part of the activities of the PROMISE EU FP7 Network of Excellence [1].

By employing this "black box application evaluation", we perform comparative evaluation based on an estimate of user perception. The choice of the notion of "user perception" fits the limitation of only being able to assess aspects of the IR application which typical users can access and experience (due to the black box nature of the approach). More importantly, however, we also feel that the targeted audience of such evaluation results (e.g. corporate decision makers) has an interest in assessing and improving the user perception of these applications.

2   Related Work

The evaluation of IR systems in the narrower sense (systems for ranked retrieval) is a well-researched field, and mature methods are widely employed. To briefly summarize the most important approach, it helps to reflect the basic problem addressed by IR systems. The goal of IR systems is "[...] to retrieve all and only those documents that the inquiring patron wants (or would want)" [2]. This is a difficult problem for a number of reasons. Typically, IR systems allow access to large, potentially heterogeneous, document collections that contain unstructured free-text (or, in the case of multimedia IR systems, non-textual items). The documents are usually written by a range of authors, and can stem from a variety of sources. These authors have considerable freedom in expressing information: there is no set vocabulary, and paraphrasing, metaphors etc. are used. Linguistic phenomena such as homonyms, synonyms, morphology etc. complicate matters further. Users search such a body of documents based on "information needs" - aiming to solve problems for which they are missing information. It would be paradox to expect the users to be able to form perfect queries: they would have to effectively "predict" the formulation used by the author of a matching document. This would require the user to read the document itself – before it was found. As a consequence, an "exact match" strategy (as used in database management systems), whereby the system matches a set of keywords exactly as entered with the documents, is rarely an effective strategy for information retrieval. "Best match" strategies dominate IR approaches, where query terms are weighted, and retrieval scores RSV(q,dj) (the retrieval status value for document j given query q) are calculated. Instead of returning a set of (exactly) matching documents, a ranked list sorted in descending order of the RSV scores is returned. The effectiveness of obtaining these "best matches" (the "retrieval effectiveness") directly depends on the mechanisms employed for processing documents and queries, and for later matching them. These mechanisms have to consider all the phenomena described above. However, further complicating things is a subjective notion of how users would judge the relevance of these partially matching items that are returned by the system. The same document may well be judged as either relevant or irrelevant by different users with respect to the same query, depending on the context, background, or personal preferences.

No retrieval mechanisms can therefore in practice deliver optimal results (i.e. all relevant items, and only relevant items, for all queries). The different popular strategies, such as vector-space retrieval, probabilistic retrieval, language models, etc. present the user with differing results that need to be assessed for effectiveness. It is thus not surprising that evaluation of information retrieval (IR) systems is an extensively researched problem. Starting all the way back in the 1960s the foundation for today's most prominent IR system evaluation methodology ("the Cranfield paradigm") was laid [3]. In a nutshell, the evaluation is conducted in a "lab style" environment, where the documents are fixed (in the form of a "test collection"), and the users are abstracted (in the form of "information needs", which are attributed to those users). To conduct a retrieval experiment using the Cranfield paradigm, queries are derived from the information needs, and then run against an index of the documents. The scalability of this approach is limited directly by the capacity to judge the results – conceptually, every document in the collection has to be assessed for relevance for every query – i.e. an effort of the order number of queries times number of documents[1].

The Cranfield paradigm has been highly successful in driving progress in the academic field of information retrieval, substantially aiding the development of more effective term weighting schemes, stemmer components, indexing pipelines, among others. Catalyst for this has been the formation of large evaluation campaigns that bundle the evaluation efforts of IR academics and system developers worldwide (TREC, CLEF, NTCIR, FIRE, etc.). Despite its success, the paradigm's applicability for evaluation of entire IR applications is limited, since retrieval effectiveness is but one aspect that influences a user's perception of IR applications.

Log file analysis is an alternative strategy to evaluate search engines. Transaction logs collect significant amounts of user behavior such as their clicks and queries. Later the logs are used to evaluate the quality of the search engine [5]. However the users' perception is only deduced from the logs [6].

Two IR applications can be compared using A/B testing, where users are randomly assigned to one of two systems [7]. By analyzing user behavior it can be seen which system is preferred. A very similar evaluation methodology was suggested by Radlinski. Instead of assigning users to one of two search engines, the result lists of both engines are interleaved and presented [8].

User based evaluation aims to measure user perception. Dunlop's evaluation framework accounts for user experience by evaluating surface interactions and system usability [9]. Borlund's work on interactive information retrieval (IIR) describes how to measure IR application performance when considering the humans cognitive perspective [10].

The methodology for "black box application evaluation" discussed in this tutorial paper is partially based on earlier work that is presented in two studies [11; 12]. Those studies describe an evaluation based on a grid of scripted tests in an attempt to identify the state of Swiss and German enterprise Web portal search, and are much

---

[1]   There are encouraging signs that in spite of the subjectivity of relevance, multiple assessments of relevance per document/query pair are not necessary for many evaluation scenarios.[4].

narrower in focus We adapted the main criteria categories from this earlier work, whereas the individual tests themselves were developed from scratch. The previous studies furthermore omit the discussion of different domains and use case scenarios and do not explore the question of the underlying measures in detail, both discussion topics of the present report.

3   Black Box Application Evaluation

The methodology aims to evaluate entire IR applications without any further knowledge of their inner workings or the components employed. This makes the methodology broadly applicable to large range of IR applications. Further, it eases the use of the methodology on live, operational applications, which was an important design goal ("evaluation in the wild"). Specifically, the main guidelines for the evaluation are:

1. The evaluation is performed in a "black box mode", or minimally invasive
2. The evaluation is performed on operational applications ("in the wild")
3. The evaluation is performed in a clearly defined use case domain context

The third guideline determines the applicability of different tests employed during evaluation. Varying influence of different criteria on user perception may make comparison across different use case scenarios difficult. Information retrieval applications for the purpose of this paper are defined to consist of

1. a specific data/document collection
2. an information retrieval (IR) system, and
3. a business application/GUI layer,

as well as the specific configuration of these components. The following figure (figure 1) shows the named components and configuration, highlighting the latter's equal importance to operational performance.

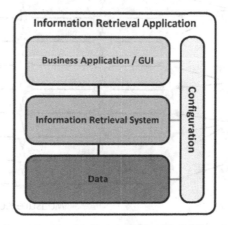

Fig. 1. Information Retrieval Application Model, based on [14]

For the purpose of the black box evaluation, we do not incorporate specific users directly into this model of information retrieval applications. Instead, prototypical users are modeled to the extent as their actions and their preferences are reflected in the criteria that are chosen to be evaluated, influencing the weight that each criterion has on the overall scores.

The modus operandi of the evaluation process is to employ a comprehensive set of all identified "quality" criteria that are believed to be tied to user perception or the user's search experience (at presence, 43 criteria). This is an ambitious goal: it is a large undertaking to identify and define the individual tests, elaborate the correspond-ing testing steps, and assign both scoring procedures and overall weights for later aggregation. Clearly, there is much room for the methodology to develop over time, as new insights are gained into many of the issues addressed by the tests. For the time being, we employ "simple" tests, which we organized hierarchically. For the present iteration of the methodology, the design goal was a maximum number of coarse, or-thogonal tests that should ideally cover most aspects of the IR application that may influence the defined evaluation metric. Note that depending on the use case domains served by an IR application, the resulting hierarchical tree of tests may have to be pruned before evaluation, as a number of tests may not be applicable. The following figure (figure 2) shows a schematic view of the criteria/test hierarchy and applications when set up for an actual evaluation.

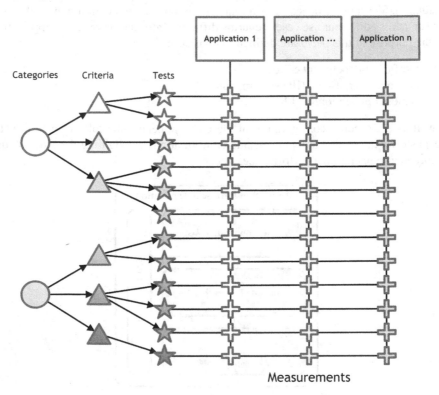

Fig. 2. Evaluation Grid for Multiple Applications

The methodology in its current form groups the criteria and associated tests into four main categories (derived from [12]):

1. **Indexing**: Contains all tests addressing the indexing component of an IR application, specifically how documents are processed and stored to allow later retrieval
2. **Matching**: Contains all tests covering the matching between queries and documents
3. **User Interface**: Contains all tests that address user interface criteria, such as presentation, usability and others
4. **Search Result**: Contains all tests that address the "quality" of search results, such as overall retrieval effectiveness

4 Conducting the Evaluation

The evaluation is conducted according to a test script, containing all necessary information for performing the individual tests. The script contains step-by-step instructions for the tester that are designed to minimize the necessity of testers to resort to "creative" testing, i.e. the outcome of the tests should ideally be as independent as possible from the person of the actual tester. It is a stated goal to automate as many of the tests as possible in the future; however, for the time being, most tests contain steps that require intellectual effort, such as for example the selection of small excerpts from a document. The tests further contain clear definitions as to how to determine if a test can be conducted at all (abort conditions), and if so, how to score its outcomes. The complete reproduction of the test script lies outside of the scope of this paper. However, a comprehensive description of all tests can be found in [1].

To start with the evaluation, the set of tests is determined by pruning the individual tests that do not apply to the use case domain underlying the IR application. There is a field in each test description that gives indications on the applicability of the test to different domains. If the application addresses use case domains not yet considered in the development of the methodology, this step requires more effort. Discussions with domain experts need then be held, to assess the merits of the tests and their likely contributions to the overall user perception. Alternatively, some tests may be adapted to the new use case domain. Next, each test is carried out according to the script. It is important to carefully check the abort conditions given for each test: there are preconditions recorded for the tests which must be met to calculate corresponding scores.

Overall evaluation scores for IR applications are computed based on the aggregated scores of the individual criteria. The weights should be defined in advance based on the practical significance of any criterion in the evaluated application's use case domain. How to weight the individual criteria is still matter of on-going research. For the time being, we resort to uniform weighting across all criteria. Where tests operate on a different level of granularity, multiple, associated tests are bundled, and assigned a weight as a whole. Experience gathered so far seems to indicate that this "coarse" approach works well enough, possibly due to use of a large number of tests (see below for a discussion of the preliminary results of applying the methodology).

The calculated scores lend themselves directly to comparative evaluation of IR applications (or different incarnations of one particular IR application), but by choosing scoring methods that are based on absolute counts, there is a well-defined maximum score, which allows assessment and monitoring of single applications as well. Finally, it is possible to use the methodology in an evaluation campaign style, spanning many different IR applications, restricted by the use case domains that they serve.

5   Individual Tests

This section outlines the test description structure, a list of tests with short summaries and finally, selected examples of criteria and tests for each main category. The full description of all tests can be found in [1]. The individual tests are structured according to a template containing the following main sections (table 1):

Table 1. Test Description Structure

Section	Content
Assumption	Assumptions/preconditions for the tests to be valid. Also, in this field, the expected behavior (attributed to the preferences of the prototypical user) is described
Irregularity	A description of unwanted behavior tied to the test.
Root causes	A description of possible causes for irregularities
Test	Description of the actual step-by-step testing procedure, includes scoring and abort conditions
Use case domain adaption	Any information necessary to decide on adaptions for specific use cases and/or decide on the applicability of a test to a specific use case.

5.1   Criteria List

The following table (table 2) gives a full list of all criteria that have tests currently defined for the black box IR application evaluation methodology. The tests have been compiled in two steps. In a first step four main categories (indexing, matching, user interface and search results) have been adopted, analogous to earlier work [11; 12]. In a second step a board of use case domain stakeholders assembled the quality criteria for their domains. We are confident that this process has given us a reasonable base set of criteria. Most criteria have been included in the test script, with few exceptions, most notably a criterion for the evaluation of informational queries, where no simple mechanism for measurement has been found. We plan to publish the criteria list as a living document where stakeholders from research and industry can participate in order to have a broader basis in the future.

Table 2. Criteria List

Criterion Name	Description
INDEXING	
Completeness	Are all (browsable) documents findable through the search functionality?
Freshness	Are the newest documents findable through the search functionality?
Special Characters	Does the application handle diacritics and special characters correctly?
Tokenization	Are terms and names with complex punctuation and/or hyphenation treated correctly?
Decompounding	Are complex terms (such as used in agglutinative languages) handled correctly?
Named Entities	Are named entities handled and disambiguated correctly?
Stemming	Does the system normalize word forms?
Meta-Data Quality	Are meta data fields correct and complete?
Office Document Handling	Are binary office documents (PDF, Office formats etc.) handled correctly?
Separation of Actual Content and Representation	Are structural elements (such as headers, footers) excluded from searches for document content?
Duplicate (Content) Documents	Are duplicate entries removed from result lists?
MATCHING	
Query Syntax	Does the application offer query operators (e.g. Boolean operators)?
Phrasal Queries	Does the application offer phrasal querying (e.g. by using quotes)?
Over- and under-specified Queries	Are over- and under-specified queries (e.g. too many specific search terms or too few, too broad search terms) handled gracefully?
Feedback	Does the application allow the user to give feedback on a document's relevance, with the search result influenced by such feedback?
Multimedia	Does the application offer search for videos, images or audio content?
Cross-Language Information Retrieval	Does the application allow querying across different languages?
USER INTERFACE	
Performance/Responsiveness	Does the application provide fast response times?
Browsing	Are users able to efficiently navigate (browse) the content without using ad-hoc querying?

Table 2. (*continued*)

Field Search (Facets)	Can search results be filtered by categories?
Query Term Highlighting	Are matching query terms highlighted in documents?
Document Summarization	Are suitable document summarizations („snippets"? presented in the result lists?
Result List Presentation	Is the result list presentation well organized?
Exception Handling	Is the application stable?
Term Suggestions	Does the application provide term suggestions? (potentially for technical terms)
User Guidance	Are users assisted in query formulation?
Related Content	Is content related to searches automatically shown?
Context Information	Is context additional to the search results presented (e.g. derived from corpus statistics etc.)
Personalization	Does the application manage user profiles?
Localization	Is the application adapted to different regional audiences?
Result List Import/Export	Can search results be imported and/or exported?
Sorting of Result List	Can result lists be (re-)sorted according to metadata or other criteria?
Justification of Results	Is there any supplementary information on how results were generated? (explanation of weighting, of matches etc.)
Monitoring	Can long-standing queries be monitored over time?
System Override/User Control	Can features, such as spelling correction, stemming etc. be turned off?
Navigational Aids	Can users navigate between different queries?
Social Aspects	Can search results be shared with other users?
Entertainment/Fun	Is the user experience good?
Mobile Access	Is there a mobile version of the user interface?
SEARCH RESULT	
Navigational Queries	Can users easily locate "entry points" into subsections of the website?
Factual Queries	Can users effectively find factual information?
Known/Suspected Item Retrieval	Can users effectively (re-)find a document in the application that they have accessed before or expect to be present?
Diversity	Are different aspects of ambiguous queries covered in the search results?

It is beyond the scope of this paper to present the full version of the test script, detailing all the tests for the different criteria above. For the complete details, see [1]. We will restrict the discussion to four specific, illustrative examples (one per category) in the following.

We begin with a test designed to evaluate whether the IR application uses domain knowledge to treat named entities (often core business entities) in a special way. This test is filed in category "Indexing". To execute the test, it is required that the tester has gained some knowledge about the underlying application domain in order to identify the named entities. The test is repeated for five named entities to compensate for named entities that are not handled. Resulting scores are in a range of 0 to 5.

Indexing Criterion Example: Named Entities	
Assumption	Users want to search for named entities where the respective entity is very clearly defined within the context of the application. Inability to find documents pertaining to the entities at a high rank in the result list is disruptive to the user experience.
Irregularity	Clearly defined entities from the application context cannot be directly found using their names as a short query.
Root Cause	The document indexing process does not consider named entities and thus tokenizes them in less informative bits.
Test	1. Identify 5 named entities (preferably composed of 2 or more terms) based on the applications context. Usually you are able to deduce these from the content. 　(a) Abort if less than 5 named entities can be found 2. Search for the entities using only their name 3. Score success (0, 1, 2, 3, 4, 5) for each query which returns results that clearly refers to the correct entity, and not to other entities that share parts of the name.
Use Case Domain Adaptations	N/A

The second test we discuss focuses on the issue of over- and underspecified queries. It is filed in category "Matching". The test can be carried out without any knowledge about the application domain or even information retrieval mechanisms. The score consists of two parts. One point each is given for correct handling of over-specified and underspecified queries, respectively. The resulting score for this test is in a range of 0 to 2.

Matching Criterion Example: Over- and Underspecified Queries	
Assumption	Users feel irritated if long queries return very few or no results and short queries return almost the entire collection.
Irregularity	Missing the application's unknown "sweet spot" in terms of query length returns an undesirable number of results. Users receive no indication of what went wrong.
Root Causes	• No user guidance when result set has an unusual number of hits • Matching model punishes verbose descriptions
Test	1. Copy and paste a sentence from any document within the application into a query and add some out-of-context terms 2. Score success (1) if the document can still be found, score failure (0) otherwise 3. Use 2 terms from the application's context as a query, which should return a very large number of results 4. Score success (1) if the application offers suggestions or facilities to improve your search, e.g. further terms, browsing, etc. Score failure (0) otherwise for a total of (0, 1, 2)
Use Case Domain Adaptations	N/A

The criterion on query term highlighting is an example for a set of criteria that test for the presence or absence of features. It is filed under category "User Interface". The test script is easy to follow for a human, but hard to automate since the terms can be highlighted in different ways; e.g. color, bold, italic. The resulting score is either 0 or 1.

User Interface Example: Query Term Highlighting	
Assumption	Highlighted query terms in a result list help users to preliminarily assess the relevance of documents.
Irregularity	Query terms are not highlighted or otherwise marked in the result list.
Root Cause	Feature not implemented
Test	Score success (1) if query terms are marked in any way in the result list. Otherwise score failure (0).
Use Case Domain Adaptations	N/A

Lastly, we discuss a criterion filed under category "Search Result". The criterion on factual queries is not applicable to the search for innovation use case. In that domain querying general facts leads to a lot of results, while querying very specific facts returns the document itself. However the search for a specific document is already covered in the known item retrieval criterion. Resulting scores are in a range of 0 to 5.

Search Result Example: Factual Queries	
Assumption	Users enter queries to find a single fact. A single trustworthy document is sufficient to satisfy the information need.
Irregularity	Factual information cannot be found by suitable queries.
Root Causes	• Freshness and completeness of index are lacking • Bad treatment of binary documents (e.g. PDF) • Missing document summaries or snippets in result list
Test	1. Pick 5 facts from the application's content, examples: (a) Company's year of incorporation (b) Number of branches (c) Revenue (d) CEO (e) Product lines (f) etc. 2. Build short queries for these facts from the context 3. Score success for each query which retrieved the sought for fact in the top 10 results (0, 1, 2, 3, 4, 5)
Use Case Domain Adaptations	Search for Innovation: Criterion not applicable. Cultural Heritage: Criterion not applicable

6   Validation of Methodology

To validate the methodology, a campaign was conducted by the Promise EU FP7 Network of Excellence to evaluate a number of public websites that offer search functionality, and thus qualify for our definition of an IR application. The websites were chosen according to the following criteria:

1. Only publicly accessible web sites were considered
2. The website offers search functionality, and functions as an IR application in the sense of the definition of this paper

3. The website fits one of the following four use case domains: "enterprise/extranet search", "cultural heritage", "search for innovation", "visual clinical support"
4. The website addresses users in one of the countries represented by the PROMISE partners that conducted the tests: Germany, Switzerland, France, Italy and Sweden. Some exceptions were made for websites run by European organizations (mainly in order to get good coverage for the use case domains mentioned above)

In total, 62 websites conformant to the above criteria were evaluated. The time to evaluate a single website was roughly of the order of half a person day, i.e. approximately 4 working hours. In addition to following the test script and recording the respective scores, testers were also asked to record their user experience. They provided a coarse score (0 to 2) for the "fun" they had using the application and a more finely grained score (0 to 10) for their overall user experience. This gives the possibility to correlate this subjective experience by testers with the estimates of user perception calculated through the evaluation methodology. As a working title, the campaign was run jokingly under the title of "guerilla campaign", to express the fact that any website can potentially be a target of this evaluation, with direct involvement by the operators not being necessary.

7   Results and Lessons from Guerrilla Campaign

Aside from validating the feasibility of the evaluation methodology, and giving input for improvements to the test script, the guerrilla campaign also gives insight into the state-of-the-art of public websites in the use case domains covered. Please note that this was not a primary motivation for the campaign, and we did not strive for the necessary "completeness" in the websites covered to get a real "overview of the state of the art". The amount of websites evaluated was strictly limited by the effort that partners had available for validating the methodology itself. Even so, the number of websites is large enough to give interesting insights, and possibly guidance for later applications of the methodology by practitioners.

We present the overall results in the form of a boxplot in figure 3. The aggregated scores are given for the four main categories. For each category, it is therefore possible to read the maximum, minimum and median performance from the graph. To summarize the overall results, we found:

— A high scatter in the results for all the categories. There has been no deep analysis into the cause of this yet, but the websites we have evaluated have certainly shown different degrees of maturity in the search functionalities they offer, which likely is one of the contributing factors.
— The median performance is 0.5 or lower, indicating that a lot of potential for improvement still exists for many of the IR applications we evaluated.
— The category "User Interface" has lowest mean and smallest standard deviation. This is somewhat surprising, given that there are well-known examples from the field of Web search services, which are good blueprints for what users expect from search functionalities today.
— "Search Result" is the only category where the maximum score is reached.

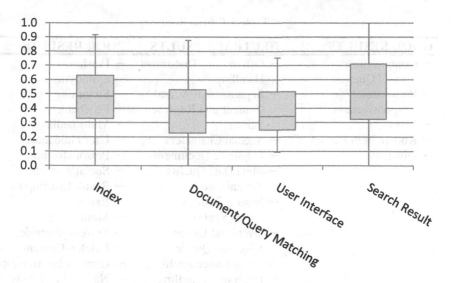

Fig. 3. Overall results from guerrilla campaign

Further exploration shows that no website scored consistently high for all categories. Again, this is testament to the potential for improvement of the underlying IR applications.

We can partition the results for the individual criteria in three groups (see Table 3):

— good results (generally the tests are passed by most of the sites)
— poor results (most of the sites failed these tests)
— neutral (no general tendency, some sites pass, some fail)

Some of the preliminary conclusions we draw from the observations during the guerilla campaign include:

For the category "Indexing", we found applications lacking in terms of "freshness". Operators should pay care to keeping the index fresh, i.e. to choose an appropriate interval for updates. Further, stemming is still not employed in many applications, and can help to boost both retrieval effectiveness and make handling more transparent for users.

For the category "Matching", few applications provide strong functionality for users to give feedback about the search results (and thus, ultimately, influence the search mechanism) – which seems counter to the idea of modern Web services involving the user more deeply. Multimedia retrieval has not found widespread adoption in the applications we tested so far.

For the category "User Interface", we found a lack of functionality for user guidance – i.e. tools such as term suggestion or spell checking components. Across all applications, functionalities that let users benefit from other users (such as display of related content or context information; or provisions for sharing results) are still not widely adopted.

Table 3. Criteria Results

GOOD RESULTS	NEUTRAL RESULTS	POOR RESULTS
– Completeness	– Office Document Handling	– Freshness
– Phrasal Queries		– Synonyms
– Performance/ Responsiveness	– Separation of Actual Content and Represen- tations	– Stemming
– Browsing		– Feedback
– Known Item Retrieval		– Multimedia
– Diversity	– Special Characters	– User Guidance
	– Duplicate Documents	– Personalization
	– Meta Data Quality	– Social Aspects
	– Tokenization	– Result List Import/ Export
	– Named Entities	
	– Query Syntax	– Monitoring
	– Over- and Under Specified Queries	– System Override
		– Related Content
	– Cross-Language IR	– Context Information
	– Exception Handling	– Navigational Aids
	– Result List Presenta- tion	– Mobile Access
		– Geo-Location
	– Entertainment	
	– Localization	
	– Facets	
	– Sorting of Result List	
	– Justification of Results	
	– Navigational Queries	

The scores in the category "Search Result" were overall the best of the main cate-gories. Still, ample opportunities for improvement remain, such as the inclusion of geo-location information into the ranking of results.

When looking at the scores that testers assigned for their subjective experience, we find a correlation of 0.53 between this "user experience" and the overall scores. This is an encouraging indication that scores derived from the evaluation methodology are actually useful estimates of user perception.

8   Outlook / Future Work

There are two logical next steps to improve the presented methodology. First and foremost, the limitations of the methodology should be more closely examined and remedied, if possible. More precisely, the scoring of individual tests is to be re-visited. A scientific rationale for score ranges needs to be elaborated. As it stands, scoring has been designed to be very coarse to facilitate result aggregations and weighting. While the design was shown to be practical in the validation campaign, some tests might benefit from more granular scoring, according to estimated degrees of user satisfaction probabilities. Such estimations can be based in part on our work on best practices for information retrieval applications [11].

Another worthwhile effort is the description of test automation possibilities, including guides as to how automation of individual tests can be achieved. An envisioned result of that effort is a tool suite which can be used to instrument applications and run automated tests, providing an evaluation and monitoring tool for industry practitioners.

Acknowledgements. Most of the work reported in this paper has been supported by the PROMISE network of excellence[2] (contract n. 258191) project as a part of the 7th Framework Program of the European commission (FP7/2007-2013). The authors would like to acknowledge the contributions and support of all the different Promise partners, mainly to use case specific adaptations, criteria selection and conducting the validation of the methodology, among other points. See also [1] for a list of contributors to the methodology. The work is based on two earlier studies on the evaluation of the search functionality of enterprise web portals, see [12] and [13].

References

1. Rietberger, S., Imhof, M., Braschler, M., Berendsen, R., Järvelin, A., Hansen, P., García Seco de Herrera, A., Tsikrika, T., Lupu, M., Petras, V., Gäde, M., Kleineberg, M., Choukri, K.: PROMISE deliverable 4.2: Tutorial on Evaluation in the Wild (2012)
2. Robertson, S.E., Maron, M.E., Cooper, W.S.: Probability of relevance: a unification of two competing models for document retrieval. Info. Tech: R. and.D 1, 1–21 (1982)
3. Cleverdon, C.W.: The Cranfield tests on index language devices (1967)
4. Voorhees, E.M.: The philosophy of information retrieval evaluation. In: Peters, C., Braschler, M., Gonzalo, J., Kluck, M. (eds.) CLEF 2001. LNCS, vol. 2406, pp. 355–370. Springer, Heidelberg (2002)
5. Jansen, B.J.: Search log analysis: What it is, what's been done, how to do it (2006)
6. Blecic, D., Bangalore, N., Dorsch, J., Henderson, C., Koenig, M., Weller, A.: Using transaction log analysis to improve OPAC retrieval results (1998)
7. Kohavi, R., Henne, R., Sommerfield, D.: Practical Guide to Controlled Experiments on the Web: Listen to Your Customers not to the HiPPO (2007)
8. Radlinski, F., Kurup, M., Joachims, T.: How Does Clickthrough Data Reflect Retrieval Quality? (2008)
9. Dunlop, M.: Reflections on Mira: Interactive evaluation in information retrieval. J. Am. Soc. Inf. Sci. 51, 1269–1274 (2000)
10. Borlund, P.: User-centered evaluation of information retrieval systems. In: Information Retrieval: Searching in the 21st Century, pp. 21–37 (2009)
11. Braschler, M., Rietberger, S., Imhof, M., Järvelin, A., Hansen, P., Lupu, M., Gäde, M., Berendsen, R., García Seco de Herrera, A.: PROMISE deliverable 2.3: Best Practices Report (2012)
12. Braschler, M., Herget, J., Pfister, J., Schäuble, P., Steinbach, M., Stuker, J.: Evaluation der Suchfunktion von Schweizer Unternehmens-Websites (2006)
13. Braschler, M., Heuwing, B., Mandel, T., Womser-Hacker, C., Herget, J., Schäuble, P., Stuker, J.: Evaluation der Suchfunktion deutscher Unternehmens-Websites (2009)
14. Peters, C., Braschler, M., Clough, P.: Multilingual Information Retrieval: From Research to Practice. Springer (2012) ISBN 3642230075

---

[2] http://www.promise-noe.eu/

Twinder: Enhancing Twitter Search

Ke Tao[1], Fabian Abel[1,2], Claudia Hauff[1],
Geert-Jan Houben[1], and Ujwal Gadiraju[1]

[1] TU Delft, Web Information Systems
PO Box 5031, 2600 GA Delft, The Netherlands
wis@st.ewi.tudelft.nl
[2] XING AG, Gänsemarkt 43, 20354 Hamburg, Germany
fabian.abel@xing.com

Abstract. How can the search process on Twitter be improved to better meet the various information needs of its users? As an answer to this question, we have developed the *Twinder* framework, a scalable search system for Twitter streams. Twinder contains algorithms to determine the relevance of tweets in relation to search requests, as well as components to detect (near-)duplicate content, to diversify search results, and to personalize the search result ranking. In this paper, we report on our current progress, including the system architecture and the different modules for solving specific problems. Finally, we empirically determine the effectiveness of Twinder's components with experiments on representative datasets.

1 Introduction

Since the launch of Twitter in 2007, microblogging sites have gained immensely in popularity and have become important information sources for exploring and discussing news-related topics [1]. The number of posts published per day typically exceeds several hundred million[1]. Thus, searching and retrieving tweets that are relevant to a user's search request (or query) is a non-trivial research challenge. Previous studies [2,3] have investigated users' search behaviour on microblogging sites and compared them to typical Web search behaviour. For example, queries are often shorter on microblogging sites (1.64 words) than on the Web (3.08 words). The limited length of microblog messages is likely to be the main reason for this observation: the longer a query, the less likely that all query terms are contained within a microblog message (on Twitter the limit is 140 characters). This also implies that queries are more likely to be overly general, making it difficult for users to express their specific information needs. Moreover, many of the microblog posts convey the same semantic information in slightly different syntactic forms which adds to the user's burden when searching for new information.

Recently, we introduced our solution, the Twinder framework [4], to overcome some of the drawbacks of keyword search as provided by microblogging sites.

---

[1] http://goo.gl/vZlnf

N. Ferro (Ed.): PROMISE Winter School 2013, LNCS 8173, pp. 208–217, 2014.

In this paper, we briefly introduce our latest architecture of Twinder and its components - those that have already been implemented as well as the components we plan to include in the future.

2 Twinder

Twinder (*Twitter Finder*) [4] is a search system for Twitter streams that enhances search for Twitter messages by going beyond keyword-based matching for determining the relevance of tweets. We incorporate semantic information, both in the content of tweets and the external resources mentioned, as well as contextual information to improve the search result ranking.

Figure 1 shows the general architecture of Twinder. The pre-processing components, such as *Feature Extraction* and *Feature Extraction Task Broker*, support the search & analysis modules including *Relevance Estimation, Near-Duplicate Detection and Diversification,* and *Personal Adaptation.* Given the huge amount of tweets that are published every day, Twinder makes use of typical cloud computing infrastructures for processing-intensive tasks such as feature extraction and indexing in order to achieve scalability.

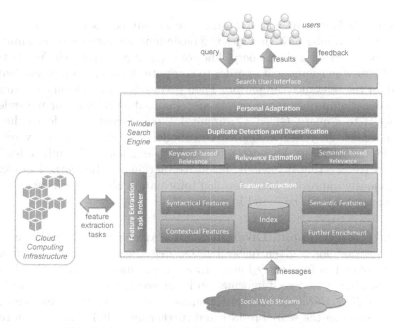

Fig. 1. Architecture of the Twinder search system

2.1 Pre-processing Components

Feature Extraction. The *Feature Extraction* component receives Twitter messages and extracts the features that are used by the search & analysis components. Twinder exploits syntactical elements, the semantics in tweets and the content of referred Web pages, as well as contextual information about tweets and users sending the tweets. The computation of some features requires external services which offer additional functionalities (e.g. named-entity recognition). The contextual features describing the author of the tweet and the multifaceted index of Twinder are periodically updated in order to reduce the system load. To ensure scalability, the component of *Feature Extraction Task Broker* takes charge of orchestrating the feature extraction tasks with the consideration of system performance, resources, and customized needs from administrators.

Feature Extraction Task Broker. MapReduce-based implementations are efficient at processing batch tasks with large volumes of data and are typically executed on large cloud computing infrastructures. Twinder is designed to take advantage of this to allow for high scalability and to allow for the availability of a most up-to-date multifaceted index. The *Feature Extraction Task Broker* coordinates feature extraction tasks as well as indexing tasks and dispatches them to cloud computing infrastructures.

2.2   Search and Analysis Components

Relevance Estimation. The *Relevance Estimation* component is the essential component of Twinder as it provides the basic functionality for determining the relevance of tweets for a given query. The component passes search queries to the *Feature Extraction* component in order to compute the query-dependent features required for the relevance estimation. Then it considers the relevance estimation as a classification problem; the tweets are classified as relevant or non-relevant with respect to a query. Given a training dataset, Twinder can learn the classification model. At runtime, the learned model is applied to identify relevant tweets. Furthermore, as Twinder receives both explicit and implicit feedback from users (re-tweeting behaviour, favourite markings), the learned model can be continuously improved. More detailed information about the *Relevance Estimation* component can be found in Section 3.

Duplicate Detection and Diversification. Among the tweets that are classified as relevant for a given query by the *Relevance Estimation* component, duplicate content is frequently found. In a sample dataset, the ratio of tweets that repeat already observed information is on average 20%. The *Duplicate Detection and Diversification* component aims at detecting the (near-)duplicate information among the search results and further diversifying the search results in order to reduce the information load for users and to better satisfy their information need.

In order to achieve this, the component is capable of classifying a pair of tweets as duplicate or non-duplicate. With the features extracted for tweet pairs and a training dataset with duplicate labelling, a binary model can be learned to classify the tweet pairs as duplicate or non-duplicate. A second model can be derived for detecting the duplicity level between a pair of tweets (tweets can be weak duplicates or strong duplicates). The details of (near-)duplicate detection are described in Section 4.

Teevan et al. [2] found that queries submitted to microblogging search engines are shorter than on the Web, therefore these queries are more likely to be underspecified. As it is impossible to know the exact information need of every user, a common practice for search engines is to adopt a diversification strategy so that the retrieved search results can cover as many aspects of the given query as possible. Twinder has been designed with this goal in mind as well.

Personalization. With short queries, users have limited space for specifying their personal preferences. Moreover, it is a non-trivial challenge to deal with the cold-start problem while building an adaptive system. However, it has been shown that the microblogging posts from users can be a good resource for profiling their personal preferences [6]. Given this fact, the component of *Personal Adaptation* enables Twinder to provide its users with search results that are tailored to their individual preferences. Technically, the de-duplicated results will be processed to prioritize the ones that match the preferences indicated in the profiles of the users.

2.3 Cloud Supported Scalability

As described in Section 2.1, Twinder leverages a cloud computing infrastructure to execute processing-intensive tasks. In order to demonstrate this, we compare the efficiency of creating an inverted index on Amazon ElasticMapReduce (EMR)[2] and a multi-core server[3]. We evaluated the runtime of four different Twitter corpora, ranging in size from 100,000 to 32 million tweets. On EMR, the indices were built by using ten instances[4], where each instance contains one virtual core, in contrast to the 8 cores in the multi-core server.

As shown in Table 1, if the corpora are small, the index can be efficiently created with a dedicated toolkit on a single machine. However, as the corpus size increases, utilizing cloud infrastructures offers significant speed gains.

Table 1. Comparison of indexing times: Amazon EMR vs. a single multi-core machine

Corpus Size	Mainstream Server	EMR (10 instances)	Speedup Ratio
100k (13MBytes)	0.4 min	5 min	0.08
1m (122MBytes)	5 min	8 min	0.625
10m (1.3GBytes)	48 min	19 min	2.526
32m (3.9GBytes)	283 min	47 min	6.021

---

[2] http://aws.amazon.com/elasticmapreduce/
[3] We wrote our own indexer in Hadoop and relied on the Lemur Toolkit for Information Retrieval to create the index on the single server: http://www.lemurproject.org/.
[4] Specifically, we used ten instances of type m1.small.

3   Relevance Estimation

As we mentioned in Section 2.2, we interpret the task of relevance estimation as a classification problem. While building the classification model, Twinder considers not only the retrieval scores but also additional features that could be predictive of the relevance between a tweet and a given topic.

3.1   Features of Microposts

We re-visited a number of features that were proposed by Duan et al. [7]. Moreover, a number of novel semantic measures were constructed to further boost the retrieval effectiveness of Twinder. The features that are currently adopted in Twinder are listed in Table 2. Each of them is constructed with a hypothesis in mind [4] for its score tendency in the relevance estimation process.

Table 2. The features extracted from tweet pairs for relevance estimation

Category	Feature	Remarks
keyword relevance	keyword-based	retrieval score given by language modelling
semantic relevance	semantic-based isSemanticallyRelated	retrieval score (*semantically expanded query*) whether same entity in both tweet and query
syntactical	hasHashtag hasURL isReply length	whether the tweet contains a #hashtag whether the tweet contains a URL whether the tweet is a reply the length of the tweet
semantics	#entities diversity positive sentiment neutral sentiment negative sentiment	the number of entities extracted from the tweet the number of types of entities extracted from the tweet whether the tweet is sentimentally positive whether the tweet is sentimentally neutral whether the tweet is sentimentally negative
contextual	#followers #lists Twitter age	the number of followers that the author of the tweet has the number of lists that the author appears in how long has the author of the tweet been on Twitter

Depending on whether the query is required while extracting the features, we categorize the features into (i) query-dependent features and (ii) query-independent features. The query-dependent features contain two features that are based on the retrieval scores and one feature that indicates whether there is semantic overlap between the query and the tweet. The query-independent features represent the syntactical, the semantic, as well as the contextual characteristics of the tweets.

3.2   Methodology and Analysis

Given 15 features that are used to represent a tweet and its relation to the query, a classification model can be learned. The Tweets 2011 corpus [8], which is designed to be a reusable test collection for investigating Twitter search and

Table 3. Performance results of relevance estimations for different sets of features

Features	Precision	Recall	F-Measure
keyword relevance	0.3036	0.2851	0.2940
semantic relevance	0.3050	0.3294	0.3167
query-dependent	0.3135	0.3252	0.3192
query-independent	0.1956	0.0064	0.0123
without semantics	0.3410	0.4618	0.3923
without sentiment	0.3701	0.4466	0.4048
without context	0.3827	0.4714	0.4225
all features	0.3725	0.4572	0.4105

ranking, has been adopted for this purpose. The corpus contains 16 million original tweets and relevance judgement for 49 search queries.

To analyse the efficiency of the *Relevance Estimation* component, we employ logistic regression to classify tweets as relevant or non-relevant. Due to the relatively small size of the query set (49 queries), we use 5-fold cross validation to evaluate the learned model. We experimented with various sets of feature subsets to analyse their importance in estimating the relevance. The results of the analysis are shown in Table 3. Unsurprisingly, query-independent features on their own cannot be used to estimate a tweet's relevance. However, the performance is boosted when combining them with query-dependent features. As a result, Twinder can achieve a precision and recall of 36% and 47% respectively by employing all features.

4 Near-Duplicate Detection

The problem of (near-)duplicate detection has been well studied in the context of the Web. However, little research has focused on techniques for detecting near-duplicate content on microblogging platforms. In Twinder, we implemented a microblog-specific component for *Duplicate Detection and Diversification* [5].

4.1 Duplicate Content on Twitter

We consider a pair of tweets as duplicates when they convey the same information either syntactically or semantically. The duplicate tweets can be classified into 5 levels:

Exact copy. The duplicates at the level of *exact copy* are identical in terms of characters.

Nearly exact copy. The duplicates of *nearly exact copy* are identical in terms of characters except for *#hashtags*, *URLs*, or *@mentions*.

Strong near-duplicate. A pair of tweets is *strong near-duplicate* if both tweets contain the same core messages syntactically and semantically, but at least one of them contains more information in form of new statements or hard facts.

Weak near-duplicate. Two *weak near-duplicate* tweets either (i) contain the same core messages syntactically and semantically while personal opinions are also included in one or both of them, or (ii) convey semantically the same messages with differing information nuggets.

Low-overlapping. The *low-overlapping* pairs of tweets semantically contain the same core message, but only have a couple of common words.

If a tweet pair does not match any of the above definitions, it is considered as *non-duplicate*.

To analyse the duplicate content on Twitter, we again take the Tweets 2011 corpus as our sample dataset. We manually labelled[5] all the possible pairs of relevant tweets (recall that in this corpus relevance judgements exist for 49 topics) within each topic as *duplicate* or *non-duplicate* along with the duplicate level (for duplicate pairs). As can be seen from Figure 2(a), 48.71% of the duplicates are *Weak near-duplicate* while only about 10% are *Exact copy* or *Near exact copy*. It is also shown in Figure 2(b) that on average about 20% of the items over Top 10, 20, 50, full range of search results are duplicates on different levels.

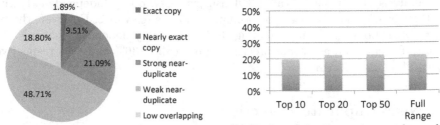

(a) Ratios of duplicates in five different lev- (b) Ratios of duplicates in search results
els

Fig. 2. Analysis of duplicate content on Twitter with the Tweets 2011 corpus

4.2   Features of Micropost Pairs

To determine whether a pair of tweets are duplicates or not (binary detection) is the main function provided by Twinder. Besides that, Twinder is also capable of determining the duplicate level (level detection). Both problems are considered as classification problems. Different features constructed for tweet pairs are used to train the model. Given a pair of tweets (t_a, t_b), four sets of features are extracted as shown in Table 4. The hypotheses that led us to include them in our strategies are detailed in [5]. As an example consider the *temporal difference* feature; we hypothesize that a smaller difference in posting time between a pair of tweets increases the likelihood of it being a duplicate pair.

---

[5] The labels are publicly available on our website [9].

Table 4. The features extracted from tweet pairs for near-duplicate detection tasks

Category	Feature	Remarks
Syntactical	Levenshtein Distance overlap in terms overlap in hashtags overlap in URLs overlap in expanded URLs length difference	Jaccard coefficient (similarly hereinafter) the shortened URLs are expanded
Semantics	overlap in entities overlap in entity types overlap in topics overlap in WordNet concepts overlap in WordNet Synset concepts WordNet similarity	extracted by DBpedia Spotlight extracted by DBpedia Spotlight extracted by OpenCalais service based on the work by Lin et al. [10]
Enriched semantics	overlap in entities overlap in entity types overlap in topics overlap in WordNet concepts overlap in WordNet Synset concepts WordNet similarity	
Contextual	temporal difference difference in #followees difference in #followers same client	

4.3 Methodology and Analysis

Twinder employs logistic regression classifiers to classify tweet pairs as (non-) duplicates and to determine the duplicate level if applicable. Different combinations of features yield different strategies. Twinder supports a *Baseline strategy* and six *Twinder strategies*: *Sy* (only syntactical features), *SySe* (including tweet content-based features), *SyCo* (without semantics), *SySeCo* (without enriched semantics), *SySeEn* (without contextual features), and *SySeEnCo* (all features). Twinder can be configured according to the hardware and the network limitations.

Table 5. Performance results of duplicate detection for different sets of features

Task	Binary Detection			Level Detection		
Strategies	Precision	Recall	F-measure	Precision	Recall	F-measure
Baseline	0.5068	0.1913	0.2777	0.5553	0.5208	0.5375
Sy	0.5982	0.2918	0.3923	0.6599	0.5809	0.6179
SyCo	0.5127	0.3370	0.4067	0.6747	0.5889	0.6289
SySe	0.5333	0.3679	0.4354	0.6708	0.6151	0.6417
SySeEn	0.5297	0.3767	0.4403	0.6694	0.6241	0.6460
SySeCo	0.4816	0.4200	0.4487	0.6852	0.6198	0.6508
SySeEnCo	0.4868	0.4299	0.4566	0.6739	0.6308	0.6516

We evaluate our methodology on the Tweets 2011 corpus and our manual duplicate labelling. As shown in Table 5, both tasks benefit from considering more sets of features. By applying the *SySeEnCo* strategy (using all features), we can achieve a precision and recall of 48% and 43% respectively in the binary detection task; as well as 67% and 63% in the level detection task.

5 Conclusions

In this paper, we introduced our updated architecture of the Twinder search system, which enhances the search on microblogging services by boosting the accuracy of the relevance estimation, by diversifying the search results, and by supporting personalization. We briefly summarized the components Twinder consists of and the results of the empirical evaluations we conducted.

In the future, we plan to continue our work on search result diversification and personalization.

Acknowledgements. The research has received funding from the European Union Seventh Framework Programme, grant agreement no ICT 257831 (ImREAL project).

References

1. Kwak, H., Lee, C., Park, H., Moon, S.: What is twitter, a social network or a news media? In: Proceedings of the 19th International Conference on World Wide Web, WWW 2010, pp. 591–600. ACM, New York (2010)
2. Teevan, J., Ramage, D., Morris, M.R.: #TwitterSearch: a comparison of microblog search and web search. In: Proceedings of the International Conference on Web Search and Web Data Mining (WSDM 2011), pp. 35–44. ACM, New York (2011)
3. Golovchinsky, G., Efron, M.: Making sense of twitter search. In: Proc. CHI 2010 Workshop on Microblogging: What and How Can We Learn From It? (2010)
4. Tao, K., Abel, F., Hauff, C., Houben, G.-J.: Twinder: A search engine for twitter streams. In: Brambilla, M., Tokuda, T., Tolksdorf, R. (eds.) ICWE 2012. LNCS, vol. 7387, pp. 153–168. Springer, Heidelberg (2012)
5. Tao, K., Abel, F., Hauff, C., Houben, G.J., Gadiraju, U.: Groundhog day: Near-duplicate detection on twitter. In: Proceedings of the 22nd International Conference on World Wide Web, WWW 2013, pp. 1273–1284. International World Wide Web Conferences Steering Committee (2013)
6. Abel, F., Gao, Q., Houben, G.-J., Tao, K.: Analyzing User Modeling on Twitter for Personalized News Recommendations. In: Konstan, J.A., Conejo, R., Marzo, J.L., Oliver, N. (eds.) UMAP 2011. LNCS, vol. 6787, pp. 1–12. Springer, Heidelberg (2011)
7. Duan, Y., Jiang, L., Qin, T., Zhou, M., Shum, H.Y.: An empirical study on learning to rank of tweets. In: Proceedings of the 23rd International Conference on Computational Linguistics, COLING 2010, pp. 295–303. Association for Computational Linguistics, Stroudsburg (2010)

8. McCreadie, R., Soboroff, I., Lin, J., Macdonald, C., Ounis, I., McCullough, D.: On building a reusable twitter corpus. In: Proceedings of the 35th International ACM SIGIR Conference on Research and Development in Information Retrieval, SIGIR 2012, pp. 1113–1114. ACM, New York (2012)

9. Tao, K., Abel, F., Hauff, C., Houben, G.J., Gadiraju, U.: Supporting website: datasets and additional findings (2012), http://wis.ewi.tudelft.nl/duptweet/

10. Lin, D.: An information-theoretic definition of similarity. In: Proceedings of the 15th International Conference on Machine Learning, vol. 1, San Francisco, pp. 296–304 (1998)

Domain-Driven News Representation Using Conditional Attribute-Value Pairs

Mihail Minev and Christoph Schommer

Interdisciplinary Lab for Intelligent and Adaptive Systems
Computer Science and Communications Research Unit
University of Luxembourg
{mihail.minev,christoph.schommer}@uni.lu

Abstract. Financial news carry information about economical figures and indicators. However, these texts are mostly unstructured and consequently hard to be processed in an automatic way. In this paper, we present a representation formalism that supports a linguistic composition for machine learning tasks. We show an innovative approach to structuring financial texts by extracting principal indicators. Considering announcements in the monetary policy domain, we distinguish between attributes and their values and argue that attributes are to be represented as an aggregated set of economic terms, keeping their values as corresponding conditional expressions. We close with a critical discussion and future perspectives.

Keywords: Feature Extraction, Text Representation, Financial News.

1 Introduction

Written text is the most common used format for the announcement of financial news. It usually includes several standard elements, in particular a title, a date, a location, an author, and a content, respectively. While a coherent text can normally be read and interpreted by humans (quite easily), an associative text analysis requires a complete and logical formal representation. Although many electronic publications feature structural metadata as well, such specifications do not cover the annotation of economic terms: moreover, these remain hidden in the text.

In this paper, we focus on a single class of documents, which is financial news related to *monetary policy* and being conducted by the *Federal Reserve*[1] (Fed). The corresponding news documents are provided by Thomson Reuters NewsScope. In particular, we examine the time period 2007–2012, which captures the development of the subprime mortgage crisis in the United States. We consider only official press releases, which are issued periodically by the Fed and which include the latest economic information as well as the arranged decisions by the *Federal Open Market Committee* (FOMC, the liable subdivision of the Fed).

---

[1] This is the central bank on the United States; its main goals are to monitor the price stability and to foster maximum output and employment [1].

N. Ferro (Ed.): PROMISE Winter School 2013, LNCS 8173, pp. 218–226, 2014.

In general, financial news address a single company or an industrial branch, whereas Fed announcements have a significant impact on the entire [2] economy of a country. Typically, the FOMC announcements comply to a specific structure concerning the past and the current state of the economy as well as the promoted committee decisions. In addition, the documents comprise a high number of principal indicators, e.g., numbers for the labor market and the housing sector as well as the target range for the federal funds rate. Referring to the text composition a concrete example is available in Section 3.1.

The purpose of this work is to describe a novel approach for accumulating economic information in *monetary policy* news by incorporating linguistic aspects. First, we apply a shallow parser on the input and identify key attributes (features)[2]. We define an attribute as a *noun phrase* (NP), which is a phrase with a noun as a head word [3]. In this way, determined features are aggregated and ranked by frequency. Next, this feature list is likewise filtered and confirmed by financial domain experts. In a second step we obtain candidate *attribute values* (instances), which are either a *verb phrase* (VP), an *adverb phrase* (AdvP), or an *adjective phrase* (AdjP). For example, a valid combination is *'unemployment rate'* (attribute) and *'went down'* (value). Finally, the output is annotated for machine learning tasks, such as the analyzis of the correlations between the *monetary policy* decisions and particular stock market volatilities.

The paper is organized as follows: Section 3 provides a literature overview focusing on financial text representation methods. It also describes the model requirements in regard to the *monetary policy* domain along with the addressed linguistic aspects. In Section 4 we present an extraction and annotation model for the selected *attribute-value* pairs. We close with a critical discussion and prospective future works (Section 5).

2 Related Works

Studies concerning financial text representation distinguish between two main approaches: *unigrams* (or single terms) and *compositions* (or multi-word terms). Whereas *unigrams* are mainly used as individual, independent features, the second approach concerns features that are a composition of one or more words (following context-free grammars) and statistical measures. Since we emphasize on high information retention in the *monetary policy* domain, this is also the focus of the following literature survey.

2.1 Single-Word Terms

Representing documents as isolated words has been initially described by [4] as the *Vector Space Model*. The approach is also known as *Bag-of-Words* (BoW) and is preferred in many studies due to its ease of use. Among others, [5,6] apply this model to financial texts. A main requirement for the operation of a learning

---

[2] In this work the words *attribute* and *feature* are used as synonyms.

algorithm is that all feature constructs should be explicitly defined. Features are the linguistic counterpart of concepts in a particular domain. In the *Bag-of-Words* model, each of the features corresponds to a single term, which is assumed to be the meaningful unit in a sentence. Many comparative studies approved the high yields of *Bag-of-Words* for document classification [7,8]. However, BoW generates numerous (and noisy) features disregarding multi-word terms, which are typical for financial texts. Another main disadvantage of the single term representation is the information, which is discarded from the original text. The word order in sentences is not considered, but also the syntactic and semantic structures of word compounds are abolished. In spite of preserving the last, several alternative approaches are discussed in the next section.

2.2   Multi-word Terms

A second text representation method incorporates *multi-word terms* and – with them – domain affiliations and word relationships. This is why *multi-word terms* are a strong candidate technique for retaining as much semantics as possible. However, there is no evidence for a straightforward analogy between the length of a feature, which in this case is a compound, and the vocabulary in a particular domain [9]. In [10], a categorization scheme for *multi-word terms*, which is based on part of speech analysis, is suggested. According to the results, the most expressive compounds are the noun phrases, which also include the adjective-nouns and the phrasal compounds [9]. On the other hand, not all of these are terminology-relevant for the financial domain. Therefore, a thorough field expertise for the candidate assessment is still indispensable.

More lexical issues with multi-word term recognition are explained by [9]. The authors claim that even though a direct juxtaposition may indicate a terminology, it does not guarantee it. Composite terms can not be determined only by a set of formal syntactic rules. The English language structures and parsing ambiguities inhibit a clear distinction between *multi-word terms* and general language compounds. Variations like hyphenations and abbreviations hinder likewise the process and hence the comparability of the results. In contrast, *n-grams* are a language independent method for text representation. Word bi- and tri-grams are a popular topic of recent scientific studies, though some specific research focused also on character and byte n-grams [11]. Word n-grams are defined as adjoined strings in texts. To reduce the number of candidates, which may be huge for a large document set, a number of statistical measures may be applied: Likelihood ratio, Chi-square, and Pointwise Mutual Information. Besides the high dimensionality, n-grams lack the complete representation power, which noun phrases have [12]. Obviously due to the non-consideration of lexical structures. The information they capture is insufficient and can be used only partially (in combination with some other method) for an extended text abstraction.

In a comparative study [13] examines three widespread financial news representation techniques including Bag-of-Words, Noun Phrases and Named Entities. The latter is an extension of Noun Phrases, which assigns a particular category to a subset of its terms like date, location, money, organization, percentage, person, and time. The evaluation upon a stock price prediction task were ambiguous as none of the methods dominated the field. Nevertheless Noun Phrases achieved the best results in two out of tree prediction metrics. Further attempts for an independent term selection and their ranking include the application of statistical methods as Mutual Information [6] and Chi-Square [14]. Nevertheless, none of the previous studies concerns the discrete relationships between the extracted features and their instances. In the next section we introduce the model requirements for such an approach.

3 Model Requirements

The model requirements are indicated by two aspects. The first aspect involves the understanding of the *monetary policy* domain and the corresponding press releases. The second aspect concerns the study of the content and the structure of the documents as well as the formal identification of the candidate attribute-value pairs.

3.1 Domain Understanding

Monetary policy news are packed with indicators, e.g., the recent developments on the labor market, the average interest rates, and the latest economic barometers. Accordingly, our goal is to transform such stories into a structured format using feature-value pairs, which enclose one or more coherent words. Logically, the first step is to examine the official press releases (issued by the Federal Reserve) in a concrete time period. To demonstrate, we have chosen a time interval between 2007 until 2013, because the year of 2007 has been recognized by many officials [15] as the begin of the *subprime mortgage crisis* in the United States. In the six year time interval, 55 FOMC statements (21520 tokens) for the tracking the eminent *monetary policy* are considered.

The *Federal Open Market Committee*, which is responsible for setting the *monetary policy*, meets regularly eight times per year. Subsequently, the committee releases an official statement; afterwards the chairman of the Federal Reserve, Ben Bernanke, stages a question and answer session. The released records comprise the latest principal indicators, but also the short-term economy expectations as well as proposed measures for interventions. Evidently, the conclusions disclosed by the *Federal Open Market Committee* have a significant influence on the entire US industry [2] and as a result the information is greatly anticipated by politicians and investors.

In this work we describe a method to extract the facts from the Fed announcements and to enable dedicated economic surveys, for instance—an analysis of the correlations between the federal funds rate and the unemployment rate; or between the asset purchase programs and the stock markets. In order to do so, we first need to quantify the information before we can apply learning algorithms to identify associated patterns. We begin with examining the structure and the content of a random FOMC document (June 20, 2012). Here is a snippet from the first paragraph:

"Business fixed investment has continued to advance. Household spending appears to be rising at a somewhat slower pace than earlier in the
year. Despite some signs of improvement, the housing sector remains
depressed. Inflation has declined, mainly reflecting lower prices of crude
oil and gasoline, and longer-term inflation expectations have remained
stable."

Clearly, the fragment provides information about the current economy state
and includes at least one principal indicator per sentence (marked below in
bold). The next part of the message is devoted to the committee expectations
such as the *labor market conditions*, *long-term inflation*, and *economic growth*.
The third and fourth paragraphs give information about the *Federal Funds Target Rate*, the *Maturity Extension Program* (alias *Operation Twist*) and the *Asset
Purchase Program* (alias *Quantitative Easing*). The attendees' names and their
voting *pro/against* the proposed measures come at the end. Empirically, all *Federal Open Market Committee* announcement within the examined period share
similar structure:

*"**Business fixed investment** has continued to advance. **Household
spending** appears to be rising at a somewhat slower pace than earlier
in the year. Despite some signs of improvement, the **housing sector**
remains depressed. **Inflation** has declined, mainly reflecting lower prices
of **crude oil and gasoline**, and **longer-term inflation expectations**
have remained stable."*

As mentioned previously, our objective is to create a method for the identification and extraction of attributes, which are equal to economic indicators. In
line with our analysis, the attributes are noun phrases, with a high frequency
distribution over the text collection. Furthermore we look for their conditional
values in the text, which are labeled consistent with syntactic rules..

3.2 Linguistic Processing

Each document in our collection is annotated corresponding to the process shown
in Fig. 1 [16]. In the first part of the workflow, we carry out the sentence segmentation, the tokenization and the part-of-speech (POS) tagging. The output
is a set of tuples, where each word is assigned to a lexical class, e.g., (investment, NN). The tag NN hereby refers to a *noun, singular or mass*. This is a
standard preprocessing step before the phrasal category detection (also *chunking*). Second, a *maximum entropy*-based chunker evaluates the input pairs and
assigns labels to each syntactic word group. Currently, four types of phrases are
detected: *noun phrase, verb phrase, adverb phrase*, and *adjective phrase*. For example, the construct [business, NN fixed, VBN investment, NN] is a noun phrase.
In this case it is a multi-word attribute with a verb in past participle surrounded
by two singular nouns. All syntactic rule definitions for the phrase annotation
are summarized by [17].

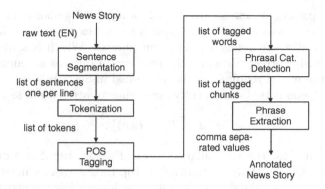

Fig. 1. This workflow describes how the document annotation process works: starting from a news story, the text is firstly linguistically preprocessed (Sentence Segmentation, Tokenization, Part-Of-Speech tagging). Next, the phrasal category detection is completed using a trained model. The annotated news story is received by filtering the four tagged chunks (NP, VP, AdvP, AdjP).

In the extraction phrase, we separate the chunks (per sentence) and file them as comma separated values. The output accumulates all identified phrases in a document. Based on our experiments with the training data, four words per phrase are not exceeded. In order to determine the attributes (economic indicators) from the data, we collect all noun phrases (in total 705). According to [18,19], the noun phrase is the most expressive construct in a sentence, ergo suitable as a candidate for a domain vocabulary. However, our list aggregates also personal and location names as well as roughly 15% incorrectly identified noun phrases. In order to trim the candidate attributes we rank the NPs using the *C-Value* [20,21] algorithm, which incorporates assorted frequency measures. Despite some improvements[3] in the feature distribution, the false positive values remain high. External domain knowledge is, therefore, explicitly needed, which evokes us to ask financial experts to select those noun phrases, which represent economic indicators. Based on their votes, we aggregate all matching attributes to a domain specific vocabulary T (here, 153 unique records are listed).

With respect to the linguistic annotation, we utilized the *OpenNLP* machine learning toolkit [22]. Due to the data similarity we measured the *OpenNLP* chunking performance on the *CoNLL-2000* [23] test set with 47377 tokens. *CoNLL-2000* contains syntactically annotated sentences from 'The Wall Street Journal'. The results for precision and recall were respectively 0.93% and 0.92%.

4   Attribute-Value Representation

For the text representation, we extend a formalism initially proposed by [24] for improving the retrieval performance in search queries. The author describes

---

[3] Setting the *C-value* rate to one and above, which is a typical threshold, reduces the number of noun phrases to 509.

a method for parsing search strings by adopting their semantic and syntactic features. The study assumes, that the queries are not expressed as full sentences, but built up of distinct nouns and/or noun phrases. Which is a divergence to the grammatically correct texts and the four lexical phrases we encounter.

Following the model requirements as presented in Section 3, we acquire a set of annotated documents. Consequently, we define an attribute a as

$$\{a \mid a \in T \wedge P(a)\}. \tag{1}$$

where T stands for the vocabulary we use. $P(a)$ is true if and only if a set of terms exists, which satisfy a condition a [16]. In this case, a must be a noun phrase, as requiered for the domain specific vocabulary. For the attribute values av we apply the definition

$$\{av \mid av \in P(av)\}. \tag{2}$$

Here, the property $P(av)$ is true if and only if av is either a verb phrase, or an adverb phrase, or an adjective phrase. For each *attribute* per sentence the matching *attribute values* are retrieved. Accordingly, we outline a representation schema, which incorporates the three integrals:

1. *attribute* $\in T$;
2. *attribute value* $\in (VP \vee AdvP \vee AdjP)$;
3. a class C, which describes the time-variant type of the *attribute value*.

We can determine the time frame C based on the token's POS tags, which are available for the *verb phrases*. Each *attribute* has one or more expressions of an *attribute value*. An *attribute value* exists only in a combination with an *attribute* and is assigned to zero or one class C. In a composition, an *attribute* and an *attribute value* establish an unique pair for each sentence. For example, the sentence

> *"However, growth in employment has slowed in recent months, and the unemployment rate remains elevated."*

is annotated with the values

[*attribute*: employment]
[*attribute_value$_{past\_state}$*: has_slowed]
[*attribute*: unemployment_rate]
[*attribute_value$_{present\_state}$*: remains]
[*attribute_value*: elevated].

For longer sentences the identification of the attribute instance(s) can be ambiguous. To avoid redundant value allocations we apply syntax-based rules, which use lexical delimiters like a comma or a dash and support partitioning. In the latter example we split the sentence in three parts (delimiter is a comma) and determine the attribute-value pairs in each case.

5   Conclusions

A strong limitation of our approach is its domain dependency. Although practicable for the financial text representation, it correlates also with contributions in other areas like medicine (see [25]). In the same context, its application on more generic news is still challenging: this is because of the natural ambiguity and the linguistic complexity of universal texts. Besides that, for a more precise *attribute-value* identification we also plan to conduct experiments using dependency trees.

A quantitative model evaluation is targeted in a future work. Typical text classification measures like *Precision/Recall* are barely applicable due to the specific attribute-value format. Clustering and similarity techniques sound more promising, though further definitions of the comparability parameters are necessary. At present, our alternative idea is to add time series data and to juxtapose the prediction results of stock market trends with analog studies.

In this work, we have proposed a fresh approach for representation of *monetary policy* news in the context of machine learning applications. In order to quantify a Federal Reserve document, we have considered the lexical structure of the texts as well as the semantic relationships between the terms. In this context, we acquire a set of four phrase types, which enable multi-word term identification in financial texts. Correspondingly, we have designed an annotation model to capture the domain-specific information as conditional attribute-value pairs. One future application of this work is to facilitate economic surveys. For example, we may track the *monetary policy* implementation over a dedicated time period and/or measure the correlations between principal indicators, e.g., the policy instruments, the various interest rates and the economy state.

References

1. Federal Reserve Bank of New York,
   http://www.newyorkfed.org/aboutthefed/fedpoint/fed48.html
2. Bernanke, B.S., Kuttner, K.N.: What explains the stock market's reaction to federal reserve policy? Working Paper 10402. National Bureau of Economic Research (April 2004)
3. Radford, A.: English Syntax: An Introduction. Cambridge University Press (May 2004)
4. Salton, G., Wong, A., Yang, C.S.: A vector space model for automatic indexing. Commun. ACM 18(11), 613–620 (1975)
5. Lavrenko, V., Schmill, M., Lawrie, D., Ogilvie, P., Jensen, D., Allan, J.: Language models for financial news recommendation, pp. 389–396 (2000)
6. Gidófalvi, G., Elkan, C.: Using news articles to predict stock price movements. Technical report, Department of Computer Science and Engineering, University of California (2003)
7. Fengxi, S., Liu, S., Yang, J.: A comparative study on text representation schemes in text categorization. Pattern Anal. Appl. 8(1), 199–209 (2005)
8. Scott, S., Matwin, S.: Feature engineering for text classification. In: Proceedings of ICML 1999, 16th International Conference on Machine Learning, pp. 379–388. Morgan Kaufmann Publishers (1999)

9. Frantzi, T.K., Ananiadou, S.: Automatic term recognition using contextual cues. In: Proceedings of 3rd DELOS Workshop (1997)
10. Sager, J.C., Dungworth, D., McDonald, P.F.: English special languages: principles and practice in science and technology. Brandstetter (1980)
11. Shafiei, M., Wang, S., Zhang, R., Milios, E., Tang, B., Tougas, J., Spiteri, R.: Document representation and dimension reduction for text clustering. In: ICDE Workshops, pp. 770–779 (2007)
12. Radford, A.: Syntactic Theory and the Structure of English: A Minimalist Approach (Cambridge Textbooks in Linguistics). Cambridge University Press (August 1997)
13. Schumaker, R.P., Chen, H.: Textual analysis of stock market prediction using breaking financial news: The AZFin text system. ACM Trans. Inf. Syst. 27(2) (2009)
14. Hagenau, M., Liebmann, M., Hedwig, M., Neumann, D.: Automated news reading: Stock price prediction based on financial news using context-specific features. In: Hawaii International Conference on System Sciences, pp. 1040–1049 (2012)
15. Federal Reserve Bank of St. Louis, http://timeline.stlouisfed.org/pdf/CrisisTimeline.pdf
16. Bird, S., Klein, E., Loper, E.: Natural Language Processing with Python, 1st edn. O'Reilly Media (July 2009)
17. Marcus, M., Santorini, B., Marcinkiewicz, M.A.: Building a large annotated corpus of English: The penn treebank. Computational Linguistics 19(2), 313–330 (1993)
18. Schwarzschild, R.: The role of dimensions in the syntax of noun phrases. Syntax 9(1), 67–110 (2006)
19. Pazienza, M.T., Pennacchiotti, M., Zanzotto, F.M.: Terminology extraction: An analysis of linguistic and statistical approaches. In: Sirmakessis, S. (ed.) *Knowledge Mining.* STUDFUZZ, vol. 185, pp. 255–279. Springer, Heidelberg (2005)
20. Frantzi, K., Ananiadou, S., Mima, H.: Automatic recognition of multi-word terms: the c-value/nc-value method. Int. J. on Digital Libraries 3(2), 115–130 (2000)
21. Java Automatic Term Extraction toolkit, http://code.google.com/p/jatetoolkit/wiki/JATEIntro
22. Apache OpenNLP library, http://opennlp.apache.org/
23. CoNLL-2000, http://www.cnts.ua.ac.be/conll2000/chunking/
24. Li, X.: Understanding the semantic structure of noun phrase queries. In: Proceedings of the 48th Annual Meeting of the Association for Computational Linguistics, ACL 2010, pp. 1337–1345. Association for Computational Linguistics, Stroudsburg (2010)
25. Milios, E., Zhang, Y., He, B., Dong, L.: Automatic Term Extraction and Document Similarity in Special Text Corpora, pp. 275–284 (August 2003)

Knowledge Graphs as Context Models: Improving the Detection of Cross-Language Plagiarism with Paraphrasing*

Marc Franco-Salvador[1,2], Parth Gupta[1], and Paolo Rosso[1]

[1] Natural Language Engineering Lab - ELiRF, DSIC
Universitat Politècnica de València, Valencia, Spain
{mfranco,pgupta,prosso}@dsic.upv.es
[2] Linguistic Computing Laboratory (LCL)
Sapienza Università di Roma, Roma, Italy
francosalvador@it.uniroma1.it

Abstract. Cross-language plagiarism detection attempts to identify and extract automatically plagiarism among documents in different languages. Plagiarized fragments can be translated verbatim copies or may alter their structure to hide the copying, which is known as paraphrasing and is more difficult to detect. In order to improve the paraphrasing detection, we use a knowledge graph-based approach to obtain and compare context models of document fragments in different languages. Experimental results in German-English and Spanish-English cross-language plagiarism detection indicate that our knowledge graph-based approach offers a better performance compared to other state-of-the-art models.

Keywords: Cross-language plagiarism detection, textual similarity, paraphrasing, knowledge graphs, BabelNet.

1 Introduction

One of the biggest problems in literature and science is plagiarism: unauthorized use of the original content. Plagiarism is very difficult to detect, especially when the web is the source of information due to its size. The detection of plagiarism is even more difficult when it concerns documents written in different languages. Recently a survey was done on scholar practices and attitudes [2], also from a cross-language (CL) plagiarism perspective which manifests that CL plagiarism is a real problem: only 36.25% of students think that translating a text fragment and including it into their report is plagiarism.

Plagiarized fragments can be translated verbatim copies, or can be hidden by their authors altering its structure, which is known as paraphrasing. In the recent study on paraphrasing in plagiarism [1] it has been shown that paraphrase mechanisms make

---

* The research has been carried out in the framework of the European Commission WIQ-EI IRSES (no. 269180) and DIANA-APPLICATIONS - Finding Hidden Knowledge in Texts: Applications (TIN2012-38603-C02-01) projects as well as the VLC/CAMPUS Microcluster on Multimodal Interaction in Intelligent Systems. We thank Roberto Navigli for offering help to get familiar with the BabelNet API.

N. Ferro (Ed.): PROMISE Winter School 2013, LNCS 8173, pp. 227–236, 2014.

plagiarism detection more difficult. Moreover, this study also shows that lexical substitutions are the paraphrase mechanisms most used in plagiarism, shortening the plagiarized text. This may be used in future to develop more effective plagiarism detectors.

In recent years there have been a few approaches to CL similarity analysis that can be used for CL plagiarism detection. A simple, yet effective approach is the cross-language character n-gram (CL-CNG) model [9] which is based on the syntax of documents, which uses character n-grams, and offers remarkable performance for languages with syntactic similarities. Cross-language explicit semantic analysis (CL-ESA) [14] is a collection-relative retrieval model, which represents a document by its similarities to a collection of documents. These similarities in turn are computed with a monolingual retrieval model such as the vector space model. The cross-language alignment-based similarity analysis (CL-ASA) model [3,2] is instead based on a statistical machine translation technology that combines probabilistic translations, using a statistical bilingual dictionary and similarity analysis. Finally, the cross-language conceptual thesaurus based similarity (CL-CTS) model [8] tries to measure the similarity between the documents in terms of shared concepts, using a conceptual thesaurus, and named entities among them. Some of these models have been compared in detecting CL plagiarism in [14]. CL-ASA and CL-CNG obtained the best results. Hence we compare our approach with them. CL setting of plagiarism detection has been also actively addressed in the PAN track[1] at the CLEF[2]. The most popular technique to handle CL plagiarism detection seems to be involving machine translation systems, where all the documents are translated to the language of comparison beforehand [15,16]. However, this put forward a heavy dependence on availability of Machine Translation (MT) systems and its quality. Hence we propose and compare to CL plagiarism detection systems which do not depend on MT system.

We propose a new approach, named cross-language knowledge graphs analysis (CL-KGA), whose goal is to exploit explicit semantics for a better representation of the documents. CL-KGA provides a context model by generating knowledge graphs that expand and relate the original concepts from suspicious and source paragraphs. Finally, the similarity is measured in a semantic graph space. In this paper we investigate how knowledge graphs as context models can help in detecting CL plagiarism when paraphrasing is employed.

The rest of the paper is structured as follows. In Section 2 we describe the cross-language similarity retrieval models we compare CL-KGA with. In Section 3 we describe the BabelNet multilingual semantic network, i.e. the resource we use to build our knowledge graphs, which are explained in Section 4. The CL-KGA model is described in Section 5. In Section 6, we evaluate our approach using the German-English (DE-EN) and Spanish-English (ES-EN) CL plagiarism cases of the PAN-PC'11 corpus and compare our results with the CL-ASA and CL-CNG models, differentiating plagiarism cases between translated verbatim copies and paraphrase translations.

---

[1] http://pan.webis.de
[2] http://www.clef-initiative.eu

2   Cross-Language Similarity Estimation Models

In this Section we describe the two state-of-the-art CL similarity retrieval models, CL-CNG and CL-ASA that perform CL plagiarism detection and against we compare.

2.1   Cross-Language Character N-Grams

Cross-language character n-gram (CL-CNG) model have shown to improve the performance of CL information retrieval immensely for syntactically similar languages. This model typically uses character trigrams (CL-C3G) to compare documents in different languages [14].

Given a source document d written in a language L_1 and a suspicious document d' written in language L_2, the similarity $S(d, d')$ between the two documents is measured as follows:

$$S(d, d') = \frac{\vec{d} \cdot \vec{d'}}{|d| \cdot |d'|}, \tag{1}$$

where $\vec{d}$ and $\vec{d'}$ are the vectorial representation of documents d and d' into character n-gram space.

2.2   Cross-Language Alignment Based Similarity Analysis

Cross-language alignment based similarity analysis (CL-ASA) model measures the similarity between two documents d and d', from two different languages L_1 and L_2 respectively, by aligning the documents at word level and determining the probability of d' being a translation of d. The similarity $S(d, d')$ between both documents is measured as in equation 2:

$$S(d, d') = l(d, d') * t(d|d'), \tag{2}$$

where $l(d, d')$ is the length factor defined in [17], which is used as normalization since two documents with the same content, in different languages do not have the same length. Moreover, $t(d|d')$ is the translation model defined in equation 3:

$$t(d|d') = \sum_{x \in d} \sum_{y \in d'} p(x, y), \tag{3}$$

where $p(x, y)$ is the probability of a word x from language L_1 being a translation of word y from L_2. These probabilities can be obtained using a bilingual statistical dictionary.

3   Multilingual Semantic Network

A multilingual semantic network (MSN) follows the structure of a traditional lexical knowledge base and accordingly, it consists of a weighted and labeled directed graph

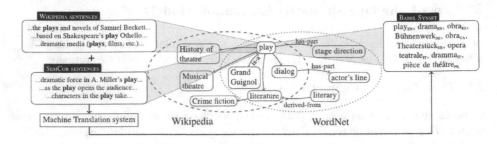

Fig. 1. Structure example of the BabelNet MSN [11]

where nodes represent the concepts and named entities while edges express the semantic relations between them. Each of the nodes contains a set of lexicalizations of the concept in different languages.

Although in this work we employ BabelNet [11], the graph-based approach we propose is generic and could be applied with other available MSNs such as EuroWordNet [21]. BabelNet is a very large MSN available in languages such as: Catalan, English, French, German, Italian and Spanish. Concepts and relations are taken from the largest available semantic lexicon of English, WordNet, and a wide-coverage collaboratively-edited encyclopedia, Wikipedia, which make BabelNet a multilingual "encyclopedic dictionary" that combines lexicographic information with wide-coverage encyclopedic knowledge. BabelNet's concept inventory consists of all WordNet's word senses and Wikipedia's encyclopedic entries, while its set of available relations comprises both semantic pointers between WordNet synsets, and semantically unspecified relations from Wikipedia's hyperlinked text. Multilingual lexicalizations for all concepts are collected from Wikipedia's inter-language links and WordNet's tagged senses in the SemCor corpus [10], using a machine translation system. A BabelNet's structure example is illustrated in Fig. 1.

BabelNet API[3] allows us to use it as a dictionary, statistical dictionary, word-sense disambiguation system and to build knowledge graphs.

4   Knowledge Graphs

A knowledge graph is a weighted and labelled graph that expand and relate the original concepts present in a set of words, providing us a "context model" of its content. Using MSN BabelNet to build the graphs, each one of them has a multilingual dimension of the concepts. Therefore, we can compare directly pairs of graphs built from document fragments in different languages and may be used to detect CL plagiarism.

We can build a knowledge graph using a MSN as follows: having a concept set C, we search the MSN for paths connecting each pair $c, c' \in C$, obtaining the set of paths P, where each $p \in P$ is a set of concepts and relations between concepts from C which include the conceptual expansion. The knowledge graph g is obtained after joining the paths from P including all its concepts and relations. Finally, to weight the concepts

---

[3] http://babelnet.org/

we use their degree of relateness, i.e. the number of outgoing edges for each node. The relation weighting is performed also in function of the degree of relateness of their source and target concepts.

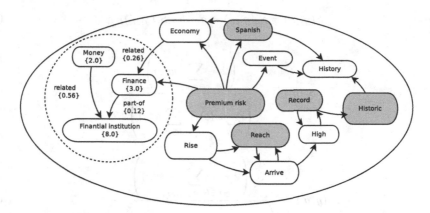

Fig. 2. Knowledge graph built from the sentence "Spanish premium risk reaches historic records", simplified without the multilingual dimension, and with labels and weights only inside the dashed circle

Example. Having the English sentence "Spanish premium risk reaches historic records", we obtain its concepts $C = \{$Spanish, premium risk, reach, record, historic$\}$. Using BabelNet to build a knowledge graph g from C, we obtain a concept set $C_g = C \cup C'$, where $C' = \{$economy, finance, history...$\}$ is the expanded concept set. In addition, we obtain a relation set $R \in \{$related-to, has-part, belong-to, is-a...$\}$ between concepts of C_g. We can observe the resulting graph g in Fig. 2.

5   Cross-Language Knowledge Graphs Analysis

Our approach, cross-language knowledge graphs analysis (CL-KGA), presented previously in [5,6], uses knowledge graphs generated from a MSN to obtain a context model of document fragments in different languages. The similarities between document fragments are computed in a semantic graph space.

Given a source document d and a suspicious document d', we compare document fragments in a four-step process:

1. We segment the original document in a set of fragments, using a 5-sentence sliding window with a 2-sentence step on the input document.
2. The paragraphs are lemmatized and tagged according to their grammatical category. For our experiments we use TreeTagger[4] [18], which supports multiple languages.
3. The knowledge graphs from the tagged fragments are built using the MSN.
4. We compare these graphs to measure similarity. The complete CL detection process using CL-KGA is shown in Fig. 3.

---
[4] http://www.ims.uni-stuttgart.de/projekte/corplex/TreeTagger/

To compare graphs we use a similarity function S for given graphs g and g' as shown in Eq. 4. It is an adapted version for MSN of flexible comparison of conceptual graphs similarity algorithm presented in [7].

$$S(g, g') = S_c(g, g') * (a + b * S_r(g, g'))$$ (4)

$$S_c(g, g') = \frac{\left(2 * \sum_{c \in g_{int}} w(c)\right)}{\left(\sum_{c \in g} w(c) + \sum_{c \in g'} w(c)\right)}$$ (5)

$$S_r(g, g') = \frac{\left(2 * \sum_{r \in N(c, g_{int})} w(r)\right)}{\left(\sum_{r \in N(c, g)} w(r) + \sum_{r \in N(c, g')} w(r)\right)}$$ (6)

where S_c is the score of the concepts, S_r is the score of the relations, a and b are smoothing variables to give the appropriate relevance to concepts and relations[5], c is a concept, r is a relation, g_{int} is the resulting graph of the intersection between g and g', and $N(c, g)$ is the set of all the relations connected to the concept c in a given graph g.

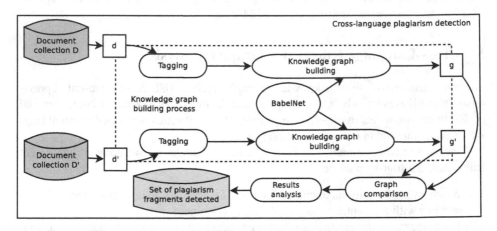

Fig. 3. CL plagiarism detection process between two sets of documents, D and D', in different languages

---

[5] In [6] we estimated the values of a and b for DE-EN and ES-EN using the MSN BabelNet.

6   Experiments and Evaluation

In this section we evaluate the performance of our approach, CL-KGA, for CL plagiarism detection, differentiating plagiarism cases between translated verbatim copies and paraphrase translations. We compare the results obtained by CL-KGA with those provided by CL-ASA and CL-C3G (CL-CNG using 3-grams) for the same task. For CL-ASA model we use two statistical dictionaries: BabelNet's statistical dictionary (CL-ASA$_{BN}$ [4]) and a dictionary trained using the word-aligment model IBM M1 [12] on the JRC-Acquis [20] corpus.

6.1   Corpus and Task Definition

Within automatic plagiarism detection scope, an international competition is celebrated annually since 2009, *Uncovering Plagiarism Authorship and Social Software Misuse*[6] (PAN), in which mono and CL plagiarism detection approaches are presented and tested. In our evaluation we use the CL plagiarism partition of PAN-PC'11[7] [15] corpus from its plagiarism task: given set of suspicious documents D in a language L_1, and their corresponding source documents D', in a language L_2, the task is to compare pairs of documents (d, d'), $d \in D$ and $d' \in D'$, to find all plagiarized fragments in D from D'. For this purpose we use a 5-sentence sliding window on the input documents to extract the fragments, and we analyze the similarities with the models listed above. Once we have the similarities between all the fragments, we use a detailed analysis and a post-processing method [19,2] to determine the plagiarism cases.

As we can see in the corpus statistics of Table 1, PAN-PC'11 corpus has plagiarism cases generated in two different ways: automatic translations (verbatim copies) and automatic translations+manual correction (paraphrase translations). In our experiments we show the results on the two types of translated plagiarism separately.

Table 1. Statistics of PAN-PC'11 external cross-language plagiarism detection partition

ES-EN documents	DE-EN documents
Suspicious 304	Suspicious 251
Source 202	Source 348
Plagiarism cases {es,de}-en	
Automatic translation 5,142	
Automatic translation + Manual correction 433	

6.2   Measures

For the evaluation, we employ the measures introduced for the PAN competition on plagiarism detection: recall and precision at character level, in addition to granularity, which accounts for the fact that detectors sometimes report overlapping or multiple detections for a single plagiarism case. The three measures were integrated together in order to obtain a overall score for plagiarism detection (plagdet):

---

[6] http://pan.webis.de/
[7] http://www.uni-weimar.de/cms/medien/webis/research/corpora/
    corpus-pan-pc-11.html

$$plagdet(S, R) = \frac{F1}{log_2(1 + granularity(S, R))},$$

where S is the set of plagiarism cases in the corpus, R is the set of plagiarism cases reported by the detector, and $F1$ is the equally weighted harmonic mean of precision and recall. A more detailed description about the corpus and the measures can be found respectively in [13] and [15].

6.3 Results and Discussion

As we can see in Table 2, for the DE-EN CL plagiarism detection, CL-C3G obtains the lowest results, being the baseline for this kind of experiments, due to the simplicity of the approach which uses n-grams. CL-ASA$_{BN}$ uses BabelNet's statistical dictionary. It obtained average results, despite many german words in the dictionary were not found. CL-ASA$_{IBMM1}$, one of the best state-of-the-art approaches for CL plagiarism detection, outperformed the baseline $plagdet$ by 365% in automatic translations and 149% in paraphrase translations. Finally, our novel approach CL-KGA, obtained the best values, surpassing the baseline $plagdet$ by 478% in automatic translations and 443% in paraphrase translations, along with better values for recall, precision and granularity.

Table 2. DE-EN cross-language plagiarism detection results for automatic and paraphrase translation cases, displayed in the decreasing order of the Plagdet score

Model	German-English							
	Automatic translations				Paraphrase translations			
	Plagdet	Recall	Precision	Granularity	Plagdet	Recall	Precision	Granularity
CL-KGA	**0.5296**	**0.4671**	**0.6306**	**1.0188**	**0.1006**	**0.2101**	**0.0661**	**1.0**
CL-ASA$_{IBMM1}$	0.4230	0.3690	0.6019	1.1163	0.0462	0.0978	0.0303	1.0
CL-ASA$_{BN}$	0.3019	0.2363	0.5962	1.1753	0.0275	0.0796	0.0166	1.0
CL-C3G	0.0909	0.0564	0.3414	1.0913	0.0185	0.0389	0.0121	1.0

Table 3. ES-EN cross-language plagiarism detection results for automatic and paraphrase translation cases, displayed in the decreasing order of the Plagdet score

Model	Spanish-English							
	Automatic translations				Paraphrase translations			
	Plagdet	Recall	Precision	Granularity	Plagdet	Recall	Precision	Granularity
CL-KGA	**0.6087**	**0.5399**	**0.7036**	**1.0050**	**0.0993**	**0.1979**	**0.0662**	**1.0**
CL-ASA$_{BN}$	0.5793	0.5245	0.6631	1.0154	0.0738	0.1909	0.0457	1.0
CL-ASA$_{IBMM1}$	0.5339	0.4728	0.6911	1.0729	0.0612	0.1501	0.0384	1.0
CL-C3G	0.1756	0.1336	0.6158	1.3796	0.0289	0.0587	0.0192	1.0

As we can see in Table 3, for ES-EN CL plagiarism detection, the models performance was quite similar to DE-EN. CL-C3G is the baseline with the lowest values. CL-ASA$_{BN}$ increased the baseline $plagdet$ by 230% in automatic translations and 155% in paraphrase translations. This time CL-ASA$_{BN}$ obtain better results than CL-ASA$_{IBMM1}$ showing that using BabelNet's statistical dictionary for ES-EN plagiarism detection allowed to obtain a good performance. CL-KGA obtained the best values with all the measures, increasing the baseline *plagdet* by 246% in automatic translations and 243% in paraphrase translations. The *granularity* for CL-KGA is the closest to 1.0, the best possible value.

Notice that in both tables, values for paraphrase translation detections remain fairly low in general. All models benefit from the simplicity of the automatic translation cases, obtaining much higher values in all the values of *plagdet*, *recall* and *precision*. The *precision* values remain especially low and, looking at the statistics in Table 1, we can see that there are ten times more automatic than paraphrase cases, which may have influenced the false positive detection, with few cases in a large corpus in comparison. This fact explains the *granularity* value of 1.0 in all the paraphrase detections: due to the small number of paraphrase cases, all the plagiarism cases detected are isolated, making impossible overlappings between detections. Despite the low values, CL-KGA obtained the best performance in detecting paraphrase too, increasing CL-ASA *plagdet* by 34% in ES-EN and by 118% in DE-EN, which highlights its potential for DE-EN.

All these results exhibit the accuracy of the approach CL-KGA in identifying CL plagiarism. The model benefits from the context model obtained through MSN to measure CL similarity. This provides a tighter bound in estimation and leads to better results. We point out that the knowledge graph construction used in CL-KGA is more time-consuming compared to the other two models and, if time is the priority, the fastest approach is CL-ASA.

7   Conclusions and Future Work

In this study we have shown the good performance and potential of knowledge graphs to detect CL plagiarism even when paraphrasing is employed. CL-ASA using BabelNet's statistical dictionary also has shown his potential for ES-EN plagiarism detection. CL-KGA model obtained better results than CL-ASA and CL-CNG in detecting verbatim copies and paraphrase on the DE-EN and ES-EN CL plagiarism cases of the PAN-PC11 corpus. Nevertheless, experimental results indicate that automatic translations are much easier to detect than translations with paraphrasing. There are many aspects to be improved in order to make plagiarism detectors efficient in the CL task.

In the future we will investigate how the task of CL plagiarism detection can be approached using other MSNs. Moreover, we would like to investigate the knowledge graph suitability for CL information retrieval.

References

1. Barrón-Cedeño, A., Vila, M., Martí, M., Rosso, P.: Plagiarism meets paraphrasing: insights for the next generation in automatic plagiarism detection. Computational Linguistics 39(4) (2013)
2. Barrón-Cedeño, A.: On the mono- and cross-language detection of text re-use and plagiarism. Ph.D. thesis, Universitat Politènica de València (2012)
3. Barrón-Cedeño, A., Rosso, P., Pinto, D., Juan, A.: On cross-lingual plagiarism analysis using a statistical model. In: Proc. of the ECAI 2008 Workshop on Uncovering Plagiarism, Authorship and Social Software Misuse, PAN 2008 (2008)

4. Franco-Salvador, M., Gupta, P., Rosso, P.: Cross-language plagiarism detection using BabelNet's statistical dictionary. Computación y Sistemas, Revista Iberoamericana de Computación 16(4), 383–390 (2012)
5. Franco-Salvador, M., Gupta, P., Rosso, P.: Cross-language plagiarism detection using a multilingual semantic network. In: Serdyukov, P., Braslavski, P., Kuznetsov, S.O., Kamps, J., Rüger, S., Agichtein, E., Segalovich, I., Yilmaz, E. (eds.) ECIR 2013. LNCS, vol. 7814, pp. 710–713. Springer, Heidelberg (2013)
6. Franco-Salvador, M., Gupta, P., Rosso, P.: Graph-based similarity analysis: a new approach to cross-language plagiarism detection. Journal of the Spanish Society of Natural Language Processing (Sociedad Espaola de Procesamiento del Languaje Natural) (50) (2013)
7. Montes-y-Gómez, M., Gelbukh, A., López-López, A., Baeza-Yates, R.: Flexible comparison of conceptual graphs. In: Mayr, H.C., Lazanský, J., Quirchmayr, G., Vogel, P. (eds.) DEXA 2001. LNCS, vol. 2113, pp. 102–111. Springer, Heidelberg (2001)
8. Gupta, P., Barrón-Cedeño, A., Rosso, P.: Cross-language high similarity search using a conceptual thesaurus. In: Catarci, T., Forner, P., Hiemstra, D., Peñas, A., Santucci, G. (eds.) CLEF 2012. LNCS, vol. 7488, pp. 67–75. Springer, Heidelberg (2012)
9. Mcnamee, P., Mayfield, J.: Character n-gram tokenization for European language text retrieval. Information Retrieval 7(1), 73–97 (2004)
10. Miller, G.A., Leacock, C., Tengi, R., Bunker, R.T.: A semantic concordance. In: Proceedings of the Workshop on Human Language Technology, HLT 1993, pp. 303–308. Association for Computational Linguistics, Stroudsburg (1993)
11. Navigli, R., Ponzetto, S.P.: BabelNet: The automatic construction, evaluation and application of a wide-coverage multilingual semantic network. Artificial Intelligence 193, 217–250 (2012)
12. Och, F.J., Ney, H.: A systematic comparison of various statistical alignment models. Computational Linguistics 29(1), 19–51 (2003)
13. Potthast, M., Barrón-Cedeño, A., Stein, B., Rosso, P.: An evaluation framework for plagiarism detection. In: Proc. of the 23rd Int. Conf. on Computational Linguistics, COLING 2010, Beijing, China, pp. 997–1005 (2010)
14. Potthast, M., Barrón-Cedeño, A., Stein, B., Rosso, P.: Cross-language plagiarism detection. Language Resources and Evaluation, Special Issue on Plagiarism and Authorship Analysis 45(1), 45–62 (2011)
15. Potthast, M., Eiselt, A., Barrón-Cedeño, A., Stein, B., Rosso, P.: Overview of the 3rd int. competition on plagiarism detection. In: CLEF (Notebook Papers/Labs/Workshop) (2011)
16. Potthast, M., Gollub, T., Hagen, M., Kiesel, J., Michel, M., Oberländer, A., Tippmann, M., Barrón-Cedeño, A., Gupta, P., Rosso, P., et al.: Overview of the 4th international competition on plagiarism detection. In: CLEF (Online Working Notes/Labs/Workshop) (2012)
17. Pouliquen, B., Steinberger, R., Ignat, C.: Automatic linking of similar texts across languages. In: Proc. Recent Advances in Natural Language Processing III, RANLP 2003, pp. 307–316 (2003)
18. Schmid, H.: Probabilistic part-of-speech tagging using decision trees. In: Proc. Int. Conf. on New Methods in Language Processing (1994)
19. Stein, B., zu Eissen, S.M., Potthast, M.: Strategies for retrieving plagiarized documents. In: Proc. of the 30th Annual Int. ACM SIGIR Conf. on Research and Development in Information Retrieval, pp. 825–826. ACM (2007)
20. Steinberger, R., Pouliquen, B., Widiger, A., Ignat, C., Erjavec, T., Tufis, D., Varga, D.: The jrc-acquis: A multilingual aligned parallel corpus with +20 languages. In: Proc. 5th Int. Conf. on Language Resources and Evaluation, LREC 2006 (2006)
21. Vossen, P.: Eurowordnet: A multilingual database of autonomous and language-specific wordnets connected via an inter-lingual index. Proc. Int. Journal of Lexicography 17 (2004)

Author Index